STRESSFUL LIFE EVENTS AND THEIR CONTEXTS

Series in Psychosocial Epidemiology
Volume 2
Series Editors
  Ben Z. Locke, M.P.H.
  Andrew E. Slaby, M.D., Ph.D., M.P.H.

SERIES IN
PSYCHOSOCIAL
EPIDEMIOLOGY
VOLUME 2

STRESSFUL
LIFE EVENTS
& THEIR
CONTEXTS

EDITED BY
Barbara Snell Dohrenwend
& Bruce P. Dohrenwend

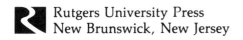

Rutgers University Press
New Brunswick, New Jersey

Originally published Neale Watson Academic Publications, Inc., 1981
Rutgers University Press edition, 1984.

Library of Congress Cataloging in Publication Data
Main entry under title:

Stressful life events and their contexts.

    (Monographs in psychosocial epidemiology ; 2)
    Includes bibliographies.
    1. Stress (Psychology)—Addresses, essays, lectures.
I. Dohrenwend, Barbara Snell. II. Dohrenwend, Bruce
Philip, 1927–   III. Series.
BF575.S75S778 1983   155.9   82-25079
ISBN 0-8135-1004-X (pbk.)

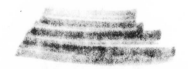

Table of Contents

251980

Foreword

Rising costs of mental health care and interest in the development of a national health insurance that should include some mental health services have heightened concern both for ways by which health planners may evaluate the extent of behavioral problems and the means by which the efficacy of various treatment modalities may be assessed. Questions of paramount importance include: If there exist two or more ways of treating an illness, which is the most effective? If two therapeutic modalities are equally effective, which is the most efficient? If equally efficient, which is the least costly? Questions regarding the prevalence and incidence rates of specific psychiatric illness in communities are being raised by those delegated with the task of making policy recommendations for programs of primary prevention and treatment. What is the natural history of a behavioral problem untreated and how is the problem affected by normal growth and development? What does a knowledge of the natural history of a disorder of mood, thought, or behavior tell us about its etiology, and how may it lead to methods of prevention? If an illness is not preventable by currently available knowledge, what interventions may be made in its natural history to arrest and possibly reverse its course? Mental health is now big business and failure to look at specific population needs when planning programs and to build in ways of evaluating cost-efficiency-effectiveness results in considerable psychological and economic cost to millions of patients and their families as well as taxpayers in general.

Epidemiology includes a number of technical skills used in answering some of the questions facing health planners today. Traditionally, epidemiology has been seen as the study of disease patterns in populations. Epidemiologists have provided data that have led to effective programs in the prevention of a number of infectious diseases including malaria, smallpox, and poliomyelitis. However, epidemiology has played a minor role in psychiatric research until relatively recently. Epidemiologic studies in mental health tended to be descriptive and focused on the prevalence and incidence rates of symptoms in broad diagnostic categories such as "neuroses" or "psychoses." In fact, some infectious and chronic-disease epidemiologists question whether epidemiology can be used to tackle psychiatric problems. The Society for Epidemiologic Research does not have a section on psychosocial epidemiology, and the publication of papers in social and psychiatric epidemiology in the main journal of epidemiology is infrequent. The principal organs for the dispersion of knowledge in psychosocial epidemiology have been *Psychological Medicine* and the *Archives of General Psychiatry*. The former journal, published quarterly, has on its editorial board members that are sophisticated in epidemiology, and probably publishes the greatest number of articles in this area. As a British journal it has limited readership in the United States. On the other hand, the *Archives of General Psychiatry*, a publication of the American Medical Association, is widely read in the United States. It publishes a number of high quality papers in epidemiology but has a broad mandate and, therefore, is limited in its ability to publish more.

The *Monographs in Psychosocial Epidemiology*, of which this is the second volume, is to serve several important functions for epidemiology, psychiatry, and related areas in public health. The objectives include:

1. Providing a forum for discussion of research strategies in the evaluation of mental health problems in the community and of assessing effectiveness of psychiatric treatment interventions;
2. Serving as a teaching tool for students in medical schools and schools of public health, hospital administration, social work and nursing as well as for students in departments of psychology and sociology and, especially, epidemiology.
3. Keeping prospective researchers alert to problems needing investigation in the area of psychosocial epidemiology;
4. Serving as a vehicle to bring together research in the area of psychosocial epidemiology;
5. Providing a means of continuing education for epidemiologists working in the field; and
6. Providing a means for discussions on how the results of epidemiologic and related behavioral research might be brought to bear on the development of state and federal health policy decisions.

To achieve these ends, each monograph will have a theme of particular interest to investigators in the field of psychosocial epidemiology, such as the study of children, the study of stressful life events, and needs assessment. Each volume of the monograph will have a guest editor with an established reputation in the field chosen by us. The guest editor will direct the selection of the individual contributors and write the introductory article. In general, the lead article will (1) contain a discussion of methodological considerations in the research of a given area (i.e., experimental design, sampling, instruments used, analysis of data, economic considerations and ethical decisions in planning studies), (2) critically review existing studies, (3) present information on the current state of the field, and (4) suggest directions for further research.

The volumes in the series, in addition to the present one on stressful life events and an earlier one on studying children epidemiologically, include ones on needs assesment, genetics, aging, alcohol use, ethics of epidemiologic research, drug use, community surveys, the methodology of natural experiments, and the interrelationships between psychological and physical responsiveness. Guest editors include Felton Earls, Carl Eisdorfer, Stanislav V. Kasl, David Mechanic, Jerome Myers, Lee N. Robins, Marc Schuckett, Laurence R. Tancredi, Ming T. Tsuang, George Warheit, and Myrna M. Weissman. In addition to the introductory article and papers by selected investigators in the field, whenever possible an issue will contain an editorial written by a representative of the World Health Organization and by ourselves. The representative of WHO, chosen by Dr. Norman Sartorius, Director of the Division of Mental Health, will discuss what is being done internationally in the topic area; what should be done cooperatively and independently to advance the field; what WHO feels are research priorities in the field; and what particular methodological research problems exist in pretechnological and Third World nations. Our editorial will address the present state of epidemiologic research in the area, the directions the Center for Epidemiologic Studies at the National Institute of Mental Health would like to see research take, and the relationship of research in the field to the formulation of health policy.

The mandate of this series is challenging and the task great, but with the help of our guest editors and other contributors, and feedback from our readership, we can make the series special and sufficient to fulfill the need for an organ to draw together researchers, students, and health-policy makers in an effort to reap from research in psychosocial epidemiology conclusions that lead to effective and consumer-responsive health policy and programs of preventive psychiatric care.

B. Z. L.
A. E. S.

Preface

A major tenet of psychoanalytic thinking has been the association of life events in the remote or recent past to current psychopathology. On a macrocosmic level, psychoanalytic researchers attempt to demonstrate a relationship between an individual's early childhood experiences and how, later in life, he feels about himself, makes choices, suffers anxiety, responds to stress, and develops psychopathology. The traditional approach to the study of the relationship of previous life events to current functioning has been the clinical case study method. This approach is fraught with biases. One of the greatest sources of bias is using selected patient populations or samples of limited size (in the extreme, Ns of one!).

Psychoanalysis has taught us how an individual's perception is distorted by anxiety, unresolved conflict, mood state, and personal psychogenetic history. Didactic analyses have as one of their functions a heightening of the analyst-in-training's consciousness to the manner in which his or her own feelings distort what is heard or seen in therapy. A training analysis helps make an analyst more objective in perception. There is no empirical evidence, however, to support this assumption. Objectivity is difficult to define. In addition, however, those entering analysis are a selected population who share biases and collude with each other to corroborate a similar world view.

The concept of loss as an antecedent event in depression, for instance, is a commonly held psychoanalytic belief. Loss may occur through death, divorce, or separation. Anger toward the lost one for going is turned inward toward the self and depression results. In the extreme, suicide may be interpreted as retroflected rage. An early therapeutic approach to depressed patients evolved around helping the individual get in touch with his or her anger. When a loss did not seem apparent, supporters of this theory said losses exist, but are not always perceived. It is true, we all have had subjective losses such as loss of self-esteem, loss of pride, and narcissistic injury. What does it all mean? Depression and its treatment are not simply nor predominantly to be understood in terms of loss and anger. Major affective illness is believed to be influenced by strong biologic and genetic factors. In addition, a number of drugs, including the antihypertensive agent reserpine, and illness such as hypothyroidism can cause alterations in personality indistinguishable from so-called psychological depressions. All depressed people look at their current and past life through blue-tinted glasses, and what they report to friends, clinicians, and researchers is not necessarily fact and cannot be considered uncritical evidence to support some causal model.

Comparably, recent genetic studies and studies of the natural history of manic-depressive illness, schizophrenia, and alcoholism have raised questions about the role of life events in these illnesses and, as Matthews and Glass discuss in this volume in their paper on Type A personality, stressful life events, and coronary heart disease, the role of life events in the genesis of all illness is still incompletely understood. Programs of prevention and treatment are contingent to some degree on an understanding of the role of life events in the genesis of illness and health.

The interest of the National Institute of Mental Health in studying stressful life events is evidenced by the research support provided through the grant programs of the Center for Epidemiologic Studies. In the past few years, and including current and committed support to research on topics covered in this monograph, the Center has awarded approximately five million dollars to ten principle investigators. The titles of their ten research projects are as follows: coping with life stress; vulnerability to the psychological consequences of stress; psychological stress and help-seeking behavior; stressful life events, social support and illness; life change and illness; a multicultural approach; resources, stress, and mental health of older persons; Shetland Isles: the effect of rapid change on mental health; epidemiology of depression and help-seeking behavior; epidemiology of recently bereaved women; and epidemiologic analysis of type A/B behavior.

Volume Two of *Monographs in Psychosocial Epidemiology* has as its editors Barbara Snell Dohrenwend and Bruce P. Dohrenwend, established researchers who have struggled for years to better understand the complex interplay of stressful life events, individual personality variables, and illness. In their overview article, the Dohrenwends tell us that the relationship between life events and changes in health is a weak one. Understanding the life stress process requires attention to the context, both the personal disposition of the individual experiencing life events and the social conditions in which these events are experienced. Subsequent contributors discuss conceptual problems in the measurement of stressful life events. Shrout explores the relative advantages of employing weighted life-event indices over unweighted counts of events in predicting health status, and Rahe evaluates the predictive power of life events as risk factors. Fairbank and Hough examine social class and culture differences in the perception of the relative importance of life events. Neugebauer questions the appropriateness of design and statistics of studies of event checklist reliability. Few investigators discuss the measurement properties of the checklist in any detail, we are told, or provide an explicit rationale for the choice of study design. Helzer compares methodological problems in studies of life events with those of interpretation of the consequences of extreme situations and finds that life-event studies have methodological problems that are not present in studies of extreme situations. The subsequent two sections of the volume address personal dispositions related to the life-stress process (i.e., the papers by Lazarus, Lefcourt, and Matthews and Glass) and the social conditions related to the life stress process (i.e., the papers by Brown, Gore, Phillips and Fischer, and the Liems). In the final section, Robert Golden and Barbara Dohrenwend review six hypotheses concerning the nature of the life stress process to determine how they can be tested. A simple path-analytic model for testing the alternative hypotheses is described and, for instances where casual effects are confirmed by the path-analytic testing, a procedure for measuring strength of association with adverse health change is provided. If the reader comes away from this volume thinking that an understanding of the role of stressful life events in the genesis of physical and psychological illness is complex and one in need of considerable methodological sophistication, he or she is correct.

B. Z. L.
A. E. S.

Life Stress and Illness:

Formulation of the Issues

BARBARA SNELL DOHRENWEND

BRUCE P. DOHRENWEND

From case studies we have learned that life stressors can play a part in causing serious illness and even death. To illustrate from the cases of sudden deaths collected by Engel (1971), "A dramatic example is the death of the 27-year-old army captain who had commanded the ceremonial troops at the funeral of President Kennedy. He died ten days after the President of a 'cardiac irregularity and acute congestion' according to the newspaper report of the medical findings" (p. 774). Two other cases from the same series that contrast with this one are, "A 56-year-old man collapsed and died while receiving congratulations for scoring his first hole-in-one" and "a 75-year-old man, who hit the twin double for $1,683 on a $2 bet, died as he was about to cash in the winning ticket" (p. 777).

In his studies of strong emotions Cannon (1929) collected a number of cases to show that life stressors can lead to pathological conditions. In one case of a pathological thyroid condition, prior to the onset of her illness, "A wife . . . saw her husband walking arm in arm with a strange woman and acting in such a way as to rouse jealousy and suspicion" (p. 255). Another case was " . . . a married woman who had had two illegitimate children and whose husband committed suicide in her presence as a rebuke to her manner of living" (p. 256).

Some more transient consequences of a stressful life event are illustrated in Mechanic's (1962) study of graduate students preparing to take their qualifying examination. About a week before the examination one student reported, "Lately I've been feeling real depressed. I don't feel that I know anything. I just feel so mentally defective, like what I have done goes into one ear and out the other . . . Instead of putting in a last-ditch effort, I can't. I'm just sort of tired of the whole business. I'm tired of studying. I'm tired of school. I'm just tired" (p. 143). Then, in the days and hours

1

immediately preceeding the examination, "severe psychosomatic symptoms seemed to appear. A few students actually become sick, probably attributable in part to the increased vulnerability resulting from the physical and mental exhaustion that had accompanied study and from keeping late hours. Many students reported having stomachaches, anxiety attacks, increased problems with asthma, and some rashes and allergies. Appetite and eating patterns also seemed affected, and a number of students reported difficulty in sleeping. On the morning of the examination most students reported stomach pains; a number reported diarrhea; and a few reported that they had been unable to hold their breakfast" (p. 162).

Taken together, these cases illustrate the wide range, in terms of the symptoms involved (Wolff et al., 1950) seriousness, of disorders that have been observed in relation to stressful life events. At the same time, the extraordinariness of most of these cases reminds us that life stressors are neither a necessary nor a sufficient condition for the occurrence of fatal or nonfatal illness. Some people whose lives appear to be ordered and gratifying do become ill, and, on the other hand, most people pass through periods of life stress without suffering illness. What we do know, then, is that life stress sometimes plays a part in the onset of a variety of psychological and somatic disorders. We do not yet understand the life-stress process well enough, however, to predict and control its pathological effects.

In trying to solve this problem, investigators have developed ideas under three rubrics: the nature of stressful life events, the nature of personal dispositions and styles of coping related to the life-stress process, and the nature of social conditions related to the life-stress process. They have also begun to develop models of life stress based on these concepts. In this chapter we will first review concepts, related evidence, and methodological problems under each of the three rubrics described. We will then present some models of the life stress process.

What is a Stressful Life Event?

The stressful life events with which we are concerned are those that are proximate to rather than remote from the onset of a disorder. This category would, for example, include the recent death of a friend or relative, but not the fact that an adult's father died when he or she was a child. The latter event is not irrelevant to life stress but is subsumed under personal dispositions since we assume that the early death of a parent can affect an adult's behavior only insofar as its impact was internalized.

Much of the debate concerning the nature of stressful life events has focused on the question of what dimensions or aspects of life events make them stressful. The most extensively studied question has been whether the stressfulness of an event is a function of the amount of change it entails, regardless of whether the change is for better or for worse, or whether only events that involve an undesirable change are stressful. The former position was most clearly developed in the early work of Holmes and Rahe (1967), who culled a list of life events "empirically observed to cluster at the time of disease onset" (Holmes and Masuda, 1974, p. 46) from the life charts of more than 5,000 medical patients. They found that, "The occurrence of each event usually evoked, or was associated with, some adaptive or coping behavior on the part of the involved individual" (p. 46). Thus, in making a list of stressful life events, "each item was constructed to contain life events whose advent is either indicative of, or requires a significant change in, the ongoing life pattern of the individual. The emphasis is on change from the existing steady state and not on psychological meaning, emotion, or social desirability" (p. 46). Holmes and his colleagues have reported statistically significant relations between a quantitative index of the amount of change entailed in recent life events and disorders or disabilities ranging from myocardial infarction and childhood leukemia to poor teacher performance and low college grade point average.

The position that the change entailed in recent life events is more strongly related than their undesirability to current psychological symptoms was weakly supported by the results of one study (B. S. Dohrenwend, 1973), but other studies of the relation between psychological symptoms and recent life event indices have found undesirable events to be more strongly correlated with these symptom inventories than total change (Crandall and Lehman, 1977; Miller et al., 1976; Ross and Mirowsky, 1979; Vinokur and Selzer, 1975). Furthermore, a number of investigators have shown that change scores based entirely on desirable events are unrelated to the onset of clinical depression (Paykel, 1974), traffic accidents (Vinokur and Selzer, 1975, p. 333), visits to physicians (Miller et al., 1976), or to elevation of psychological symptoms (Gersten et al., 1974; Johnson and Sarason, 1978; Mueller et al., 1977) of the kind included in the Langner scale (1962), and the Gurin scale (Gurin et al., 1960). However, the psychological symptoms involved need to be carefully specified since Gersten and her colleagues (1974) and Mueller and his colleagues (1977) reported associations between desirable events and measures labeled anxiety producing.

Further specification of the kinds of life events that affect health have been made in relation to certain disorders. For example, in his research on depression, Paykel (1974) identified a class of events in which a person leaves the social field of the subject (e.g., death of close family member, separation, divorce, family member leaves home, child married, and son drafted). He found that the presence of one or more events in this category was strongly related to the onset of depression. In a retrospective study of cardiac patients Theorell (1974) found that work events were closely related, and, in a subsequent prospective study, that "increased responsibility at work during the last year" was associated with subsequent myocardial infarctions (Theorell, 1976).

Although these results are not significant enough to indicate that a particular type of event leads exclusively to a particular type of disorder, they do suggest that it is a mistake to ask which dimensions or aspects of life events are stressful in general and which are not. From some studies of psychological symptom levels, onsets of episodes of clinical depression, traffic accidents, and physician visits, we might conclude that desirable events have no effect on health. However, the finding of Theorell and his colleagues for cardiac patients does not fit this generalization since "increased responsibility at work" would ordinarily involve events such as promotion or increased pay, classified as socially desirable.

The question that seems to emerge from findings reported so far is: What is the strength of the relationship between carefully specified event characteristics and health changes? An analysis by Paykel (1974) of the relation between exits and episodes of clinical depression illustrates the approach implied by this question. He first noted a difference between the proportions of depressed patients and their matched controls who reported exits in the six months prior to the onset of a depressive episode or a comparable period for controls; 25% of the patients and 5% of the controls reported events in this category. However, Paykel noted, "Most of the events reported by the depressives were in the range of everyday experience rather than catastrophic, and most often are negotiated without clinical depression" (p. 139). Making assumptions about the frequency of exits and the frequency of depressive episodes in the population, he estimated from his finding that " . . . only a small proportion of exits, less than 10 per cent, appear to be followed by clinical depression" (p. 139).

Paykel's work serves as an example of the kind of two-step analysis that needs to be done in order to clarify the nature of stressful aspects of life events. Until now almost all studies have been designed simply to test the hypothesis that a relationship exists between some aspect of life events and some indicator of health status, with apparently conflicting results. We suggest that these conflicts will be productively resolved if, in future studies, investigators take the further step of making quantitative assessments of relationships between particular aspects of life events and particular health indicators. The objective will not be to specify whether one aspect or type of life events is stressful but to examine the extent to which it puts persons at risk for specific types of disorders.

Measuring Stressful Life Events

Quantitative procedures for measuring life events have been widely adopted in research on life stress since Holmes and Rahe introduced their Social Readjustment Rating Scale in 1967. As mentioned earlier, they culled a list of events "empirically observed to cluster at the time of disease onset" from about 5,000 life charts of medical patients. These were reduced to a list of 43 events that were then rated as to the amount of readjustment each entailed by a sample of convenience of 394 judges. The instructions given to the judges were:

1. Social readjustment includes the amount and duration of change in one's accustomed pattern of life resulting from various life events. As defined, social readjustment measures the intensity and length of time necessary to accommodate to a life event, *regardless of the desirability of this event.*

2. You are asked to rate a series of life events as to their relative degrees of necessary readjustment. In scoring, *use all of your experience* in arriving at your answer. This means personal experience where it applies as well as what you have learned to be the case for others. Some persons accommodate to change more readily than others; some persons adjust with particular ease or difficulty to only certain events. Therefore, strive to give your opinion of the average degree of readjustment necessary for each event rather than the extreme.

3. The mechanics of rating are these: Event 1, Marriage, has been given an arbitrary value of 500. As you complete each of the

remaining events think to yourself, 'Is this event indicative of more or less readjustment than marriage?' 'Would the readjustment take longer or shorter to accomplish?' If you decide the readjustment is more intense and protracted, then choose a *proportionately larger* number and place it in the blank directly opposite the event in the column marked 'Values.' If you decide the event represents less and shorter readjustment than marriage, then indicate how much less by placing a *proportionately smaller* number in the opposite blank. (If an event requires intense readjustment over a short time span, it may approximate in value an event requiring less intense readjustment over a long period of time.) If the event is equal in social readjustment to marriage, record the number 500 opposite the event (Holmes and Masuda, 1974).

The mean ratings for the events were used to calculate the total Life Change Unit score for subjects who reported which events they had experienced in a given recent time period, usually the last six months or the last year. It is these scores that were found to correlate with a wide variety of illnesses and disabilities (Holmes and Masuda, 1974).

Many criticisms have been leveled at Holmes and Rahe's Social Readjustment Rating Scale, most of them revolving around three general questions: What populations of events should be studied? Should event-specific weights be used to compute measures of recent life events? If so, should these weights be person-specific or standard across persons? Unfortunately, much of the discussion of these questions has been carried on at cross purposes. Specifically, differences about what procedure is best often seem to emerge from an underlying difference as to whether the measure should be designed to maximize the strength of its relationship with indicators of illness and disability or whether it should be designed to test hypotheses about relations between specific aspects of life stress and illness. The former aim dictates packing as much information as possible that might be relevant to occurrences of illness into life-event measures. The latter aim, in contrast, dictates using measures that indicate as cleanly as possible single aspects or dimensions of life events.

What populations of events should be studied—The major issue here is partly evident in the distinction between objective and subjective events made by some investigators (e.g., Thurlow, 1971). Subjective events, for example, "sexual difficulties," "major change in number of arguments with spouse," and "major changes in sleeping habits" (Holmes and Masuda, 1974) may be manifestations of or responses to an underlying disorder rather than causes of a disorder. Moreover, particularly when the investigator is concerned with psychological disorder, the problem is not limited to "subjective" events since many objective events such as "divorce" or "being fired from work" (e.g., Holmes and Masuda, 1974), which are included in many life event lists, are as likely to be consequences as causes of psychopathology. By Hudgens's count, for example, 29 of the 43 events on the list constructed by Holmes and Rahe (1967) and 32 of the 51 events on the list developed by Paykel and his colleagues (1971) "are often the symptoms or consequences of illness" (Hudgens, 1974, p. 131). As Brown (1974) and B. P. Dohrenwend (1974) pointed out, when investigators are concerned with etiological questions this kind of a sample of life events seriously limits the kinds of inferences that can be drawn from a correlation between the number or magnitude of events experienced and illness. The limitation on causal inference is especially severe in investigations of disorders that have an insidious onset, and is likely to be most serious in studies of psychological disorders. Only if the investigator can date the onset of an event in relation to the onset of the pathology and learn something about whether the event was within or outside the control of the subject can he make relatively unambiguous inferences about the etiological role of such events.

Most samples of events also include major physical illness or injury, understandably enough since these are negative events and entail serious disruption of usual activities. However, it is a basic proposition of psychosomatic medicine that physical disorders are accompanied by some degree of emotional disturbance and emotional disorders by some degree of somatic disturbance. There is no instance of which we are aware in which investigations of relations between physical illness and emotional disturbance have failed to report a strong positive correlation between the two (cf., Lipowsky, 1975). And, as Hinkle (1974) pointed out with reference to various types of physical illness, "the presence of one disease may imply the presence of others and beget yet other diseases" (p. 39), a fact that accounts in part for his finding that risk of disease is not randomly distributed in groups of similar people who share similar experiences over periods of ten to twenty years. Thus, once again, a sample of events that includes physical illness and injury, and most lists do, can lead to further problems of etiological interpretation when the events are summed to provide scores for the amount of stress experienced by particular individuals. The additional problem of interpretation centers on the extent to which a positive correlation indicates the impact of life stress or, instead, the relation among physical illnesses, or between physical and psychiatric symptomatology, which are important problems in their own right.

We suggest, therefore, that there are at least three populations of life events that should be kept distinct in studies whose aim is to investigate etiological questions concerning life events and illness (B. P. Dohrenwend, 1974; Dohrenwend and Dohrenwend, 1974). These populations are: (1) events that may be confounded with the physical health and the psychiatric condition of the subject; (2) events consisting of physical illnesses and injuries to the subject; and (3) events whose occurrences are independent of either the subject's physical health or his psychiatric condition.

As a general principle, the more a sample of events in a particular measure of stressful life events represents a summated mixture from these three event populations, the higher is the correlation with health indicators, and the more difficult it is to assess the etiological implications of a relationship between such a measure and various types of pathology. Thus, if an investigator's aim is to maximize the strength of the observed relationship between life events and illness, he or she should indiscriminately combine all populations of events or, better still, emphasize events that may be confounded with physical health and the psychiatric condition of the subject, and events consisting of physical illnesses and injuries to the subject. If, however, the investigator's aim is to investigate the etiological role of life events, the various populations of events should be included but kept distinct in analyses of relations between life events and illness.

Should event-specific weights be used to compute measures of recent life events?—With their Social Readjustment Rating Scale, Holmes and Rahe (1967) introduced into research on life stress and illness a procedure for quantifying the different amounts of stressfulness of different life events. On its face this procedure seems reasonable, since it involves, for example, giving greater weight to the death of a child than to a son or daughter leaving home. However, critics have questioned whether event-specific weights offer any empirical advantage over simply counting life events, that is, giving each event a weight of one. Their most telling point is that the correlation between recent event scores based on the weighted sum of recent life events and scores based on the unweighted sum is likely to be so high that they will yield essentially the same results (Lorimer et al., 1979). On the assumption of equal and positive correlations between events, this correlation is given by Ghiselli's (1964) formula:

$$\rho ss' = \sqrt{\frac{1 + (k - 1)r}{(\sigma_w/\overline{w})^2 (1 - r) + 1 + (k - 1)r}}$$

For this purpose, k is the number of events, r is the correlation between events, $\overline{w}$ is the standard deviation of the event specific weights and w is the mean of these weights. Even if r is very small, .001, this formula applied to Holmes and Rahe's event weights or those of the PERI Life Events Scale (B. S. Dohrenwend et al., 1978) predicts correlations on the order of .90 (Lorimer et al., 1979). If r is larger the predicted correlation will be even higher. Moreover, when this correlation was calculated from data about their recent life events reported by several different samples of subjects it was generally on the order of .90 (Lorimer et al., 1979; B. S. Dohrenwend et al., 1979). Should we then infer that useful information is not provided by giving different weights to different life events?

This conclusion involves a premature simplification of the measurement of stressful life events. First, if an investigation concerns subsets of events rather than only the aggregate of all kinds of life events, the observed correlations in some subsets between weighted and unweighted scores may not be anywhere near .90. For example, an observed correlation between weighted and unweighted recent life event scores for the subset of events concerning childbearing and child rearing on the PERI Life Events Scale (B. S. Dohrenwend et al., 1978) was .36. By Ghiselli's formula, if r is assumed to be .001, the correlation between unweighted and weighted scores for this subset of events was predicted to be .93.

Another problem with unweighted life event scores is the implicit assumption that meaningful group differences in perceptions of the stressfulness of specific life events do not exist. Yet our review of studies involving ratings by different social class and ethnic groups suggested that there are meaningful differences in their judgments of the change entailed in some life events (Askenasy et al., 1977). We also found sex differences, as well as class and ethnic differences, when we collected ratings of the change entailed in life events from a sample of New York City residents. For example, men and women differed in their ratings of "marital infidelity," with men rating it higher, and social class was inversely related to ratings of "expanded business or professional practice" (B. S. Dohrenwend et al., 1978). These findings argue against adopting unweighted scores, which preclude measuring group differences in evaluation of the various aspects of life events.

Another assumption implicit in the suggestion that unweighted event scores are as efficient as weighted scores is that only one form of life event measure, the total additive score, will prove useful. Yet in a study of age differences in recent life event experience, Mulvey (1979) found that the number of events experienced in one year did not vary with age. Nor did weighted event totals differ. However, the average weight of events reported by individuals did vary, increasing significantly with age.

In general, we suggest that life-event weights are a useful research tool for some purposes. When events are simply aggregated over an entire list of the usual length of 40 or more in the same way for all individuals, unweighted as well as weighted scores should be tested and the former, simpler score adopted if it yields equivalent results. However, event-specific weights may provide valuable information concerning subsets of different types of life events and group differences in perceptions and experiences of these events.

Should event-specific weights be person-specific or standard across persons?—The measurement of differences in the stressfulness of particular life events must take two facts into account. First, it is not possible to measure the stressfulness of an event in terms of physical units such as volts or decibels as it is when electric shock or noise is the stressor. Second, stressful life events are not limited to extremely severe, life threatening events which, as Appley and Trumbull (1967) noted, are universal stressors. The consensus that such events are highly stressful is, presumably, largely biologically determined. For most life events, such as losing a job or getting a divorce, however, there is no such biological reality underlying the perception of the event. Yet most people have ideas about how positive or negative an event such as divorce or loss of a job is, and how much change it entails. These ideas must be learned. The question of how they are learned is central to resolution of the issue of person specific versus standard weights for particular life events.

In dealing with this question it is crucial to distinguish between the meaning of an event to an individual after he or she has experienced it and become ill compared to its meaning to him or her beforehand. If we rely on its meaning after it has been associated with illness to define the stressfulness of a life event, we risk becoming ensnared in an etiological tautology: events that are followed by dysfunctional behavior or illness are stressful; stressful events induce dysfunctional behavior or illness. In practice, some investigators advocating personal measures of the stressfulness of particular life events have done just this, since they have taken their measures of stressfulness after subjects have experienced particular events in association with, for example, an automobile accident (Vinokur and Selzer, 1975) or a heart attack (Theorell, 1974). These investigators have, moreover, further confused the issue in relation to etiological research by arguing for personal measures of the stressfulness of particular life events on the ground that they yield higher correlations with outcomes than a standard measure, a result to be expected from the tautology involved (Paykel and Uhlenhuth, 1972).

Thus, for etiologically oriented research, we must reject post hoc personal measures of the stressfulness of particular life events. We come, then, to the question of what is learned that would give personal meanings to stressful life events before they are experienced. Our reading of the literature indicates that this question has not been answered directly since, among those who advocate personal measures, it is not the perception of the event as such that is conceived in personal terms but, instead, the relation between the individual's acquired coping skills, among other resources (Lazarus and Launier, 1978), and the demands of the event. Thus, for example, one group of investigators who advocated personal scoring as "more accurate" argued that, "It may also reflect the subject's perception as well as his way of coping with life change events" (Ander et al., 1974, p. 123). When we think about testing etiological hypotheses concerning life stress and illness, this relational type of conception handicaps us because it provides no basis for measuring stressful life events apart from the context of personality and the social situations in which they occur. Its limitations are, moreover, indicated in the rationale for it offered by Lazarus and Launier (1978): "The continuous flow of person-environment relationships in stress, emotion, and coping cannot comfortably be encompassed within the traditional S-O-R, linear causation models . . . such a flow, and the changing relationships involved in it, need to be examined in purely descriptive terms before one asks the more analytic questions about the respective causal roles of variables of person and environment". Contrary to Lazarus and Launier, we think that analytic studies complement descriptive studies. On this assumption these analytic questions should be asked now rather than postponed to some unknown future when descriptive work has been completed.

We return, then, to the question of the learned basis for defining the stressfulness of life events. As a general principle we know that much learning that occurs in a social context depends on vicarious rather than direct experience. Moreover, this vicarious experience can be transmitted through many persons or generations as social norms (Bandura and Walters, 1963). In this way individuals who have not personally experienced an event could come to have definite expectations concerning its stressfulness.

We are likely to recognize the existence of culturally determined expectancies about the meaning of certain events in the case of exotic phenomena such as voodoo and hex deaths (Seligman, 1975). We are, however, not as likely to be aware of less dramatic expectancies that also appear to be culturally determined. For example, Miller and his colleagues (1974) found that the amount of readjustment required by marriage was ranked much lower by residents of a rural area than by residents of urban areas in the United States. In interpreting their finding Miller and his coauthors noted, "In rural North Carolina when one marries the expectation is to move only a few miles and to stay where you move—or at least to stay in the locale. In an urban area marriage may mean the uprooting of one or the other of the couple, a change in living abode for more space, and a change in recreation because of a change in expenses" (p. 271).

As part of the answer to the question of how to measure the stressfulness of particular life events, we hypothesized that the stressfulness of most life events is defined by group norms (Hinkle, 1973, Redfield and Stone, 1979). We are, therefore, proposing a standard conception of the stressfulness of life events, but one that implies that the stressfulness of a particular life event may vary from group to group and may change over time.

Given this conception of what is to be measured, one must choose between two different procedures that were designed to detect group differences in the stressfulness of life events. One calls for collecting direct ratings of life events from representative samples of judges from different social groups and applying statistical tests to determine whether these judgments indicate group differences in perceptions of particular events (B. S. Dohrenwend et al., 1978). The other, descriptively labeled the effect-proportional measure of life events, proposes to develop weights for particular life events from observations of their relations to health indicators in different groups (Ross and Mirowsky, 1979). The argument for the latter measure of life events is that it is more highly correlated with symptoms than any of a wide variety of other measures. However, the effect-proportional measure of life events achieves a high correlation with health indicators by including information about the vulnerabilities of individuals who experienced a particular event as well as about the qualities of the event that determined its effects on health. Therefore, the effect-proportional index might be used for purely predictive purposes, but is not suitable for etiological analysis. For that purpose, the procedure of obtaining ratings of qualities of events by judges chosen from the appropriate groups is more suitable since it is designed to provide a measure of group norms uncontaminated by other factors in the life stress process.

Note that in emphasizing the conceptual importance of the normative expectancy concerning an event we are not suggesting that this expectancy will necessarily be the major determinant of the impact of life stress on an individual. Personality and social situational factors may be more important. However, other things being equal, we hypothesize that the impact of a life event on an individual will be determined by a learned normative expectancy concerning the stressfulness of that event.

What Personal Dispositions are Related to the Life Stress Process?

In general, the magnitude of the relationship between stressful life events and illness has been found to be small. As we noted earlier, Paykel (1974) estimated that despite a statistically significant association, no more than 10% of exits are followed by clinical depression. In their review of the literature on life events and illness Rabkin and Struening (1976) estimated from reported correlations that stressful life events "may account at best for nine per cent of the variance in illness" (p. 115). Even more conservatively, on the basis of studies of U.S. Navy personnel, Rahe and Arthur (1978) estimated that the correlation between stressful life events occurring in a six-month period and illness reporting over the next six months to one year was .12. Given these findings, investigators have become concerned with explaining the substantial differences among individuals in responses to the same or similar life events. One approach to solving this problem is to consider what personal dispositions may account for these individual differences.

Much has been learned in the last two decades from clinical observations, observations in natural settings, and experimental studies about effective psychological defense and coping responses to stressful events (Lazarus, 1966; Hamburg and Adams, 1967; Horowitz, 1976). At the same time several hypotheses have been developed and tested concerning the nature of individual differences in disposition that account for pathological outcomes related to stressful life events.

One hypothesis, developed by Friedman and Rosenman (1974), is that persons with what they call Type A behavior pattern are more prone to develop heart disease than those with Type B behavior pattern. The Type A pattern is characterized by competitive achievement striving, a sense of time urgency, and a proneness to respond with hostility when frustrated. Friedman and Rosenman suggested that the Type A behavior pattern is elicited by events whose import is to lower others' esteem for the Type A individual. Further analyses of measures of AB behavior patterns suggest that they are multidimensional (Zyzanski and Jenkins, 1970) and that critical dimensions may relate to maintaining control over the environment (Matthews et al., 1977).

In a program of experimental studies related to the work of Friedman and Rosenman, Glass (1977) has shown that when persons prone to Type A behavior are faced with threatening events they tend first, as expected, to exert themselves strongly to achieve control. However, if they fail to achieve control they are likely to react with extreme helplessness.

Glass's finding concerning the association of a helpless response with the Type A behavior pattern suggests a link between the work of Friedman and Rosenman and another conceptual theme in the research literature on stress and illness. A research group in the Department of Psychiatry at the University of Rochester developed a multistage model of stress-induced illness in which, given a stressful life event involving loss, those with a particular constitution or personality are prone to a helpless/hopeless response. This response is part of the giving up–given up complex which, in the presence of environmental pathogens or constitutional vulnerability to disease, becomes the final common pathway to illness (Schmale, 1972). While sharing the concept of helplessness with Glass's extension of the hypothesis developed by Friedman and Rosenman, the model proposed by the Rochester group differs in that the helpless/hopeless response to stressors predicts general vulnerability to illness rather than a specific vulnerability to cardiovascular disease.

Another hypothesis related to helplessness as a basis for individual differences in vulnerability to stress-induced illness grows out of

Rotter's (1966) social learning theory and his concept that individuals have a generalized expectancy concerning the extent to which they control the rewards, punishments, and, in general, the events that occur in their lives. Rotter conceived this expectancy, which he labeled locus of control, as varying on a dimension from internal to external. Persons at the extreme internal end of the locus of control dimension expect to be in control of their life events to a high degree. In contrast, persons at the extreme external end of the locus of control dimension expect that their life events will generally be controlled by others or by fate. Although there is some controversy concerning the relation of locus of control expectancy to vulnerability to pathology, the hypothesis with the most extensive empirical support is that persons with an external locus of control expectancy have greater proneness to pathology, particularly psychopathology, than those with an internal locus of control expectancy (Lefcourt, 1976). In some studies, internal locus of control expectancy has been equated with competence, coping ability, and relative invulnerability to debilitating effects of stressful events (Campbell et al., 1976). The person with the external locus of control expectancy may be the social learning theorist's version of the Rochester group's helpless/hopeless person, especially when experiencing a life event involving loss.

Laboratory research on physiological and psychological responses to stressful stimuli has supported the idea that individuals differ in the extent to which they repress awareness of threatening stimuli or, alternatively, are highly sensitive to such stimuli (Epstein and Fenz, 1967; Lazarus, 1966). Studies of these response styles in relation to recovery from illness suggest that repression leads to a better recovery (Brown and Rawlinson, 1976; Cohen and Lazarus, 1973). At the same time, in the face of a threat against which the individual must act to escape or avoid harm, repression would be dysfunctional. Some of the work on Type A and B behavior patterns suggests that Type A may involve repression of responses to threatening stimuli (Glass, 1977).

One possibility, then, is that researchers coming from varied theoretical and empirical backgrounds may be converging on a central conception of factors in the individual that are related to stress induced illness. The person who exhibits what Friedman and Rosenman called the Type A behavior pattern may, when observed in the Rochester group's frame of reference, be seen as responding to loss with helplessness and, when examined from a social learning perspective, be found to have an external locus of control expectancy. Finally, his cognitive style may be to repress rather than to be sensitive to threatening stimuli and events. To date, however, these constructs concerning modes of stress-related responses have been developed largely by separate disciplines and subdisciplines so that their interrelationships have not been examined.

A finding that apparently diverse conceptions of personal dispositions related to life stress represent different views of a single central construct would greatly simplify the task of understanding how personality functions in the life-stress process. Empirical studies of the role of various dispositions must, however, allow for another possibility that would complicate rather than simplify this task. This possibility is signified by the terms state and trait. So far our discussion of the possible role of personality in the life stress process has only considered traits or stable dispositions to respond in particular ways to a variety of specific situations. Thus, for example, an individual was implicitly assumed to have a particular locus of control expectancy regardless of the immediate situation. Close observations of individuals in diverse situations has shown, however, that some dispositions are states that are situation specific or at least modified in intensity or level by the immediate situation (Kendall et al., 1976; Spielberger et al., 1970; Lefcourt, 1976). Thus, a person who exhibits an internal locus of control expectancy in relation to some life events may nevertheless exhibit a realistic external expectancy in relation to events that are inherently difficult to control.

In order to test this alternative in research on life stress and illness, personal dispositions should be measured not only at one time using an instrument that assumes stability across situations, but also should be measured in relation to specific life events. Thus, in studying the effects of personal control for each life event that a subject reported, we have probed the extent to which he or she anticipated and controlled the occurrence of that life event (B. S. Dohrenwend, 1977). Our results so far suggest that individuals' perceptions of the extent to which they control the occurrence of their life events is influenced at least as much by characteristics of the particular event as by the personality of the individual (B. S. Dohrenwend and Martin, 1979). Further work along this line will be necessary to determine the extent and stability of the effects of personality differences on the life-stress process.

We have been concerned with stressful life events that are proximate to rather than remote from the onset of a disorder. However, that we were not assuming that remote events were irrelevant, but only that it was more convenient to consider such events as they might influence personal dispositions later in life. Is there evidence, then, that stressful events early in life do in fact render the individual more or less vulnerable to stressful events later in life?

There are quite consistent findings that homes broken by divorce or separation in childhood are associated with later antisocial behavior (Rutter, 1974). The results of research on the later effects of death of one or both parents during childhood appeared to be much less consistent (Granville-Grossman, 1968). It seems possible, however, that the apparent inconsistency has been due to insufficient attention to whether bereavement took place earlier or later in childhood. There are now at least three studies whose results suggest that death of one or both parents before age 11 is associated with vulnerability to depression (Brown and Harris, 1978) and/or severe psychological distress (B. P. Dohrenwend and deFiguerido, 1980; Langner and Michael, 1963) among adults in samples from the general population who experience stressful life events. There is considerably less information on whether early experience with some types of events tends to decreased vulnerability to later stressful events. It is intriguing to consider whether there may be such inoculation effects (Bornstein et al., 1973).

What Social Conditions are Related to the Life Stress Process?

Complementing efforts to find factors within the individual that affect his risk of illness related to stressful life events are more recent attempts to identify social factors in the individual's environment that affect this risk. One of the most influential hypotheses in the recent literature on life stress states that social support mitigates the effects of stressful events (Caplan and Killilea, 1976). Secondary analysis of data not specifically designed to test this hypothesis has shown that highly stressful events combined with low social support are significantly more pathogenic than highly stressful events combined with high social support or less stressful events with high or low social support (Cobb, 1976; Eaton, 1978; Gore, 1978). Similarly, Theorell (1976) reported on the basis of a prospective study that stressful life events were followed by illness only for persons in a state of discord and dissatisfaction. It should be noted, however, that these measures of social environmental conditions are probably also measuring level of personal competence in such a way that the two are positively associated.

As with life-event measures that confound objective events with symptoms of illness, social support measures that confound environmental supports with personal competence will probably be more strongly related to health indicators than social support measures not thus confounded. For etiological investigations the former are poor measures, however, since they do not provide an accurate assessment of the strength of the effect of social support as an element in the life-stress process.

Despite measurement problems, the results of studies of social support to date do indicate that a full understanding of individual differences in response to life events will not be achieved without examining the social situations in which these events are experienced in some detail. Some of the questions that need to be addressed for this purpose are discussed below.

What is the structure of the support systems available to an individual? Although early efforts to conceptualize social supports tended to focus on formal helping agencies, such as mental health centers (Bloom, 1977; Caplan and Killilea, 1976), work has also been done on analysis of the structure of varied forms of informal support systems, particularly family, neighborhood, and friendship networks (Caplan, 1976; Fischer et al., 1977; Litwak and Szelenyi, 1969). What is needed now in measures to be used in etiological research is objective information about structures and networks unconfounded with the quality of an individual's participation in those structures. Without this separation the relative contribution to the life-stress process of an individual's personality compared with his or her social situation cannot be assessed.

What functions can be performed by the various structures in an individual's support systems? Although most studies to date of social support have, by implication, emphasized emotional support, some exploratory studies suggest that it is equally important to investigate the availability of instrumental support during life events (Carveth and Gottlieb, 1979; Kaplan et al., 1977). Financial support is probably an important type of instrumental support in many life events. For example, if there is illness in the family, is there adequate insurance available or if not, is there someone in the person's informal network who will help out, or a community agency to serve this purpose? Other types of instrumental support may be specific to particular life events. For example, in the case of serious illness can the person obtain adequate medical care? Does the new mother have someone to turn to for advice about the care of her baby (Carveth and Gottlieb, 1979)? Exploratory studies suggest that different functions may be served by different support structures (Litwak and Szelenyi, 1969). For example, friends and acquaintances may be able to do more than family about helping a person find a new job, but family may be a better source of help with problems in personal relationships. Thus, at least in our present state of ignorance about how support systems function in the life-stress process it is important to obtain as complete a description as possible of potentially supportive structures.

The fact that a particular type of structure, such as the family, or a network of neighborhood acquaintances, can, in general, provide support does not mean that it can do so in every individual case. On the contrary, conflicts within the family may potentially aggravate rather than mitigate life stress (Croog, 1970), and life events involving certain types of illness, particularly mental illness, as well as some other socially undesirable events may lead to rejection and stigmatization rather than support from neighbors and the surrounding community. A full picture of the potential support available to an individual would, therefore, include an assessment of norms and expectations that are applied to that individual by those in the family and other networks that are possible sources of support in the time of stressful life events.

Finally, to evaluate the actual effect of social support in the life-stress process we must answer the question: to what extent does an individual avail himself of potential supports or avoid potential stigmatization and rejection? Although available evidence suggests that the mere presence of sympathetic persons does not mitigate the effects of a stressor (Epley, 1974), we have yet to learn what kind of action in what circumstances may be needed to convert a potentially supportive system into one that is actually supportive.

Hypotheses about the Life-Stress Process

The great majority of studies of life stress and illness have been concerned primarily or exclusively with one or another of the three types of constructs that we have discussed: stressful life events, personal dispositions, or social conditions. The task now is to integrate these constructs into hypotheses about the life-stress process, a task that has received increasing attention recently. In theoretical and empirical studies investigators have developed at least seven different hypotheses (fig. 1).

The first hypothesis (fig. 1A) indicates that occurrence within a relatively brief time of a number of severely stressful life events can

FIGURE 1

A. Victimization Hypothesis

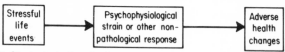

B. Stress-strain Hypothesis

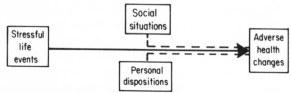

C. Vulnerability Hypothesis

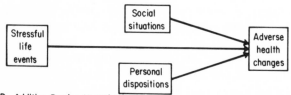

D. Additive Burden Hypothesis

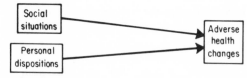

E. Chronic Burden Hypothesis

F. Event Proneness Hypothesis

Six Hypotheses About the Life Stress Process

cause adverse health changes. This model was developed empirically in studies of extreme situations such as combat and concentration camps. It has been generalized to normal civil life in terms of a pathogenic triad of concomitant events and conditions that involve physical exhaustion, severe physical illness or injury, loss of social support, geographical relocation, and the fateful negative events other than physical illness or injury over whose occurrence the individual has no control, e.g., death of a loved one (B. S. Dohrenwend and B. P. Dohrenwend, 1978; B. P. Dohrenwend, 1979). It is also the model that underlies and was supported by the early work of Holmes and Rahe and their coworkers (Holmes and Masuda, 1974). This is the victimization hypothesis.

The next hypothesis (fig. 1B) is exemplified by the work of Garrity, Marx, and Somes (1977). They tested the model in a college student population using an instrument similar to Holmes and Rahe's Schedule of Recent Events to measure the change entailed in recent life events, the Langner 22-item symptom scale to measure psychophysiological strain, and a number of general illness indicators. They found that when Langner scale scores were partialed out, correlations between life-event scores and illness indicators were sharply reduced, evidence that they interpreted as supporting their hypothesis that psychophysiological strain mediates the impact of life events.

The hypothesis diagramed in fig. 1B also describes the general form of Friedman and Rosenman's theory that certain self-esteem threatening life events elicit from predisposed individuals the Type A response pattern, which is a risk factor for coronary heart disease. It also underlies the Rochester group's theory that loss events elicit a helpless/hopeless response from some individuals that, in the presence of environmental pathogens or physiological vulnerability to a particular disorder, leads to illness. In a general form, it was proposed by Langner and Michael (1963) as the stress-strain hypothesis.

The third hypothesis (fig. 1C) indicates that stressful life events, moderated by preexisting personal dispositions and social conditions that make the individual vulnerable to the impact of life events, cause adverse health changes. A version of this hypothesis was developed by Rahe (1974). This hypothesis also underlies the literature on vulnerability involving conceptions such as coping ability (Hamburg and Adams, 1967), and social support (Caplan and Killilea, 1976; Cobb, 1976; Gore, 1978). It was also used by Zubin and Spring (1977) in their model of the etiology of schizophrenia and by Brown and Harris (1978) in their social model of the etiology of depression. This is the vulnerability hypothesis.

The fourth hypothesis (fig. 1D) states that, rather than moderating the impact of stressful life events, personal dispositions and social conditions add to the impact of stressful life events. This hypothesis is labeled the additive burden hypothesis. It received empirical support in a study of psychological symptoms by Andrews and his colleagues (1978) and was also proposed by Tennant and Bebbington (1978) as a better fit than the third hypothesis to the data presented by Brown and Harris (1978) in their study of social factors in the etiology of depression.

Figure 1E, the chronic burden hypothesis, is another and further modification of the third hypothesis. It proposes that stable personal dispositions and social conditions rather than transient stressful life events cause adverse health changes. This hypothesis was presented by Gersten and her colleagues (1977) as an explanation of changes in children's psychological symptom patterns. The method used in developing the empirical basis for this hypothesis is, however, open to criticism (Link, 1978).

The proneness hypothesis (fig. 1F) raises the crucial issue of the direction of the causal relation between life events and symptoms of illness. It proposes that the presence of a disorder leads to stressful life events which in turn exacerbate the disorder. In empirical studies this hypothesis was supported by a study of chronic mental patients (Fontana et al., 1972) but not by a study of neurotics (Tennant and Andrews, 1978). It should be tested for other chronic illnesses as well. For example, Fox (1978) emphasized the need to consider this alternative, among others, in his critical review of research on the etiological role of life stress in cancer. This might be called the proneness hypothesis, in the sense that proneness to stressful events is the central mechanism posited.

Conclusion

Up to now the overwhelming number of studies of life stress and illness have simply asked: does life stress relate to changes in health? Since the answer to this question is clearly affirmative, we can now move on to the question: how does life stress relate to changes in health? The purpose of this chapter has been to indicate some of the procedures that we believe will help to answer this question. We argued, first, for development of quantitative estimates of relations between various aspects of life events and different kinds of health changes. Second, we proposed that the conception of the nature of these relations be expanded in terms of a life-stress process composed of life events and the psychological and social contexts in which they occur. Finally, we suggested some alternative hypotheses about this process to be tested against each other.

Acknowledgments

The work reported in this chapter has been supported in part by Research Scientist Award K05-MH 14663 from the National Institute of Mental Health, U.S. Public Health Service, and by the Foundations' Fund for Research in Psychiatry.

References

Ander, S., Lindstrom, B., & Tibblin, G. (1974), Life changes in random samples of middle-aged men. In: *Life stress and illness*, ed. E. K. G. Gunderson & R. H. Rahe. Springfield, Ill.: Charles C Thomas, pp. 121–124.

Andrews, G., Tennant, C., Hewson, D. M., & Vaillant, G. E. (1978), Life event stress, social support, coping style, and risk of psychological impairment. *J. Nerv. Ment. Dis.*, 166:307–317.

Appley, M. H. & Trumbull, R. (1967), On the concept of psychological stress. In: *Psychological stress*, ed. M. H. Appley & R. Trumbull. New York: Appleton.

Askenasy, A. R., Dohrenwend, B. P., & Dohrenwend, B. S. (1977), Some effects of social class and ethnic group membership on judgments of the magnitude of stressful life events: a research note. *J. Hlth. Soc. Behav.*, 18:432–439.

Bandura, A. & Walters, R. H. (1963), *Social Learning and Personality Development*. New York: Holt, Rinehart, & Winston.

Bloom, B. L. (1977), *Community Mental Health.* Monterey, Calif.: Brooks/Cole.

Bornstein, P. E., Clayton, P. J., Halikas, J. A., Maurice, W. L., & Robins, E. (1973), The depression of widowhood after thirteen months. *Brit. J. Psychiat.*, 122:561–566.

Brown, G. W. (1974), Meaning, measurement, and stress of life events. In: *Stressful Life Events: their nature and effects*, ed. B. S. Dohrenwend & B. P. Dohrenwend. New York: Wiley, pp. 217–243.

Brown, G. W., & Harris, T. (1978), *Social origins of depression: a study of psychiatric disorder in women.* New York: The Free Press.

Brown, J. & Rawlinson, M. (1976), The morale of patients following open-heart surgery. *J. Hlth. Soc. Behav.*, 17:135–145.

Campbell, A., Converse, P. E., & Rodgers, W. L. (1976), *The Quality of American Life.* New York: Russell Sage Foundation.

Cannon, W. B. (1929), *Bodily Changes in Pain, Hunger, Fear and Rage.* New York: D. Appleton and Company.

Caplan, G. (1976), The family as a support system. In: *Support Systems and Mutual Help: Multidisciplinary Explorations*, ed. G. Caplan & M. Killilea. New York: Grune & Stratton, pp. 19–36.

Caplan, G., & Killilea, M. (eds.). (1976), *Support Systems and Mutual Help: Multidisciplinary Explorations.* New York: Grune & Stratton.

Carveth, W. B. & Gottlieb, B. H. (1979), The measurement of social support and its relation to stress. *Canad. J. Behav. Sci.*, 11:179–188.

Cobb, S. (1976), Social support as a moderator of life stress. *Psychosom. Med.*, 38:300–314.

Cohen, F. & Lazarus, R. S. (1973), Active coping processes, coping dispositions, and recovery from surgery. *Psychosom. Med.*, 35:375–389.

Crandall, J. E. & Lehman, R. E. (1977), Relationship of stressful life events to social interest, locus of control and psychological adjustment. *J. Coun. Clin. Psychol.*, 45:1208.

Croog, S. H. (1970), The family as a source of stress. In: *Social Stress*, ed. S. Levine & N. Scotch. Chicago, Ill.: Aldine, pp. 19–53.

Dohrenwend, B. P. (1974), Problems in defining and sampling the relevant population of stressful life events. In: *Stressful Life Events: Their Nature and Effects*, ed. B. S. Dohrenwend & B. P. Dohrenwend. New York: Wiley, pp. 275–310.

Dohrenwend, B. P. (1979), Stressful life events and psychopathology: some issues of theory and method. In: *Stress and Mental Disorder*, ed. J. E. Barrett, R. M. Rose, & G. L. Klerman. New York: Raven Press, pp. 1–15.

Dohrenwend, B. P., & de Figurerido, J. M. (1980), Remote and recent life events and psychopathology. In: *Life History Research in Psychopathology*, ed. D. Ricks & B. S. Dohrenwend. New York: Cambridge University Press, in press.

Dohrenwend, B. S. (1973), Life events as stressors: a methodological inquiry. *J. Hlth. Soc. Behav.*, 14:167–175.

Dohrenwend, B. S. (1977), Anticipation and control of stressful life events: an exploratory analysis. In: *Origins and Course of Psychopathology*, ed. J. S. Strauss, H. M. Babigian, & M. Roff. New York: Plenum, pp. 135–186.

Dohrenwend, B. S., & Dohrenwend, B. P. (1974), Overview and prospects for research on stressful life events. In: *Stressful Life Events: Their Nature and Effects*, ed. B. S. Dohrenwend & B. P. Dohrenwend. New York: Wiley, pp. 313–331.

Dohrenwend, B. S., & Dohrenwend, B. P. (1978), Some issues in research on stressful life events. *J. Nerv. Ment. Dis.*, 166:7–15.

Dohrenwend, B. S., Krasnoff, L., Askenasy, A. R., & Dohrenwend, B. P. (1978), Exemplification of a method for scaling life events: the PERI life events scale. *J. Hlth Soc. Behav.*, 19:205–229.

Dohrenwend, B. S., & Martin, J. L. (1979), Personal versus situational determination of anticipation and control of the occurrence of stressful life events. *Amer. J. Commun. Psychol.*, 7:453–468.

Eaton, W. W. (1978), Life events, social supports, and psychiatric symptoms: a re-analysis of the New Haven data. *J. Hlth. Soc. Behav.*, 19:230–234.

Engel, G. L. (1971), Sudden and rapid death during psychological stress, folklore or folkwisdom? *Ann. Intern. Med.*, 74:771–782.

Epley, S. W. (1974), Reduction of the behavioral effects of aversive stimulation by the presence of companions. *Psychol. Bull.*, 81:271–283.

Epstein, S. & Fenz, W. D. (1967), The detection of areas of emotional stress through variations in perceptual threshold and physiological arousal. *J. Exper. Res. Personality*, 2:191–199.

Fischer, C. S., Jackson, R. M., Stueve, C. A., Gerson, K., McCallister Jones, L., & Baldassare, M. (1977), *Networks and Places: Social Relations in the Urban Setting*. New York: Free Press.

Fontana, A. F., Marcus, J. L., Noel, B., & Rakusin, J. M. (1972), Prehospitalization coping styles of psychiatric patients: the goal-directedness of life events. *J. Nerv. Ment. Dis.*, 155:311–321.

Fox, B. H. (1978), Premorbid psychological factors as related to cancer incidence. *J. Behav. Med.*, 1:45–133.

Friedman, M. & Rosenman, R. H. (1974), *Type A Behavior and Your Heart.* New York: Fawcett Crest Books.

Garrity, T. F., Marx, M. B., & Somes, G. W. (1977), Langner's 22-item measure of psychophysiological strain as an intervening variable between life change and health outcome. *J. Psychosom. Res.*, 21:195–199.

Gersten, J. C., Langner, T. S., Eisenberg, J. G., & Simcha-Fagan, O. (1977), An evaluation of the etiologic role of stressful life-change events in psychological disorders. *J. Hlth. Soc. Behav.*, 18:228–244.

Glass, D. C. (1977), *Behavior Patterns, Stress and Coronary Disease.* Hillsdale, N.J.: Lawrence Erlbaum Associates.

Gore, S. (1978), The effect of social support on moderating the health consequences of unemployment. *J. Hlth. Soc. Behav.*, 19:157–165.

Granville-Grossman, K. L. (1960), The early environment in affective disorder. *Brit. J. Psychiat.*, Special Publication, No. 2, 65–79.

Gurin, G., Veroff, J., & Feld, S. (1960), *Americans View Their Mental Health.* New York: Basic Books.

Hamburg, D. & Adams, J. (1967), A perspective on coping behavior: seeking and utilizing information in major transitions. *Arch. Gen. Psychiat.*, 17:277–284.

Hinkle, L. E., Jr. (1973), The concept of "stress" in the biological and social sciences. *Soc. Sci. Med.*, 1:31–48.

Hinkle, L. E., Jr. (1974), The effect of exposure to culture change, social change, and changes in interpersonal relationships on health. In *Stressful Life Events: Their Nature and Effects*, ed. B. S. Dohrenwend & B. P. Dohrenwend. New York: Wiley, pp. 9–44.

Holmes, T. H. & Masuda, M. (1974), Life change and illness susceptibility. In: *Stressful Life Events: Their Nature and Effects*, ed. B. S. Dohrenwend & B. P. Dohrenwend. New York: Wiley, pp. 45–72.

Holmes, T. H. & Rahe, R. H. (1967), The social readjustment rating scale. *J. Psychosom. Res.*, 11:213–218.

Horowitz, M. J. (1976), *Stress Response Syndromes.* New York: Jason Aronson.

Hudgens, R. W. (1974), Personal catastrophe and depression: a consideration of the subject with respect to medically ill adolescents, and a requiem for retrospective life-event studies. In: *Stressful Life Events: Their Nature and Effects*, ed. B. S. Dohrenwend & B. P. Dohrenwend. New York: Wiley, pp. 119–134.

Johnson, J. H. & Sarason, I. G. (1978), Life stress, depression and anxiety: internal-external control as a moderator variable. *J. Psychosom. Res.*, 22:205–208.

Kaplan, B. H., Cassel, J. C., & Gore, S. (1977), Social support and health. *Med. Care*, Supplement, 15(5):47–58.

Kendall, P. C., Finch, A. J., Jr., Auerbach, S. M., Hooke, J. F., & Mikulka, P. J. (1976), The State-Trait Anxiety Inventory: a systematic evaluation. *J. Counsel. Clin. Psychol.*, 44:406–412.

Langner, T. S. (1962), A twenty-two item screening score of psychiatric symptoms indicating impairment. *J. Hlth. Hum. Behav.*, 3:269–276.

Langner, T. S. & Michael, S. T. (1963), *Life Stress and Mental Health.* New York: Free Press.

Lazarus, R. S. (1966), *Psychological Stress and the Coping Process.* New York: McGraw-Hill.

Lazarus, R. S., & Launier, R. (1978), Stress-related transactions between person and environment. In: *Perspectives in Interactional Psychology*, ed. L. A. Pervin & M. Lewis. New York: Plenum, pp. 287-327.

Lefcourt, H. M. (1976), *Locus of Control: Current Trends on Theory and Research*. New York: Lawrence Erlbaum Associates.

Link, B. (1978), On the etiological role of stressful life-change events (comment on Gersten et al., September 1977). *J. Hlth. Soc. Behav.*, 19:343-345.

Lipowsky, S. J. (1975), Psychiatry of somatic diseases: epidemiology, pathogenesis, classification. *Comp. Psychiat.*, 16:105-124.

Litwak, E. & Szelenyi, I. (1969), Primary group structures and their functions: kin, neighbors and friends. *Amer. Sociol. Rev.*, 34:465-481.

Lorimer, R. J., Justice, B., McBee, G. W., & Weinman, M. (1979), Weighting events in life-events research (comment on Dohrenwend et al., June 1978). *J. Hlth. Soc. Behav.*, 20:306-307.

Matthews, K. A., Glass, D. C., Rosenman, R. H., & Bortner, R. W. (1977), Competitive drive, pattern A, and coronary heart disease: a further analysis of some data from the Western Collaborative Group Study. *J. Chron. Dis.*, 30:489-498.

Mechanic, D. (1962), *Students Under Stress: A Study in the Social Psychology of Adaptation*. New York: Free Press.

Miller, F. T., Bentz, W. K., Aponte, J. F., & Brogan, D. R. (1974), Perception of life crisis events: a comparative study of rural and urban samples. In: *Stressful Life Events: Their Nature and Effects*, ed. B. S. Dohrenwend & B. P. Dohrenwend. New York: Wiley, pp. 259-273.

Miller, P. M., Ingham, J. G., & Davidson, S. (1976), Life events, symptoms and social support. *J. Psychosom. Res.*, 20:515-522.

Mueller, D. P., Edwards, D. W., & Yarvis, R. M. (1977), Stressful life events and psychiatric symptomatology: change or undesirability? *J. Hlth. Soc. Behav.*, 18:307-317.

Mulvey, M. A. (1979), The relationship of life events, gender and age: a community study of adulthood. Ph.D. dissertation, The City University of New York.

Paykel, E. S. (1974), Life stress and psychiatric disorder: applications of the clinical approach. In: *Stressful Life Events: Their Nature and Effects*, ed. B. S. Dohrenwend & B. P. Dohrenwend. New York: Wiley, pp. 135-149.

Paykel, E. S., Prusoff, B. A., & Uhlenhuth, E. H. (1971), Scaling of life events. *Arch. Gen. Psychiat.*, 25:340-347.

Paykel, E. S. & Uhlenhuth, E. H. (1972), Rating the magnitude of life stress. *Canad. Psychiat. Assn. J.*, 17:5593-55100.

Rabkin, J. G. & Struening, E. L. (1976), Life events, stress, and illness. *Science*, 194:1013-1020.

Rahe, R. H. (1974), The pathway between subjects' recent life changes and their near-future illness reports: Representative results and methodological issues. In: *Stressful Life Events: Their Nature and Effects*, ed. B. S. Dohrenwend & B. P. Dohrenwend. New York: Wiley, pp. 73-86.

Rahe, R. H. & Arthur, R. J. (1978), Life change and illness studies: past history and future directions. *J. Hum. Stress*, 4:3-15.

Redfield, J. & Stone, A. (1979), Individual viewpoints of stressful life events. *J. Coun. Clin. Psychol.*, 47:147-154.

Ross, C. E. & Mirowsky, J., II. (1979), A comparison of life-event-weighting schemes: change, undesirability, and effect-proportional indices. *J. Hlth. Soc. Behav.*, 20:166-177.

Rotter, J. B. (1966), Generalized expectancies for internal versus external control of reinforcement. *Psychol. Monogr.*, 80(609).

Rutter, M. (1974), *The Qualities of Mothering: Maternal Deprivation Reassessed.* New York: Jason Aronson.

Schmale, A. H. (1972), Giving up as a final common pathway to changes in health. *Adv. Psychosom. Med.*, 8:20–40.

Seligman, M. E. P. (1975), *Helplessness: On Depression, Development, and Death.* San Francisco: W. H. Freeman.

Spielberger, C. D., Gorsuch, R. C., & Lushene, R. E. (1970), *Manual for the State-Trait Anxiety Inventory.* Palo Alto, California: Consulting Psychologists Press.

Tennant, C. & Andrews, G. (1978), The cause of life events in neurosis. *J. Psychosom. Res.*, 22:41–45.

Tennant, C. & Bebbington, P. (1978), The social causation of depression: a critique of the work of Brown and his colleagues. *Psychosom. Med.*, 8:565–575.

Theorell, T. (1974), Life events before and after the onset of a premature myocardial infarction. In: *Stressful Life Events: Their Nature and Effects,* ed. B. S. Dohrenwend & B. P. Dohrenwend. New York: Wiley, pp. 101–117.

Theorell, T. (1976), Selected illness and somatic factors in relation to two psychosocial stress indices—a prospective study in middle-aged construction building workers. *J. Psychosom. Res.*, 20:7–20.

Thurlow, H. J. (1971), Illness in relation to life situation and sick-role tendency. *J. Psychosom. Res.*, 15:73–88.

Vinokur, A. & Selzer, M. L. (1975), Desirable versus undesirable life events: their relationship to stress and mental distress. *J. Pers. Soc. Psychol.*, 32:329–337.

Wolff, H. G., Wolf, S. G., Jr., & Hare, C. C. (eds.) (1950), *Life Stress and Bodily Disease.* Baltimore: Williams and Wilkins.

Zubin, J. Spring, B. (1977), Vulnerability—a new view of schizophrenia. *J. Abnorm. Psychol.*, 86:103–126.

Zyzanski, S. J. & Jenkins, C. D. (1970), Basic dimensions within the coronary-prone behavior pattern. *J. Chron. Dis.*, 22:781–795.

Conceptualization and Measurement
of Stressful Life Events

Explicit conceptualization and systematic measurement of stressful life events was initiated by Holmes and Rahe with their 1967 publication of the Social Readjustment Rating Scale. This scale and others of the same type developed subsequently have been widely adopted as research instruments. At the same time, a variety of methodological problems concerning conceptualization and measurement of stressful life events have emerged from critical analyses of these studies. These problems are addressed in this section.

In the next chapter Patrick E. Shrout deals with the theory and method underlying alternative procedures for deriving weights for life events, and discusses the conditions under which these weights are useful. Next, Richard Rahe raises questions about earlier work on life-event weighting, including his own, and proposes the Subjective Life Event Unit Scaling technique as an alternative. He then reports results from a study of the effects of life events in which this technique was used.

Fairbank and Hough review studies of group differences in ratings of life events. They argue that investigations on this topic will be more productive if they are based on explicit conceptualization of psychosocial processes underlying these group differences.

Studies concerning the effects of stressful life events depend on reports by subjects of the events that they have experienced. Richard Neugebauer reviews the evidence concerning the accuracy of this reporting and presents a clarification of the problem. John E. Helzer relates the study of life stress to research on extreme situations. He reports results concerning the effects of one such situation, American military service in Vietnam. In this study he anticipates the next section by introducing the concept of personal predisposition as a component of the life-stress process.

Scaling of Stressful Life Events

PATRICK E. SHROUT

The fact that health can be affected by life events is becoming well accepted. Research on the general relationship between life events and health changes, however, is complicated by the multivariate nature of the problem; in order to characterize the general relationship a very large number of specific events must be considered. One strategy used to avoid these difficulties is to limit research to a single event, such as divorce, that has considerable significance in its own right. Another strategy is to include a large list of events in the research study, but to extract from this list a single index which can be studied in relation to health variables. The simplest index of this kind is a count of life events experienced by a person within a specified period of time. In what is now a classic paper, Holmes and Rahe (1967) suggested a more intricate index which is formed by weighting life events according to the degree of social adjustment each event requires, and by summing these weights for the events experienced by a person within a specified period of time. In order to obtain social readjustment weights, Holmes and Rahe devised a procedure for scaling life events.

In this chapter I review the rationale for the use of a weighted life-event index instead of an unweighted index and then discuss the possible interpretations of the weighted indices and the assumptions made in forming such indices. Finally, I will review the issues involved in choosing a scaling procedure for future life event scaling.

Weighted Indices vs. an Unweighted Index

What advantage does the use of a weighted life-event index offer over the unweighted count of life events? Holmes and Rahe (1967) stated that weights should be associated with life events "to bring greater precision to this area of research and to provide a quantitative basis for new epidemiologic studies of diseases" (p. 213). Precision in this context may mean both predictive, empirical precision and also conceptual precision. One might assume that if a life-event index incorporates more information, it should be more highly predictive of health indices than cruder indices. Moreover,

29

since weights allow theoretically important events to be distinguished from less important events it might be possible to define conceptually what it is about life events that relates them to health.

The disadvantage of using life-event weights are (1) determining the weights involves time-consuming and expensive research, and (2) under many circumstances the weighted indices are almost identical to the simple unweighted index. This last point, which has been raised by Lorimer et al. (1979), makes the cost of weighting events even more serious; let us consider this second point first.

Let u stand for an unweighted life-event index for a person who has filled out an extensive life-event checklist; this is simply the sum of the checks made by the respondent. Let w be a weighted life-event index for the same person, computed by summing the weights associated with the events checked. If we assume that the events occur independently, and that the occurrence of events has the same variability across events [assumptions consistent with Brown (1973), for example], we can describe the expected correlation between the weighted and unweighted index as

$$\rho_{wu} = \sqrt{\frac{1}{(\sigma_w/\overline{w})^2 + 1}} \qquad (1)$$

where ρ_{wu} is the expected correlation between w, the weighted index, and u, the unweighted index, and where σ_w and w are the standard deviation and mean of the weights. A more general form of this formula can be found in Ghiselli (1964). Notice from equation 1 that if the standard deviation of the weights is small relative to the mean of the weights, ρ_{wu} approaches one. This is reasonable since a small standard deviation indicates that the weights are similar to each other, and thus are like unit weights. If, on the other hand, σ_w is large relative to the mean of the weights, ρ_{wu} will approach zero.

Thus, in order to make the weighted index distinct from the simpler unweighted index, weights must be found which have a wide range, but a small average magnitude. One way to achieve this ideal is to use weights, half of which are negative and half of which are positive. In actual practice, however, life-event weights have been established using scaling techniques described by Holmes and Rahe (1967) which produce only positive values; the resulting correlations between weighted and unweighted indices tend to be of the order of 0.90. With strictly positive weights the only way to increase weight variability without increasing the mean is to introduce life events with weights near zero. I will return to this idea in the next section when I discuss the conceptual advantages offered by the determination of weights by scaling.

A straightforward method for weighting life events in a way that allows negative weights (and hence lowers the weighted index-unweighted index correlation) is the application of standard multiple regression techniques. If, for example, one wished to estimate weights for 100 life events that could be used to relate the events to a given health index, one could collect from a very large sample of persons (say 2000 or more) information concerning their health and the occurrence or nonoccurrence of the 100 life events within a specified period. Presuming that each of the 100 life events occurred to at least one subject, the occurrence-nonoccurrence of life events could be assigned dummy variable codes of 1/0, and least squares estimation could be used to estimate life-event scale values (i.e., weights) in the metric of the health index used. With so many coefficients being estimated, presumably one would want to verify the estimates on another random sample of the same size. Statistically speaking, this least squares procedure produces weights that optimally predict the health index of interest. Thus, such weights will provide predictive precision, but they will not necessarily provide conceptual precision since the interpretation of the weights is post hoc. Moreover, in the context of a change theory of life events, it is unclear how negative weights could be interpreted, since by definition there cannot be negative change. The very presence of negative weights would require a new perspective on the mechanism of the effect of life events on health. No doubt because the regression method of estimating life event weights is expensive due to the sample sizes needed, it has been utilized rarely. However, this approach offers some advantages and it deserves more attention in future research.

If weights are all constrained to be positive, or if all are estimated to be positive by regression, the criticism that weighted indices do not add much to unweighted indices will have to be confronted. Since it might be possible to construct an unweighted index that has the same predictive precision as a weighted index (see Dawes, 1979), the argument for weighting will have to stem from the conceptual precision offered by weighted indices.

The challenge in using weighted indices is to establish weights that add conceptual clarity to the effects of life events, and that, at the same time, produce an index that is minimally correlated with the unweighted index. In the next section I will discuss how weighted events might be used to provide conceptual clarity to the relationship between life events and illness.

Interpretations and Assumptions of Weighted Life Event Indices

The Readjustment Life Event Index—The weighting of life events before combining them into an index is a mechanism for specifying which events are more important and which events are less important in terms of health. Importance can be defined conceptually, or empirically as discussed in the last section; the advance offered by Holmes and Rahe (1967) was that weights were derived from a theory of how life events affect health. Thus, these authors hypothesized that life events fall on a common continuum, and that this characteristic of life events is responsible for the onset of illness. They describe this common characteristic as follows:

The occurrence of each [life event] usually evoked or was associated with some adaptive or coping behavior on the part of the involved individual. Thus, each item has been constructed to contain life events whose advent is either indicative of or requires a significant change in the ongoing life pattern of the individual. The emphasis is on change from the existing steady state and not on psychological meaning, emotion, or social desirability. (P. 217)

Given the hypothesis that change due to life events causes illness, Holmes and Rahe (1967) were able to produce weights for each of 43 life events by having a group of raters scale the events according to the social readjustment each required. Because it was assumed that the true scale values are universal, this strategy does not require that the life events of the raters be studied. Note that relative to the multiple regression method of obtaining weights, the scaling of life events is very economical. More importantly, the scaling strategy involves a conceptual hypothesis; if an index formed using readjustment weights is more predictive of illness than indices formed using other weights, we know that it is indeed the readjustment required by life events that affects health.

The possibility of sharpening life-event theory is the greatest advantage of the scaling approach to life-event weights, but this advantage seems to get lost in much of the life-event literature. Indeed, it is common to see Holmes and Rahe's readjustment scale scores referred to as "magnitudes" without reference to the underlying dimension. Nor is it commonly recognized that the scaling approach to weighted-index construction involves a number of assumptions that affect the success of the index as a predictor of health status. Let us briefly review some of these assumptions and their implications.

Assumptions in the Scaling of Life Events—A basic assumption in Holmes and Rahe's strategy is that readjustment is such a salient dimension underlying life events that raters can unambiguously place all events on this dimension. It is also assumed that the scale values are universal, or at least consistent for individuals within a single population. (For a discussion of this assumption see Dohrenwend and Dohrenwend, 1978, and the chapter by Rahe in this volume.) That readjustment is an identifiable dimension of life events and that scale values are consistently assigned within a population can be tested by assessing the consensus among raters within a specified population and also by testing consensus between populations. It might also be worthwhile to use multidimensional scaling procedures in order to determine the salience of the readjustment dimension.

When scaling life events, researchers not only assume that the readjustment dimension is salient, they often implicitly assume that it is the *only* salient dimension of life events that is related to health status. As stated above, the fact that the use of readjustment weights implies a hypothesis about life events is often forgotten. There may in fact be another dimension, perhaps correlated with readjustment, that is more strongly related to health status. (The empirical multiple regression strategy might reveal such a dimension.) Since the use of readjustment scales as weights does imply a theory of life events, conceptual precision in the use of such scales is important. For example, while some researchers tend to use "readjustment," "change," and "stressfulness" interchangeably, Stone and Neale (1976) found that life-event ratings of "readjustment" differed consistently from ratings of "stressfulness." Which term is most appropriate is an empirical question.

As an example of the conceptual subtleties involved in using rating-scale weights, consider the hypothesis that stress affects health. One version of this hypothesis is that stress is a physiological process with physical and biochemical correlates and that health status changes as a result of physiological changes. Other versions of the hypothesis involve a more psychological interpretation of stress: that stress is a state of mind. The use of life-event weights derived from "stressfulness" ratings is more consistent with the latter hypothesis, since the weights reflect *perceived* stressfulness rather than a physiological measure of stress. Moreover, it is well known to psychophysicists that perceptions of a physical dimension tend to have a monotonic but nonlinear relationship with the actual dimension. Thus, if stress is in fact a biochemical or physiological process

that increases the risk of various dysfunctions through some physical mechanism, then the use of weights based on perceived stress
may result in an underestimate of the true relationship. If, on the
other hand, the effect of stress on health is mediated through
cognitive processes, then the use of weights based on perceived
stress may be appropriate.

Suppose that ratings of stressfulness are successfully collected for
a series of life events, and one is content to use perceived stress as a
construct. A major assumption in the construction of an index is
that the stress process is affected additively by life events. That is,
stress caused by a single severely stressful event can also be caused
by a combination of several less stressful events that occur simultaneously. Such an assumption implies that the scale values for the
life events has a consistent metric as well as an absolute zero (i.e., a
value for "no change"), which is to say that the life event weights
must form a *ratio scale* (Torgerson, 1958). This assumption will
have strong implications with regard to a choice of scaling methods,
as will be discussed later.

The explicit form of the additively weighted index is

$$W_i = X_{1i}\, b_1 + X_{2i} b_2 + \ldots + X_{pi} b_p \,, \qquad (2)$$

where W_i is the index for person i, $b_1, b_2 \ldots b_p$ are weights for the p
life events being studied, and $X_{1i}, X_{2i}, \ldots X_{pi}$ are dummy variables
for person i reflecting the occurrence ($X = 1$) or nonoccurrence
($X = 0$) of the p events within some specified period. Given that the
weights, $b_1 \ldots b$, are completely derived, equation 2 can be viewed
as a mathematical model of some process. For example, if the
weights correspond to stressfulness, and if we know what events a
person has experienced, then W_i in equation 2 is an estimate of how
much stress a person is experiencing.

There are several implications of our acceptance of equation 2 as
a model of the amount of stress a person experiences. A major one is
that the list of life events must be complete; if any event that adds to
stress is not included, our estimate of stress for the persons who
experience that event will be inaccurate. In this context, it is clear
that the notion of a "sample of life events" is misapplied to research
on stress. Since life events are largely independent of each other, we
cannot make any inferences about some life events based on
information about others for a given person. If major events are not
included on a life-event list, there may be considerable error in the
estimates of W from equation 1, and these inaccuracies could result

in a substantial underestimate of the relationship between W_i and some health index, say H_i.

While a conceptual interpretation of the weighted index in equation 2 argues for a complete list of life events in research, such a list would contain events that would obscure the causal relationship between events and health status. As Dohrenwend and Dohrenwend (1974, 1978) have pointed out, there are numerous life events that can be caused by illness (e.g., sexual difficulties or loss of job). Since these events themselves presumably add to the stress a person experiences, there exists a feedback loop between life events and health status. Clearly, the inclusion of such events in equation 2 would result in the overestimation of the causal impact of stress on illness, yet the elimination of such events from equation 2 would result in the underestimation of stress and consequently the under-estimation of the causal impact of stress. The lack of an adequate solution to this confounding remains a central unsolved problem in research involving life-event indices.

Construct Validation of Weighted Life-Event Indices—In the previous sections I have argued that the principal justification for the use of weighted indices over an unweighted index is that the former allow an investigation of characteristics of life events. As I have noted, if it is possible to show that an index formed using stress weights is more highly related to health status than other combinations of life events, we have a substantial support for the stress hypothesis. However, we have seen that unweighted life-event scores tend to correlate very highly with weighted indices; thus, it appears that gaining support for one weighting scheme over another will prove very difficult.

In the first section we saw that in order to reduce the correlation between weighted and unweighted indices the variance of the weights must be increased relative to the mean of the weights. When all weights have the same sign, this can be accomplished by adding multiple weights that are near zero. Hence, if we are interested in demonstrating that it is the stressful nature of events that causes illness, we must add to our list of events items such as "defrosted the refrigerator or freezer," "went to a movie," and "temporarily lost electricity in a storm"—items that one would expect are much less stressful than items in the Holmes and Rahe (1967) or Dohrenwend et al. (1978) lists. Note that the addition of such events will not much affect the weighted life-event index, since these events would be weighted near zero. A number of these items, however, would add considerable variance to the unweighted index.

The elimination of life events from a research list can be viewed as another way of weighting events, in which all eliminated events have weights of exactly zero. Thus, when Holmes and Rahe (1967) limited the events in their list to those "whose advent is indicative of or requires a significant change in the ongoing life pattern of the individual," they precluded an effective demonstration that readjustment was an important factor in life events, since in both the weighted and unweighted indices events requiring little readjustment were effectively weighted zero. If it is possible to show that readjustment is the crucial variable in life events, the research lists of life events may be shortened by eliminating low readjustment events *after* they have been scaled. An unweighted index of the remaining events would probably work as well as a weighted index after this elimination. Because there is evidence that the perceived stressfulness of events varies from culture to culture (Hough et al., 1976; Askenasy et al., 1977; Dohrenwend et al., 1978), the tailoring of life-event lists should be culture specific, based on separate scaling of events for each culture.

Scaling of Life Events: A Comparison of Methods

Ideally, when the stressfulness of life events is assessed in new populations, it would be done with a standardized method that would facilitate cross-cultural comparison. Unfortunately, a consensus on method does not exist. While the magnitude estimation technique used by Holmes and Rahe has been adopted by some researchers such as Dohrenwend and her colleagues (1978) in their study of New York City residents, Paykel et al. (1971), used a 21-point categorical scaling in a study of Chicago and New Haven patients, and Wainer et al. (1978) used a 10-category scale in a study of Mexicans and Americans. Because the comparison of scales derived from the various populations is of considerable interest, one must confront the question of how these different methods affect the resulting scales, and how scales derived from different methods ought to relate to each other. Moreover, since there is a continued need for the investigation of yet other populations, a question of some importance is which scaling method should be used in future research. In order to approach these questions, let us consider the methods that have been used.

Magnitude Estimation—The Magnitude Estimation (ME) method used by Holmes and Rahe (1967) requires subjects to assign scale values directly to stimuli (life events) with no restriction on range of numbers used. In order to give the scale a metric, one stimulus is arbitrarily assigned a number by the investigator (in the method of Holmes and Rahe, marriage was always assigned 500); theoretically this standard is used by the subjects to assign ratio scale values to the other stimuli. For example, if moving to a worse neighborhood is perceived to be half as stressful as marriage, it is assigned 250; if death of a family member is twice as stressful as marriage, it is assigned 1000. Scale values resulting from such a process are considered rational, i.e., the scale does have a constant scale unit and the zero point is nonarbitrary.

When Holmes and Rahe applied this method to the scaling of life events, ME was not used by many researchers, although there is now a growing literature that strongly advocates its use (Stevens, 1966, 1972, 1975; Hamblin, 1974; Lodge et al., 1975). The validity of this technique in psychophysics has been established using dozens of sensory attributes, including such sensations as loudness, brightness, warmth, and taste. In general, the magnitudes reported by the subjects in these experiments follow Stevens's power law:

$$R = kS^b, \qquad (3)$$

where R is the magnitude of the response, S is the stimulus intensity and b and k are empirically determined constants. A large literature exists on the lawfulness of this function in psychophysics. Perhaps the most compelling evidence for the validity of equation 3 comes from so-called cross modality matching experiments in which subjects estimate the magnitude of stimuli in one modality (such as brightness) by adjusting the level of a stimulus in another modality (such as loudness). That subjects are willing to attempt to make a tone as loud as a light is bright is impressive in itself, since it might imply the existence of a subjective metric. More impressively, if independent experiments are done on the two modalities to determine the form of equation 3 for each, say $R_1 = kS_1^{b_1}$ for the first modality (manipulated by experimenter in the cross modality matching study) and $R_2 = kS_2^{b_2}$ for the second (adjusted by subject in the cross modality matching study) then it is possible to predict the cross modality matching power function:

$$S_2 = S_1^{b_1/b_2}, \qquad (4)$$

where S_1 and S_2 are the actual stimulus intensity of the sensory modalities. Since the parameters b_1 and b_2 are estimated in earlier experiments, the ratio b_1/b_2 can be predicted; in fact, in psychophysics these predictions are usually very good (Stevens, 1975), lending credence to the data collection method and the power law itself.

The application of these psychophysical techniques to social scaling is done by assuming that there exists on underlying social continuum analogous to the physical stimulus intensity. Thus, the validity of this method cannot be directly tested; as Lodge et al. (1975) noted in their article championing the use of ME, "Testing the validity of magnitude estimation scales of social variables is especially problematical because there is no physical continuum (criterion) whose intensities can be plotted against magnitude estimations. Lacking a relevant physical measure of the stimulus, one can not determine a power function for a social variable" (p. 618). These authors go on to argue that stimuli should be pretested to insure (a) that they are unidimensional, and (b) that they have an unambiguous ordinal progression. They also recommend techniques for both the estimation of the power function through the use of cross modality matching, and for the corrections of so-called regression biases (see Cross, 1974) which distort the magnitude scales.

Oddly enough, there has been little written in the life-event literature on the validity of or the methodological problems involved with ME, although this method has been used widely. Indeed, very little has been written that critically evaluates the use of ME in life event research. In their original article, Holmes and Rahe (1967) only noted that ME has been successfully used in psychophysics, and other researchers have simply followed the precedent set by Holmes and Rahe. Before this technique can be recommended for further life-event scaling, both conceptual and methodological issues must be examined carefully.

When we consider the rationale for weighting life events as discussed in the first part of this chapter, we might be struck by the congruence between the assumptions made in developing a life-event index and those made for ME. It is assumed that life-event scale scores correspond to a dimension which is consistent for members within a population and that the scale values themselves have an absolute zero and a constant metric. Similarly, ME requires that a "real" dimension exists analogous to a physical dimension, and the procedure theoretically produces ratio scale values. While this congruence between application and technique is impressive, the requirement made by ME that the underlying dimension be analogous to a physical dimension may be considerably more stringent than is warranted for life-event data. From the previous results on group differences in scale scores, it is clear that the "change" dimension is not analogous to a dimension such as pitch, which is indeed universal. Because ME is designed for unambiguous universal dimensions, it makes allowances for neither group nor individual difference. Moreover, since the basic power law in equation 3 contains no individual difference or error parameters, it is assumed that all subjects will conform to the same power function with constant b and k for a given dimension. These assumptions have been questioned even for sensory dimensions (see Cliff, 1973, for review), and they certainly seem questionable in life-event research, although they have not been tested formally. Methodological research is needed to evaluate these issues fully, including assessments of the unidimensionality of the change dimension in life-event lists, and also psychophysical cross modality matching experiments of the type suggested by Lodge et al. (1975), which would give estimates of the constants in equation 3.

Besides the theoretical characteristics of ME, one must consider practical problems which might arise from the use of this technique with nonstudent populations. As we have said, the attractiveness of ME is based largely on laboratory results of psychophysics experiments, but in such studies the subjects are usually highly trained and experienced with the method. Subjects in a general population study may find the task of assigning unbounded numbers to life events abstract and difficult. Indeed, Dohrenwend et. al in 1978 have reported that:

We have strong indications that many of our judges had serious problems in making these judgments. When the completed interviews were examined, 32 sets of ratings, disproportionately from lower-class judges, had to be discarded because the judges had not followed the rating instructions. The 32 judges were eliminated on the following evidence: 15 were dropped because their ratings were highly incomplete or appeared to at least two researchers to be arbitrary or grossly failing to follow instructions. Some of these 15 respondents gave seemingly rigid responses, like many 0's and 1,000's; others wrote "less than 500" and "more than 500" still others refused to accept the modulus "marriage" as 500 points, that is, they changed it to 1,000 points, to 20 points or to 0 points. One respondent claimed the modulus did not apply to him as he was single. Some respondents reported that the task was too difficult. (P. 218)

In political science, where ME is used more frequently than in the sociomedical sciences, researchers spend up to 20 minutes of a one-hour scaling session on training. Such a procedure would probably alleviate some of the difficulties that Dohrenwend et al. reported, but it would be very costly if applied to a general population survey. Stone and Neale (1976) attempted to provide ME practice for half of their subjects in a mail-survey study, but they suspected that the training instructions were not effective. Clearly the effectiveness of the practice can only be evaluated if it is ascertained that the practice itself is done properly, which probably only can be done by an investigator present during the data collection.

These practical difficulties are encountered in the simplest ME application with untrained subjects. As I mentioned earlier, it is usually of interest to collect even more elaborate data in order to test and correct for so-called regression biases, and in order to estimate the constants k and b in equation 2 (see Cross, 1974; Stevens, 1975). These more elaborate procedures involve cross modality matching in which subjects typically scaled length of lines using ME and also using a dynomometer handgrip response. Obviously, such additional tasks make the collection of data in the general population even more difficult.

In order to evaluate fully the appropriateness of ME for scaling life events, it will certainly be necessary to conduct more method-ologically rigorous studies that reduce subject error and provide information about the assumed sensory model (i.e., equation 3) (for methods of reducing error, see Stevens, 1975, chap. 9). The reduc-tion of subject variation is especially important, since the power law includes parameters for neither individual differences nor subject error. Insofar as individual differences exist (assuming that individ-uals are from the same population) after experimental rigor has been applied, ME may be judged to be inappropriate for life-event scaling. It might turn out that only some life events are judged as unscalable; in such a case the investigator must judge what is lost by the deletion of such events. In some cases, the answer will be clear: when one psychophysicist was told that some subjects rated "death of a child" as 1,000,000 (i.e., 2000 times more stressful than marriage), he remarked that trying to scale this item was like trying to scale a dynamite blast in an auditory psychophysics experiment. If ME or any scaling procedure fails for such important events as death, it is clear that the method must be reevaluated, not the use of the item.

Categorical Scaling—Perhaps the most commonly used measure-ment technique in the social sciences is categorical scaling (CS), a method that requires a subject to select a category from a finite set of categories arranged on a continuum. Among the types of scaling procedures involving categorical scales are Likert scales (see Torgerson, 1958, p. 47), and the seven- or nine-point bipolar adjectival scales of the kind associated with Osgood's Semantic Differential (e.g., Osgood et al., 1975). Scale values are typically obtained by assigning a sequence of numbers to the categories, assuming that the categories are equally spaced, and then averaging across individual (or across responses in a within-subject design). Like magnitude estimation (ME), this method assumes that the stimuli to be scaled can be unambiguously placed on a single dimension according to a given criterion. CS seems to be more easily administered (Rippere, 1976), than ME and is apparently easily analyzed.

Paykel et al. (1971) adopted a CS procedure in which 21 categories were used with the poles identified as "least upsetting" and "most upsetting." The scale scores they developed were simply mean category weights, averaged over the sample of 373 subjects. One common criticism raised against the use of mean category weights is that the necessary assumption that category intervals are equal is unjustified. Indeed, it is often the case that extreme categories are subjectively treated as being wider than categories in the center of the continuum. One way to overcome this problem is to assign scale values using an indirect scaling method such as Thurstone's law of categorical judgment (see Torgerson, 1958). Through the application of a set of distributional assumptions this model, and others like it, create a metric for the scale from information about subject variability. For example, two stimuli that are assigned to the same category or that are ordered inconsistently across subjects are considered to be very close on the scale, while two stimuli that are never assigned the same or overlapping categories are considered to be distant from each other on the scale. Thus, the unit of the scale is one based on discriminability between stimuli rather than on direct magnitude of the stimuli. The scale location is arbitrary, unlike ratio scales which have nonarbitrary zero points. Scales that have a fixed interval but an arbitrary zero point are commonly known as *interval scales* (Torgerson, 1958).

In a study of Mexicans and Mexican-Americans, Wainer et al. (1978) have used a seven-point categorical scale to measure "change" in a set of 95 life events, and have subsequently formed scale scores using an indirect method. The measurement model they used was a logistic latent trait model (Rasch, 1960) which has been shown by Andrich (1978) to be equivalent to a variation of Thurstone's law of categorical judgment.

An interesting aspect of this indirect scaling method is that it contains an internal check on the assumptions made by the model. The Rasch model assumes that there will be individual differences among the raters as well as among the items. While item differences are represented as scale positions, rater differences are expressed in terms of the point on the scale most often used by the rater. Thus, some raters might rate most items on the high end of the change scale while others might rate most items as not involving much change. If we were interested in describing rater differences, we might characterize these differences as "sensitivity to change." The Rasch model explicitly states that the proportion of subjects at a given "sensitivity" level who rate a given item as involving change can be predicted using a linear combination of subject and item parameters. Once these parameters are estimated, the predictions can be tested, giving a test of fit for the model. For example, if an item which has a high change estimate is not judged as involving change by some subjects who typically rate most items as involving change, the item (and perhaps the subjects) will be flagged as not fitting the Rasch model. Items which fit the Rasch model will in fact be unidimensional, and thus this model provides a test of a basic assumption made by any method for simple scaling of life events.

How appropriate is CS for life event research? On the theoretical level, there seem to be several shortcomings. First, the scale values are interval not ratio scales and thus they can not be directly used to construct stress index. Another shortcoming, in contrast to ME, is that there is no model such as equation 3 which allows us to relate perceived magnitude to "true" process magnitude. Indeed, the metric for CS is that from indirect scaling models which are based on subject variability—not even on perceived magnitude.

Given the conceptual shortcomings of an interval scale, why has categorical scaling been used by investigators of life events? The main attraction of this method is that the data collection method is simple and relatively efficient. Little training is needed since the poles of rating scale can be clearly identified, and because many subjects have some experience with CS format. When subject variability exists, it is utilized by such indirect scaling procedures as the Rasch model. If there was no subject variability, these indirect methods would produce a Guttman scale, with as many classes as there are categories on the data collection form. Moreover, the problem of establishing a nonarbitrary zero point can be overcome. Wainer et al. (1978) had subjects rate pairs of life events as well as single events using an interval scaling method. If the stressfulness of events is additive, then except for the arbitrary zero point, the stress scale score for event A and the scale score for event B should equal the stress scale score for the two events judged as a compound event. In algebraic terms we can denote this

$$(X_A + K) + (X_B + K) = (X_{AB} + K),$$

where X_A, X_B, and X_{AB} are the scale scores for events A, B, and the compound event AB, and where K is the constant which adjusts for the arbitrary zero point. Using this formula, it is easy to see that K can be estimated from $K + X_{AB} - (X_A + X_B)$. Once determined, this constant can be added to all obtained interval scale scores to transform them to ratio scale scores.

An attractive aspect of the indirect scaling method is that events that do not fit on the scaling model can be readily identified; among these would be items not scalable on a single stress dimension. Such items must be examined closely, since, as we noted in the ME section, they may be of central importance to the life-event research. Certainly, if important events rejected as unscalable by the Rasch model were accepted as scalable in an ME context for the same population, we would have to reject the indirect method rather than the item under consideration. If, however, a comparison of items rejected in the two methods revealed a common set of items, and if these items were crucial to life-event theory, one would have to question the basic assumption that there is a dimension of interest underlying the events.

Comparison of Scale Values Resulting from Magnitude Estimation and Categorical Scaling—Is it possible to compare direct scale values obtained using ME to indirect values obtained using CS? There have in fact been many comparisons of direct results and indirect scaling results, particularly for psychophysics applications (Stevens and Galanter, 1975; Galanter & Messick, 1961; Ekman and Kuennapas, 1962, 1963; Eisler, 1965; Shinn, 1974). The functional relationship between direct and indirect scales seems to depend on the so-called Weber function that describes the relationship of the level of the direct scale scores to the variability of the scores at that level. This function is denoted by $V = q + hR$, where R is the direct scale score, V is the expected variability of the scale scores at level R, and q and h are constants. When the Weber function holds with $h \neq O$, then Eisler has proposed the following relationship between direct and indirect scores:

$$C = \alpha \log [R + (q/h] + \beta, \tag{5}$$

where C is the indirect scale scores, R is the magnitude score, α and β are constants that set the unit and location of the indirect score, and q and h are constants from the Weber function given above. If h is zero (i.e., variability of magnitude scores = q), equation 5 is undefined; in this case the following function relates indirect and direct scale scores:

$$C = \alpha R + \beta, \tag{6}$$

where C, R, α, and β are defined as before (Shinn, 1974). Stevens calls continua for which equation 6 is appropriate "metathetic," as opposed to "prothetic" dimensions for which equation 5 is appropriate. Masuda and Holmes (1967) have reported that there is a linear relationship between the variability of item scores and the mean magnitude of such scores. This result could indicate that Weber's law holds in this case, and therefore we would expect equation 5 to describe the relationship between magnitude and category scales. Empirically, however, this expectation has not been observed. Ruch and Holmes (1971) compared direct and indirect scaling methods and found them to be linearly related, as in equation 6.

Regardless of whether equation 5 or 6 is appropriate, it is clear from either equation that indirect scale values can be readily computed from magnitude scales using arbitrary values for α and β. It is not possible, however, to compute a magnitude scale from an indirect scale unless the values α and β for that indirect scale are known. Of course, if researchers are able to estimate α and β, and if these estimates are shown to be stable, then it will be possible to transform scale values to make results from different scaling methods comparable. Methods presented by Wainer et al. (1978) and discussed earlier can be used to set α and β to nonarbitrary values for indirect methods.

Given that the functional relationship between categorical and magnitude scales is still ambiguous, which scaling method should the applied researcher use? On theoretical grounds, ME is probably to be preferred since it directly produces values with a consistent metric and a nonarbitrary zero. Practically, however, ME presents more difficulty to the subject than CS, and the underlying model makes no provision for subject error. Therefore, if ME is to be used, efforts should be made to make the subjects' task easier and to improve the quality of the data. Suggestions have been made in the literature concerning how ME scale values can be made more error-free (e.g., Stevens, 1975; Lodge et al., 1974); in addition to training subjects in ME, simple procedures such as allowing each subject to choose his own comparison event and modulus value (instead of assigning marriage = 500 for all subjects) improve scale quality.

If practical considerations preclude the use of ME training and careful administration, the resulting error in ME scale scores probably invalidates the method's theoretical advantages. In such a case, CS may be preferable, both in terms of ease of administration and in terms of the scale scores, which can be estimated taking into account subject variability. At this time, one method can not be recommended over the other in terms of construct validity, since one set of scale scores has been shown to predict various health indices more accurately than the other.

Summary and Conclusions

Although the literature on life-event scaling is more than a decade long, there has not been conclusive proof that weighted life-event indices are superior to unweighted counts of life events in predicting health status. Given this situation and the related problem that weighted and unweighted indices tend to be highly correlated, it might be tempting to dispense with the task of scaling life events and rely on unweighted life-event indices. In this chapter I have argued that such a move would be costly in terms of the conceptual analysis of life events. The only way to discover what it is about life events that makes them related to illness is to demonstrate that some kinds of events are more related to illness than other kinds of events and to characterize theoretically the difference in the two groups of events. This differentiation among events is precisely what is achieved by weighting.

Suggestions have been made concerning how weighted indices can be constructed so that the correlation with the corresponding unweighted index is reduced. The differences and similarities between the two most popular scaling procedures, magnitude estimation and category scaling, have been discussed. While each procedure has both advantages and disadvantages, magnitude estimation seems to be preferable if efforts can be made to reduce the error in the data collection.

What seems to be the future of scaling in life-event research? The immediate research challenge is to identify the characteristic of life events (stressfulness, readjustment, etc.) that conclusively accounts for the relationship between life events and illness. Such a challenge will undoubtedly involve life-event scaling and weighted indices. If and when this is done, scaling of life events will be necessary when new populations are investigated in order to identify the most important life events with regard to the characteristic identified. In fact, once these important life events are identified, little will be lost by simply using the unweighted number of these events as a life-event index, since this sum will be very highly correlated with the weighted index. It may be that in the long run, life-event scaling will have its principal use in the description of populations, and in the formation of sets of life events appropriate for each population, rather than in determining weights for weighted indices.

References

Andrich, D. (1978), Relationships between Thurstone and Rasch approaches to item scaling. *Appl. Psychol. Measure.*, 2:449–460.

Askenasy, A., Dohrenwend, B. P. & Dohrenwend, B. S. (1977), Some effects of social class and ethnic group membership on judgments of the magnitude of stressful life events: A research note. *J. Hlth. Soc. Behav.*, 18:432–439.

Cliff, N. (1973), Scaling. *A. Rev. Psychol.*, 24:473–506.

Cross, D. V. (1974), Some technical notes on psychophysical scaling. In: *Sensation and Measurement: Papers in Honor of S. S. Stevens*, ed. H. Moskowitz. Dordrecht, Netherlands: Reidel, pp. 23–36.

Dawes, R. M. (1979), The robust beauty of improper linear models in decision making. *Amer. Psychologist*, 34:571–582.

Dohrenwend, B. S. & Dohrenwend, B. P. (1974), *Stressful Life Events: Their Nature and Effects*. New York: Wiley.

Dohrenwend, B. S. & Dohrenwend, B. P. (1978), Some issues in research on stressful life events. *J. Nerv. Ment. Dis.*, 166:7–15.

Dohrenwend, B. S., Krasnoff, L., Askenasy, A. R., & Dohrenwend, B. P. (1978), Exemplification of a method for scaling life events: The PERI life events scale. *J. Hlth Soc. Behav.*, 19:205–229.

Eisler, H. (1965), The connection between magnitude and discrimination scales and direct and indirect scaling methods. *Psychometrika*, 30:271–289.

Ekman, G. & Kuennapas, T. (1962), Measurement of aesthetic value by "direct" and "indirect" methods. *Scand. J. Psychol.*, 3:33–39.

Ekman, G. & Kuennapas, T. (1963), Further study of direct and indirect scaling methods. *Scand. J. Psychol.*, 4:77–80.

Galanter, E. H. & Messick, S. (1961). The relation between category and magnitude scales of loudness. *Psychol. Rev.*, 68:363–372.

Ghiselli, E. C. (1964), *Theory of Psychological Measurement*. New York: McGraw-Hill.

Hamblin, R. L. (1974), Social attitudes: Magnitude measurement and theory. In: *Measurement in the Social Sciences*, ed. H. M. Blalock, Jr. Chicago: Aldine, pp. 61–120.

Holmes, T. H. & Rahe, R. H. (1967), The social adjustment scale. *J. Psychosom. Med.*, 11:213–218.

Hough, R. L., Fairbank, D., & Garcia, A. M. (1976), Problems in the ratio measurement of life stress. *J. Hlth Soc. Behav.*, 17:70–82.

Lodge, M., Cross, D. V., Tursky, B., & Tanenhaus, J. (1975), The psychophysical scaling and validation of a political support scale. *Amer. J. Pol. Sci.*, 4:611–649.

Lorimor, R. J, Justice, B., McBee, G. W., & Weinman, M. (1979), Weighting events in life-event research. *J. Hlth Soc. Behav.*, 20:306–307.

Masuda, M. & Holmes, T. H. (1967), Magnitude estimations of social readjustments. *J. Psychosom. Res.*, 11:219–225.

Osgood, C. E., May, W. H., & Miron, M. S. (1975), *Cross-Cultural Universals of Affective Meaning.* Urbana: University of Illinois Press, 1975.

Paykel, E. S., Prusoff, B. A. C., & Uhlenhuth, E. H. (1971), Scaling of life events. *Arch. Gen. Psychiat.*, 25:340–347.

Rasch, G. (1960), *Probabilistic Models for Some Intelligence and Attainment Tests.* Copenhagen: Nielsen & Lydiche.

Rippere, V. (1976), Scaling the seriousness of illness: A methodological study. *J. Psychosom. Res.*, 20:567–573.

Ruch, L. O. & Holmes, T. H. (1971), Scaling of life change: Comparison of direct and indirect methods. *J. Psychosom. Res.*, 15:221–227.

Shinn, N. M., Jr. (1974), Relations between scales. In: *Measurement in the Social Sciences*, ed. H. M. Blalock, Jr. Chicago: Aldine, pp. 121–158.

Stevens, S. S. (1966), A metric for the social consensus. *Science*, 151:530–541.

Stevens, S. S. (1972), *Psychophysics and Social Scaling.* Morristown, N. J.: General Learning Press.

Stevens, S. S. (1975), *Psychophysics: Introduction to Its Perceptual, Neural and Social Prospects.* New York: Wiley.

Stevens, S. S. & Galanter, E. H. (1957), Ratio scales and category scales for a dozen perceptual continua. *J. Exp. Psychol.*, 54:377–411.

Stone, A. A. & Neale, J. M. (1976), Life event scales: psychophysical training and rating dimension effects on event weighting coefficients. Unpublished manuscript.

Torgerson, W. S. (1958), *Theory and Methods of Scaling.* New York: Wiley.

Wainer, H., Fairbank, D., & Hough, R. L. (1978), Predicting the impact of simple and compound life change events. *Appl. Psychol. Measure.*, 2:311–320.

Developments in Life Change Measurement: Subjective Life Change Unit Scaling

RICHARD H. RAHE

The observation that an individual's health may suffer following a wide variety of recent life stresses is nearly as old as the history of medicine itself. Writings from Greek and Babylonian times give several instances of such observations (Alexander and Selesnicky, 1966). Until the nineteenth century it was nearly axiomatic that physicians would evaluate their patients' life situations at the time of illness onset as part of a thorough medical examination. With the development of microbiology, twentieth century healers began to ignore the lessons of history and to think terms of microbial infection as a sufficient etiological condition for a number of disease entities. Even today, many diseases are thought to be entirely secondary to a recent environmental or microorganismic exposure rather than representing the interaction of one or more environmental agents of disease and a person's state of bodily resistance. Perhaps one of the more desirable impacts of recent life-change research has been a reestablishment in the minds of clinicians of the importance of life situation in the onset of most diseases.

Recent life-change events represent but one psychosocial dimension of an individual's life. That dimension obtains medical relevance when viewed in terms of the physiological model of homeostasis (Rahe, 1978). In the intact organism, environmental demands lead to both physiological and psychological adaptive consequences. The greater are the adaptive requirements made upon challenges, the greater are the adaptive requirements made upon the organism. Once adaptation has occurred, psychophysiological activation returns to prior or baseline levels. Thus, physiological activation with possible body dysfunction secondary to recent life-change stress occurs over a limited time span. Prolonged and/or frequently repeated stress can lead to permanent alteration in key physiological systems resulting in a wide variety of illness syndromes (Henry and Stephens, 1977).

48

Statistically significant associations between persons' recent life-change events and subsequent illness symptomatology have been found repeatedly (Rahe and Arthur, 1978). Although retrospective studies far outnumber prospectives ones, for 30 to 60 percent of subjects the relationship between recent life change and subsequent illness symptomatology is an impressive one (Gunderson and Rahe, 1974). Marked individual variability, along with some imprecision of the measures, have limited attempts to predict specific future illnesses in a large group of individuals. The goal of illness prediction remains, nonetheless.

The present chapter will first present an analogy of recent life-change events with the concept of a "risk factor" as used in epidemiology. Next, the chapter will focus on the current state of affairs in life-change measurement and scaling. Last, data will be presented from a recent study that assessed the utility of the Subjective Life Change Unit (SLCU) scaling system.

Life Change as a Risk Factor

In the field of epidemiology, a risk factor is a measureable aspect of person or environment that serves to identify those individuals in a population at higher risk to develop a disease than persons without the factor. Perhaps most familiar to us are risk factors that have been found to identify subsets of a population at increased risk for coronary heart disease (CHD). The most useful of such risk factors are cigarette smoking, serum cholesterol concentration, and blood pressure (The Pooling Project Research Group, 1978). Whereas one of these risk factors is associated with some increased CHD risk, two factors confer greater risk, and when a person has all three factors highest CHD proneness is found. Some overlap exists between these risk factors, and very few individuals in a population display all three factors.

Recent life change can be considered an environmental risk factor, in contrast to factors that represent constitutional or early life development characteristics of individuals. Recent life changes are temporary in their influence. Initial physiological activation following life change stress is time limited. Most individuals with high recent life-change totals do not remain at such levels for more than a year or two before returning to baseline levels which connote far less risk (Rahe, 1978).

Like CHD risk factors, recent life changes are disconcertingly nonspecific. Elevated serum cholesterol, for example, is not only a risk factor for CHD proneness but also identifies persons at high risk for death from all causes (Tiblin and Wilhelmsen, 1970). A student of psychology or sociology may well believe that elevated recent life change is a risk factor only for psychological disorders; in fact, initial validation studies were carried out with medical patients suffering from diseases as varied as tuberculosis and inguinal hernia. (Rahe et al., 1964).

Findings concerning life change, like those for other risk factors, are sometimes overgeneralized. For example, many more people who smoke cigarettes, or have elevated serum cholesterol levels, stay healthy over an extended follow-up period than go on to develop CHD (Rosenman et al., 1975). Similarly, as Paykel (1974) pointed out, most of the persons experiencing one of the most stressful of all life changes, death of a spouse, do not go on to develop a depression.

Risk factors can be influenced by disease processes. A recent heart attack may result in an abrupt increase in a patient's serum cholesterol level (Rahe, 1975b). Similarly, recent life changes have been shown to accrue secondarily to a recent illness, and to remain elevated over a period of a year or so before returning to baseline values (Rahe and Paasikivi, 1971).

Despite the above difficulties, the risk-factor concept remains alive and well. Combinations of psychosocial and physical risk factors may hold promise for disease prediction. Researchers also continue to search for possible refinements in life-change measurement. Oftentimes such explorations go in opposite directions. For example, some wish to restrict the number and kinds of life-change events inquired about, while others propose to increase the length of life change lists (Dohrenwend and Dohrenwend, 1974).

Life-Change Event Lists

Despite a large number of life-change event listings in the literature, there is surprising unanimity of opinion among researchers today as to which life-change events should be included in such a list. One of the first published lists was from the work of Rahe et al. (1964) and Holmes and Rahe (1967), where 42 events were compiled into the Schedule of Recent Experience (SRE) questionnaire. These events were representative of health, work, family, personal, social and community, and financial areas of life adjustment. Late in the 1960s, Brown and Birley (1968) developed a life-change event inventory from his studies of patients developing acute episodes of schizophrenia. Paykel, Prusoff, and Uhlenhuth (1971) extended the Holmes and Rahe list to 60 events. Myers, Lindenthal, and Pepper (1971) formulated a list of 62 events based on items from Holmes and Rahe as well as items mentioned by Antonovsky and Kats (1967). Rahe subsequently expanded his list to 54 life-change events, some of which had two to four options—making the actual number of life changes 76 (Rahe, 1975a). Rahe's new list retained the original 42 life-change events with new questions added to make the list applicable to both military and Scandinavian populations. Coddington (1972) revised the Holmes and Rahe list for use with children and adolescents.

In the past decade there has been a further increase in number of life-change lists. For example, Horowitz et al. (1977) published a list of 120 events, primarily derived from the revised Rahe list. Hurst, Jenkins, and Rose (1978) reported a life-change questionnaire containing 103 events. Tennant and Andrews (1976), in Australia, published a recent life-change list based on Rahe's early work with the SRE. Dohrenwend et al. (1978) recently rethought issues such as sampling of events, completeness of various categories of life adjustment, and wording of the life events themselves. This list of events, though intended to provide substantially new input from previous lists, proved to be quite similar to Rahe's revised list (Rahe, 1979).

Thus, although researchers continue to modify previously published life-change lists, the overlap between events inquired about is unexpectedly high. A simple answer to the problem of differing lists would be for life-change researchers to decide to use a standard list of events, such as the original SRE list, adding new questions as needed, but not deleting any from the original list. Such a standard list would allow for "norms" to be established as well as for interstudy comparisons to be made.

Life-Change Scaling

While unexpected agreement may be found among published life-change lists, near confusion abounds in the literature regarding how life-change events are best evaluated. The original life-change event scaling experiment was reported by Holmes and Rahe (1967). The dimension upon which they scaled life events was "change" from a "steady state" of psychosocial adjustment. This dimension of change was consistent with the concept of homeostatic balance. In this original scaling study, persons rated events at opposite poles of desirability quite similarly (Rahe, 1969). For example, the inheritance of a large sum of money was scaled to represent about as much life change and readjustment as was a severe financial setback; a marital separation was judged to represent about the same amount of life change and readjustment as was a marital reconciliation. Therefore, change was deemed the pertinent variable to scale the life events.

Paykel et al. (1971) chose to scale depressed patients' recent life changes on a dimension of "upsettingness". It is understandable that depressed patients see their recent life as having been unpleasant or upsetting. In fact, recent life-change events are important both as precipitants of disease and an influence on symptom formation in depressed and neurotic patients (Rahe, 1979).

Using the Life Change Unit (LCU) scaling system (Rahe, 1978), Dohrenwend (1973) suggested that a person's LCU values for all undesirable events be substracted from the LCU weights for all desirable events to arrive at a (usually negative) "weighted difference score." The presumption was that the greater the weighted difference score the greater is the risk of psychological dysfunction. Hough, Fairbank, and Garcia (1976) made a further modification of the Dohrenwend system. They separated the Holmes and Rahe list of events into three categories: desirable, neutral, and undesirable events. To do this they split several life-change questions into component parts. For example, change in financial state was split into improvement versus worsening of recent financial state. All events were then weighted by a panel of judges to allow for unit scores for desirable, neutral, and undesirable life events. Rahe (1978) pointed out, however, that when subjects, rather than investigators, are asked which life events are desirable, neutral, or undesirable, unanimity of opinion is not found; individual subjects do not necessarily agree with judges' ratings of the desirability of life events.

Rahe and colleagues (1972b) experimented with regression weights for recent life-change events reported by shipboard sailors in an attempt to improve the predictions of illness episodes in these men's near future. Although regression weights seemed at first to be superior to other weighting systems for this purpose, cross-validation studies showed these results were no better than LCU weights. Though Ross and Mirowsky (1979) have recently endorsed this scaling technique, they did not report any cross-validation results. Rahe (1978) has also reported that in studies of young Navy men, LCU weights correlated at a level of 0.90 with a simple counting of the number of recent life events reported.

A methodological problem that has not been addressed by researchers is that the original scaling work utilized the ratio (proportionate) method of Stevens (1966). This method is an extremely difficult one to administer to persons of below-average education. More important, results from this method cannot be assumed to give the same distribution of scores as results obtained by using a more conventional interval scaling technique. Some early as well as recent scaling studies compare lists derived by these two very different scaling techniques (Paykel et al., 1971; Horowitz et al., 1977).

Although an enormous amount of effort has gone into attempts to assign quantitative weights to life-change events, it must be emphasized that none of these systems has been proven to be a significant improvement over a simple count of events reported from a standard list. The only exception to this rule might be studies of older individuals with typically few life changes. Here, it could well be crucial to know whether two recent life-change events were changes as significant as death of spouse and retirement or events of lesser meaning such as a recent purchase and a vacation.

The Subjective Life-Change Unit Scaling Technique

The scaling technique I propose attempts to measure one of the important intervening variables that exist between environmental stress (e.g., recent life changes) and eventual symptoms and/or illnesses (Rahe, 1974).

The Subjective Life Change Unit (SLCU) method attempts to quantify an individual's own perception of his environment. Unlike the LCU system, the SLCU method requests the individual's own estimate of the "force" of his recent life change experiences rather than using mean scores derived from a panel of judges (Rahe, 1974). Various factors may influence a person's own assessment of recent life change, including his previous experience with the event, his current level of social supports, and as his level of social skills (including education and occupation) available to deal with the event (Rahe and Arthur 1978). The research question that remains is whether a person's subjective estimates of recent life change are better predictors of his subsequent symptom and/or illness experience than are the more objective life-change measures.

Vietnamese Refugees Study

With the imminent fall of South Vietnam's government in April

1975, the U.S. Department of State hastily formulated a plan to relocate approximately 150,000 South Vietnamese and Cambodian refugees into this country. As might be expected, the translocation of this group of people was a particularly stressful experience for them. The major Vietnamese refugee camp in the continental United States was located in Camp Pendleton, California (Rahe et al., 1978) from May to October 1975. The population of refugees at the camp was maintained at approximately 20,000 over six months' time; nearly 60,000 refugees in all were processed through this center.

Whereas the initial plane loads of refugees were met by friends and relatives in the United States, who rapidly sponsored them from the camp, refugees who arrived later had to remain for a few weeks to a few months prior to their sponsorship. It was in this setting of frustration over an uncertain length of stay in addition to the numerous recent stressful changes in their lives that the refugees' psychological problems first became apparent to camp personnel. In early May 1975 the Naval Health Research Center (NHRC) was requested to provide psychiatric consultation for the camp.

The medical care of refugees received prompt attention from personnel at the Naval Regional Medical Center, Camp Pendleton. As a result of input from psychiatrists at NHRC, a Vietnamese psychiatrist-refugee was selected to run a mental health crisis clinic. Though cases seen were severe, the total number of refugees found to be in crisis was amazingly small. The crisis clinic saw an average of three patients a day. Early in the first month of operation, individuals who were seen suffered from major psychiatric illnesses such as psychoses. By the second and third months of the camp's existence the most prevalent psychological disorders seen were anxiety and depression. Suicide attempts, for example, rose from a single case in June, to four in July, three in August, and two in September. Toward the closing of the camp, mental health issues referred to the clinic primarily involved consultations regarding a few depressed and potentially suicidal children who had been separated from their families.

In order to advise camp administrators of the prevalence of psychological disorders in the refugees at large, not just in those coming to the attention of the crisis clinic, NHRC physicians organized the administration of health questionnaires to a random sample of refugees (Rahe et al. 1978). Sixty-five families were selected to represent a cross section of refugees by time of arrival in camp as well as by major demographic characteristics. When the heads of households of these families were approached, only five refused to cooperate. The interviews with the 60 cooperative families resulted in a total of 298 refugees being seen. Ninety-five of this group were children under the age of 13; these children had not been given the adult questionnaires. Thus, the number of adults providing questionnaire data was 203 (99 men and 104 women, mean age 30.3 years). Forty-five percent of those interviewed had lived in Saigon most of their lives. Fifty-five percent of the sample were Catholics, 27 percent Buddhists, 11 percent Confusians, and 7 percent had no religious preference. By income classification the families appeared to be upper-middle class; by assessment of their educational achievements the families would be classified as lower-middle class (only 55% of heads-of-households were high school graduates).

Questionnaires administered were the Cornell Medical Index-Health Questionnaire (CMI), the Recent Life Changes Questionnaire (RLCQ), and the Self-Anchoring Scale (SAS) (Rahe et al., 1978). The CMI consists of 195 yes or no questions that measure the presence or absence of body symptoms in various organ systems. The CMI was specifically scored so that individuals provided us with symptoms of physical and psychological disorder experienced *since their arrival in the refugee camp.* The RLCQ has been used to estimate recent life-change incidence in a variety of cross-cultural studies. For the purposes of the present investigation, 12 new life-change events were added to the standard RLCQ—events which dealt specifically with recent life changes brought about by the war (Rahe, 1978a). The SAS was utilized to determine refugees' levels of optimism at the time they were in camp as well as for levels one year prior to becoming a refugee and for one and five years into the future (Rahe et al., 1978).

All questionnaires were translated into Vietnamese by native Vietnamese graduate students residing in the San Diego area. Family members were assured of the voluntary nature of the study and were provided with Vietnamese translations of informed consent and U.S. Privacy Act statements. The graduate students personally administered all questionnaires and recorded all answers.

Because no Life Change Unit (LCU) norms had been established for a Vietnamese population, a simple counting of the number of recent life-change events over the last six months was used as our objective measure of recent life change. Refugees were asked to give SLCU estimates for each event that they had experienced over the past six months. Tables 1, 2, and 3 present comparisons of objective and subjective life-change measures, for both men and women, in terms of the correlation between recent life change and illness symptoms.

Table 1 shows that the number of recent life changes, the RLCQ plus the 12 items about war changes, showed very similar correlations with CMI symptoms experienced in camp, for men and for women. However, women's SLCU estimates significantly increased this correlation ($p \leq 0.03$), while such SLCU estimates decreased (nonsignificant) the correlation seen for men.

Table 2 presents Pearson correlations for men for number of recent life changes and SLCU scores for the RLCQ alone, war changes alone, and for total changes with physical, mental, and total CMI symptoms. RLCQ results, using both objective and subjective scoring systems, gave similar results for physical symptoms. For mental symptoms, as well as for total symptoms, the objective life-change measure was significantly better than the SLCU measure. Table 3 presents the same analyses for women. In contrast to correlations for male refugees, the SLCU system for women significantly improved the correlation between RLCQ and war changes, with both physical and total CMI symptoms.

When number of recent life changes and SLCU were compared to SAS optimism scores, further sex differences were seen. Table 4 presents these data for men. A consistent negative correlation was seen between in-camp optimism levels and number of recent life changes. A significant positive correlation was found between the SLCU scores for war changes and recalled optimism in Vietnam one year before. Table 5 presents these analyses for women. In contrast to the men, no relationship was seen between in-camp optimism

TABLE 1

Intercorrelation Between Recent Life Changes and CMI
in Vietnamese Refugees.

RLCQ + War changes	CMI (in camp)	
	Men (N = 73)	Women (N = 74)
Number	0.23[a]	0.26[b]
SLCU	0.18	0.35[b]

[a]$P \leq 0.05$, one-tailed test.
[b]$P \leq 0.01$, one-tailed test.

TABLE 2

Intercorrelation Between Recent Life Changes and CMI
in Vietnamese Men.

Recent life changes	CMI (in camp)		
	Physical	Mental	Total
RLCQ (N = 89)			
Number	0.22[a]	0.22[a]	0.24[b]
SLCU	0.18[a]	0.16	0.19[a]
War (N = 76)			
Number	0.11	0.16	0.14
SLCU	0.13	0.04	0.10
RLCQ + war (N = 73)			
Number	0.18	0.26[b]	0.23[a]
SLCU	0.17	0.15	0.18

[a]$P \leq 0.05$, one-tailed test.
[b]$P \leq 0.01$, one-tailed test.

levels and recent life changes. A significant positive correlation was seen between degree of optimism in Vietnam one year previous and number of recent war-related changes. Also, there was a significant positive correlation between number of recent life changes on the RLCQ and women's optimism scores for five years into the future. (The correlation for one year into the future was nearly significant.)

TABLE 3

Intercorrelation Between Recent Life Changes and CMI
in Vietnamese Women.

Recent life changes	CMI (in camp)		
	Physical	Mental	Total
RLCQ (N = 87)			
Number	0.21[a]	0.14	0.21[a]
SLCU	0.29[b]	0.20[a]	0.29[b]
War (N = 79)			
Number	0.20[a]	0.12	0.19[a]
SLCU	0.34[b]	0.09	0.28[b]
RLCQ + war (N = 74)			
Number	0.27[b]	0.17	0.26[b]
SLCU	0.39[b]	0.17	0.35[b]

[a]$P \leq 0.05$, one-tailed test.
[b]$P \leq 0.01$, one-tailed test.

TABLE 4

Intercorrelation Between Recent Life Changes and Self-Anchoring
Scale in Vietnamese Men.

| | | SAS | | |
Recent life changes	1 Yr ago	In camp	1 Yr future	5 Yr future
RLCQ (N = 83)				
Number	0.02	-0.22[a]	0.08	0.02
SLCU	0.11	-0.22[a]	0.07	0.03
War (N = 70)				
Number	0.06	-0.06	0.15	0.05
SLCU	0.27[a]	-0.13	0.15	0.10
RLCQ + War (N = 67)				
Number	0.08	-0.19	0.16	0.13
SLCU	0.23	-0.22	0.13	0.14

[a]$P \leq 0.05$, two-tailed test.

TABLE 5

Intercorrelation Between Recent Life Changes and Self-Anchoring
Scale in Vietnamese Women.

| | | SAS | | |
Recent life changes	1 Yr ago	In camp	1 Yr future	5 Yr future
RLCQ (N = 81)				
Number	0.12	0.08	0.18	0.22[a]
SLCU	0.12	0.01	0.14	0.20
War (N = 75)				
Number	0.33[b]	0.15	0.17	0.18
SLCU	0.17	-0.02	0.07	0.09
RLCQ + war (N = 70)				
Number	0.24[a]	0.15	0.21	0.23
SLCU	0.14	-0.01	0.12	0.17

[a]$P \leq 0.05$, two-tailed test.
[b]$P \leq 0.01$, two-tailed test.

Conclusions

The striking differences between the data compiled for men and women for Vietnamese refugees is a new finding. We had previously reported that for the equivalent recent life change, Vietnamese women reported more CMI symptoms than men (Rahe et al., 1978b). However, among symptomatic men and women it appears that the effects of recent life change was chiefly upon mental functioning for men and upon physical symptoms for women.

For this first trial of the SLCU scoring technique a significant increase in correlation between recent life-change events and (chiefly physical) symptoms was found for women. Men's SLCU values actually decreased this correlation. Further investigation of this difference is warranted. Explanations of these findings may require a detailed knowledge of male and female illness behavior roles in the Vietnamese culture.

SAS data complemented CMI data for Vietnamese men. That is, their responses to recent life change correlated with both a fall in their levels of optimism experienced in camp and mental symptoms on the CMI. Women did not show such "mental strain" to recent life change on either the SAS or the CMI. Instead, women appeared to react somatically to recent life-change stress.

Associations between recent life change and SAS optimism levels showed that past and future optimism estimates may be influenced in part, by individuals' recent life-change stress. This relationship suggests that the tougher their life had been recently, the higher was the refugees' level of past and future optimism. Is this possibly a reflection of active coping? Do people with abundant recent life stress who react very optimistically about the future fare better than people who are less optimistic?

Many questions concerning illness prediction follow from these data. Unfortunately, our original intention to follow this Vietnamese sample has been severely curtailed by frequent residential moves of the subjects since sponsorship plus our inability to obtain their new addresses due to Privacy Act restrictions. Thus, the utility of SLCU data to predict illness could not be tested. Also, it would have been of interest to test the "optimism-coping" idea mentioned above.

Certainly future studies should consider possible differences between men and women in their perceptions of recent life change and in their illness response. The SLCU scaling technique may prove to be of particular value for women, especially in its ability to

predict subsequent physical symptoms. Admittedly, results from
Vietnamese refugees may bear little resemblance to future data
collected from individuals from other cultures and in other circumstances. Nevertheless, if sex differences are not considered in the
designs of future studies, researchers may well miss an extremely
valuable opportunity to extend these initial findings.

Acknowledgments

This is Report No. 79–40, supported by Naval Medical Research
and Development Command, Department of the Navy, under
research work unit M0096-PN001-1035. The views presented in this
paper are those of the author. No endorsement by the Department
of the Navy has been given or should be inferred.

Acknowledgements: The assistance of Linda K. Hervig, M.A.,
and LTJG Marie Wallick, MSC, USNR, in the analyses of the
Vietnamese refugee data is gratefully acknowledged.

References

Alexander, F. G. & Selesnicky, S. T. (1966), *The History of Psychiatry. An Evaluation of Psychiatric Thought and Practice from Prehistoric Times to the Present*. New York: Harper & Row.
Antonovsky, A., & Kats, R. (1967) The life crisis history as a tool in epidemiological research. *J. Hlth. Soc. Behav.* 8:15-21.
Brown, G. W. & Birley, J. L. T. (1968), Crises and life changes and the onset of schizophrenia. *J. Hlth. Soc. Behav.*, 9:203-214.
Coddington, R. D. (1972), The significance of life events as etiologic factors in the diseases of children—II. A study of a normal population. *J. Psychosom. Res.*, 16:205-213.
Dohrenwend, B. S. & Dohrenwend, B. P. (1974), *Stressful Life Events: Their Nature and Effects*. New York: Wiley.
Dohrenwend, B. S.; Krasnoff, L.; Askenasy, A. R., & Dohrenwend, B. P., (1978), Exemplification of a method for scaling life events: the PERI life events scale. *J. Hlth. Soc. Behav.*, 19:205-229.
Gunderson, E. K. E. & Rahe, R. H. (1974), *Life Stress and Illness*. Springfield, Ill.: Charles C Thomas.
Henry, J. P. & Stephens, P. M. (1977), *Stress, Health and the Social Environment*. New York: Springer-Verlag.
Holmes, T. H. & Rahe, R. H. (1967), The social readjustment rating scale. *J. Psychosom. Res.*, 11:213-218.
Horowitz, M., Schaefer, C., Hiroto, D. Wilner, N., & Lebin, B. (1977), Life event questionnaires for measuring presumptive stress. *Psychosom. Med.*, 39:413-431.

Hough, R. L., Fairbank, D. T., & Garcia, A. M. (1976), Problems in the ratio measurements of life stress. *J. Hlth. Soc. Behav.*, 17:70–82.

Hurst, M. W., Jenkins, C. D., & Rose, R. M. (1978), The assessment of life change stress: a comparative and methodological inquiry. *Psychosom. Med.*, 40:126–141.

Myers, J. K., Lindenthal, J. J., & Pepper, M. P. (1971), Life events and psychiatric impairment. *J. Nerv. Ment. Dis.*, 152:149–157.

Paykel, E. S. (1974), Life stress and psychiatric disorder: applications of the clinical approach. In: *Stressful Life Events: Their Nature and Effects*, ed. B. S. Dohrenwend & B. P. Dohrenwend. New York: Wiley, pp. 135–149.

Paykel, E. S., Prusoff, B. A., & Uhlenhuth, E. H. (1971), Scaling of life events. *Arch. Gen. Psychiat.*, 25:340–347.

Rahe, R. H. (1969), Life crisis and health change. In: *Psychotropic Drug Response: Advances in Prediction*, ed. P. R. A. May & R. Wittenborn. Springfield, Ill.: Charles C Thomas, pp. 92–125.

Rahe, R. H. (1974), The pathway between subjects' recent life changes and their near-future illness reports: representative results and methodological issues. In: *Stressful Life Events: Their Nature and Effects*, ed. B. S. Dohrenwend & B. P. Dohrenwend. New York: Wiley, pp. 73–86.

Rahe, R. H. (1975a), Epidemiological studies of life change and illness. *Int. J. Psychiat. Med.*, 6:133–146.

Rahe, R. H. (1975b), Liaison psychiatry on a coronary care unit. *J. Hum. Stress*, 1:13–21.

Rahe, R. H. (1978), Life change measurement clarification (editorial). *Psychosom. Med.*, 40:95–98.

Rahe, R. H. (1979), Life change events and mental illness: an overview. *J. Hum. Stress*, 5:2–10.

Rahe, R. H. & Arthur, R. J. (1978), Life change and illness studies: past history and future directions. *J. Hum. Stress*, 4:3–15.

Rahe, R. H., Gunderson, E. K. E., Pugh, W. M., Rubin, R. T., & Arthur, R. J. (1972a), Illness prediction studies: use of psychosocial and occupational characteristics as predictors. *Arch. Environ. Hlth.*, 25:192–197.

Rahe, R. H., Jensen, P., & Gunderson, E. K. E. (1972b), Regression analysis of subjects' self-reported life changes in an attempt to improve illness prediction. Navy Medical Neuropsychiatric Research Unit, San Diego, Report No. 71-5.

Rahe, R. H., Looney, J. G., Ward, H. W., Tung, T. M., & Liu, W. (1978), Psychiatric consultation in a Vietnamese refugee camp. *Amer. J. Psychiat.*, 135:185–190.

Rahe, R. H., Meyer, M. Smith, M., Kjaer, G., & Holmes, T. H. (1964), Social stress and illness onset. *J. Psychosom. Res.*, 8:35–44.

Rahe, R. H. & Paasikivi, J. (1971), Psychosocial factors and myocardial infarction. II. An outpatient study in Sweden. *J. Psychosom. Res.*, 15:33–39.

Rahe, R. H. & Romo, M. (1974), Subjects' recent life changes and the onset of myocardial infarction and coronary death in Helsinki. In: *Life Stress and Illness* ed. E. K. E. Gunderson & R. H. Rahe. Springfield, Ill.: Charles C Thomas, pp. 105–120.

Rosenman, R. H., Brand, R. J., Jenkins, C. D., Friedman, R., Straus, R., & Wurm, M. (1975), Coronary heart disease in the Western Collaborative Study. Final follow-up experience of 8-1/2 years. *J. Amer. Med. Assn.*, 233:872–877.

Ross, C. E. & Mirowsky, J. (1979), A comparison of life-event weighting schemes:

change, undesirability, and effect-proportional indices. *J. Hlth. Soc. Behav.*, 20:166–177.

Stevens, S. S. (1966), A metric for the social consensus. *Science*, 151:530.

Tennant, C. & Andrews, G. (1976), A scale to measure the stress of life events. *Aust. N. Z. J. Psychiat.*, 10:27–32.

The Pooling Project Research Group (1978), Relationship of blood pressure, serum cholesterol, smoking habit, relative weight and ECG abnormalities to incidence of major coronary events; final report of the pooling project. *J. Chron. Dis.*, 31:201–306.

Tiblin, G & Wilhelmsen, L. (1970), An epidemiological survey of the health of a cohort of men from Göteborg born in 1913. Personal communication.

Cross-Cultural Differences in Perceptions of Life Events

DIANNE TIMBERS FAIRBANK

RICHARD L. HOUGH

Concern about the possibility of racial, ethnic, and national variation in the perception of life-change events has been voiced since
Holmes and Rahe (1967) reported their work on the construction of
the Social Readjustment Rating Scale (SRRS) from data provided
by 394 Washington state subjects. In that article, Holmes and Rahe
reported high Pearson correlations among various subsets of the
sample, including correlations of white with black and Oriental
ratings of life events of 0.82 and 0.94 respectively. They concluded
that "the high degree of consensus . . . suggests a universal agreement between groups and among individuals about the significance
of the life events under study that transcends differences in age, sex,
marital status, education, social class, generation American, religion
and race" (p. 217).

The conclusions of several authors who administered the SRRS
to new samples perpetuated that theme. Masuda and Holmes (1967)
reported that a comparison of a Japanese sample and a matched
portion of the Holmes and Rahe sample "indicated essential similarities in their attitudes towards life events" (p. 236). Komaroff,
Masuda, and Holmes (1968) called the ratings among Mexican-
Americans, blacks, and the Holmes and Rahe sample "significantly
concordant" (p. 128), and Rahe, Lundberg, Bennett, and Theorell
(1971) found that while Swedes gave higher scores to the events than
did the Americans of the original scaling study, the rank orderings
of the events were "essentially the same" (p. 249). Each of the
investigators was impressed by the high correlation between the
scores of the particular group studied and scores of the original
Holmes and Rahe sample or portion of that sample chosen to match
the new sample on one or more characteristics such as age, sex, and
education. The authors usually tested and easily rejected a null
hypothesis of no correspondence in the ratings—a strange practice

given that the real interest was in detecting consensus, a hypothesis that is not addressed in a null hypothesis of no correspondence.

While some researchers, particularly those using the Holmes and Rahe list, have focused on agreement in the ratings, others have been concerned with the possibility of differences among various cultural groups and with the methodological and sample limitations of the data. Hough, Fairbank, and Garcia (1976) maintained that consensus in ratings decreased as cultural differences between groups increased. Janney, Masuda, and Holmes (1977) concluded that there was a "generalized increase in ranking of items dealing with bodily necessities and decrease in ranking of items dealing with the personal and interpersonal dynamics as one samples progressively less industrialized cultures" (p. 34). Askenasy, B. P. Dohrenwend, and B. S. Dohrenwend (1977) pointed to the abundance of samples of convenience in the ratings studies and to the possibility of error variance in ratings masking true differences in perceptions of life events.

In order to summarize the literature, we shall first describe the methods that have typically been used to detect similarities and differences in perceptions among various cultural groups and then describe some of the differences that have been found. A discussion of the methodological and theoretical problems in the literature follows. Particularly crucial here is the question of how to separate social class and cultural differences. Finally, we will re-analyze some of the earlier data on ratings of life events in an attempt to summarize it and to test the conclusion of several authors that economic deprivation produces more concern with creature comfort issues and less concern with interpersonal relations.

Detecting Cultural Differences

The method employed to study cultural variations and similarities in perceptions of life events has been relatively consistent. The procedure most commonly employed has been to compare the ratings of the group in question to the ratings of some criterion group. For those studies using the original Holmes and Rahe list, the criterion group has been the 1967 Holmes and Rahe raters or some subset of those raters. Studies done by Paykel, McGuiness, and Gomez (1976) used the ratings reported in Paykel, Prusoff, and Uhlenhuth (1971) as their reference point. Other studies that used special lists either made within-sample comparisons (Rosenberg and B. S. Dohrenwend, 1975; Hough et al., 1979) or tried to adjust the obtained rankings to the rankings of one or more comparison groups (Askenasy et al., 1977).

The procedures used to determine the statistical significance of observable differences between comparison groups have also been fairly consistent across researchers. For the Holmes and Rahe SRRS replications, as well as for several other studies, a *t*-test or analysis of variance was performed comparing the score a change item received in one sample to the score received in the criterion group. All items found to receive significantly different ratings were then noted. Realizing that the probability of type I error increases as significance tests are repeated, some researchers calculated the expected number of significant *t* values given the assumption of no real differences in perceptions, and showed that differences did exist because the actual number of significant *t* values was greater than the expected number. The usual procedure was then to consider each item separately or to group the items into meaningful categories (such as family or work), and to explain on an ad hoc basis the reasons for the differences (see Masuda and Holmes, 1967; Komaroff et al., 1968; Harmon et al., 1970; and Rahe et al., 1971). Miller, Bentz, Aponte, and Brogan (1974) carried their analyses farther in their comparison of the Holmes and Rahe sample to their North Carolina sample, including a factor analysis of the data from each sample. Other researchers have used a combination of latent trait, factor analysis and other techniques to examine the relative ratings of Mexican and Anglo cultural groups in the Southwest (Fairbank, 1977; Mirowsky and Wheaton, 1978; Wainer et al., 1978; Hough et al., 1979; Myjer et al., 1979). The ad hoc explanations of differences found in the studies reported above tended not to be used in predictions of differences for subsequent studies, but to remain as individual and rather idiosyncratic accounts for the differences found.

Findings Related to Differences

We shall emphasize in this section conclusions in the literature regarding cultural differences in perceptions of life events. However, most of the researchers cited below have, even when delineating differences, stressed agreements in the rating data. We do not doubt that the published data show many similarities in perceptions of life events. However, the extent of agreement and whether it can be regarded as "universal" are matters open to debate.

Judging by the literature, the list of events that has been presented most often is that of Holmes and Rahe. As noted previously, cultural variations in the perceptions of those events have often been noted and explained a posteriori. The discussion by Masuda and Holmes (1967) following their administration of the SRRS to a sample of convenience in Japan is typical of the reporting of its use. Detention in jail and minor violations of the law were given higher scores by the Japanese than by the Holmes and Rahe comparison group. This was explained as ". . . in keeping with one of the prime facets of Japanese culture, that of the concept of the obligation of the individual to his family, his name, and his position. Going to jail because of a moral transgression imposes a great sense of shame for the family and guilt for loss of prestige and status" (p. 223). The fifteen additional items on which differences were found between the Holmes and Rahe and the Japanese samples were similarly explained, sometimes by reference to the culturally defined relative importance of the event in the respective countries, and sometimes by psychological processes arising from cultural definitions and prescriptions. Similarities in ratings were explained by the shared experiences of industrialization and urbanization. Likewise, the eighteen differences found between Europeans and the Holmes and Rahe sample by Harmon et al. (1970) were explained on an item-by-item basis and then summarized with the comment that "differences in cultures and living conditions were reflected in the SRRS obtained" (p. 400). Similar analyses are found in Woon, Masuda, Wagner, and Holmes's (1971) study of Malaysian medical students, and in Rahe's (1969) summary of published and unpublished work on the SRRS.

A step in the direction of systematic analysis was provided by Komaroff et al. (1968) who, albeit ex post facto, found numerous differences between Los Angeles Mexican-Americans and blacks on the one hand, and the northwest Americans of the Holmes and Rahe study on the other. One interesting consistency appeared in the differences: eight of the fourteen items concerning labor and income were perceived by the minority groups as requiring more adjustment. Continuing the use of categories to understand the differences, Rahe et al. (1971) divided the events into family, personal, work and financial, and found that Swedes gave relatively more emphasis to work items.

Janney et al. (1977) provide, in our opinion, the most provocative attempted replication of the Holmes and Rahe ratings, and their study is worth noting in some detail. They administered the SRRS in two Peruvian cities, comparing the obtained ratings to each other, to the Holmes and Rahe ratings, and to ratings gathered earlier in Spain and El Salvador. An earthquake had occurred prior to the study in one of the Peruvian cities, Huaráz, killing half of the inhabitants and destroying 90 percent of the buildings of the city. The Huaráz ratings correlated only 0.54 with the ratings gathered in the other Peruvian city, Arequipa, and a remarkably low 0.18 with the Holmes and Rahe ratings, even though the Huaráz raters were students and thus similar to other raters. The authors concluded that the experience of the earthquake kindled anxieties about material necessities that are routinely provided in a secure, affluent society. Those anxieties led to an increased emphasis on events related to meeting those necessities, including economic events, and to a decreased emphasis on interpersonal relationships. The raters in the damaged city placed death of spouse fifteenth, not first or second in importance as all other samples have done.

The Miller et al. (1974) comparison of the Holmes and Rahe raters to a random sample of 96 rural adults of North Carolina attributed differences in ratings to the uniqueness of rural versus urban life. For example, the higher rank of the item "mortgage greater than $10,000" in the North Carolina sample occurred because "taking out a mortgage of greater than $10,000 is almost antithetical for the rural North Carolinian, whereas such a loan might be assumed with relative ease by the city dweller. In the rural South, a general pay-as-you-go philosophy still prevails" (p. 271).

Those who have developed different lists of life events have used the same analysis techniques to describe their data as have the users of the Holmes and Rahe list. Paykel et al. (1971) administered a list of 61 events to Chicago and New Haven psychiatric patients and their relatives, asking the subjects to rate the items from 1 to 20 according to how much distress or "upset" they caused. White ratings correlated with black (0.987), and upper social class ratings with lower (0.989). Statistically significant but small differences in ratings were found, but the nature of the differences was not explored. Paykel et al. (1976) then gave the same list of 61 events to English psychiatric patients and their relatives, comparing the English ratings to those of the American patients and relatives. After correcting for the English subjects' tendency to give higher scores overall, they found that only on legal items did the English and Americans differ. Since comparisons were made in ten categories, it is likely that the one significant difference was due to chance—not real—differences in the ratings.

Rahe and Romo (1974) obtained Finnish weights for a unique set of life events, but were interested in measuring the impact of life events in persons who had suffered a myocardial infarction, not in comparing the weights. Rosenberg and B. S. Dohrenwend (1975) obtained magnitude estimation ratings from 172 students of the City College of New York, and found non-Hispanic Caucasians rated four events as requiring more adjustment than had blacks, Asians, and Hispanics. Three of the four obtained differences concerned interpersonal relationships. Finally, Wyatt (1977) obtained rating data from a sample of forty black Los Angeles mothers, but took the ratings on a particular event only from those women who had experienced it in the last six months, a procedure which severely reduces the comparability of her data. She compared her findings to Komaroff et al.'s (1968) ratings by Los Angeles blacks and Mexican-Americans and to the Holmes and Rahe ratings, and found differences that she attributed to employment and economic differences in the samples.

Several researchers have conducted more systematic investigations of possible cultural and class differences in ratings. Hough et al. (1979) examined cultural variations in judgments concerning the amount of change required by 95 life events among Mexican, Mexican-American, and Anglo adults in El Paso, Texas, and Ciudad Juarez, Mexico. They found that ratings on 51 of the 95 events were sufficiently similar across the groups and of sufficient psychometric quality to be included in their Perceived Life Change Scale. That scale thus reflects a unidimensional, interval-level measurement of life change across the cultural groups represented. Note, however, that 44 (46%) of the events did not exhibit sufficiently satisfactory psychometric qualities and/or similarity of ratings across the groups to be included. This research consequently raises questions concerning the viability of any assumptions of similar rating patterns across cultural groups.

The most systematic explorations of possible cultural and class differences in ratings are provided by Askenasy et al. (1977) and B. S. Dohrenwend et al. (1978), and although they did not explore the content of those differences, they did demonstrate the existence of class and cultural variations in their samples of Puerto Ricans, blacks and non-Puerto Rican whites. Since these studies were more consciously concerned with the possibility of cultural and class differences, and since they were designed explicitly to counter some of the problems of the earlier studies, we shall return to them in more detail below.

Problems Related to Determining Differences

Several sets of methodological problems appear to be particularly thorny to investigators attempting to determine whether significant cross-cultural differences in ratings of life events exist. Difficulties arise in sampling, instrument development and translation, instrument comprehension, patterns of response bias and interpretation, and theory construction. Each set of problems will be discussed below.

Characteristics of the Samples—One problem in determining if there are cultural differences in ratings of life events is that the available comparisons across cultural groups are based on sampling procedures that make drawing decisive conclusions difficult. Ideally, sampling procedures should be such that the relative effects of culture and possible confounding variables, such as social class, can be determined. This implies the sampling of a range of cultural groups and a full range of social classes within those groups. Even more ideally, of course, sampling a full range of groups representing other potential obscuring variables (e.g., sex, age, religion) is desirable, but the social-class variable appears more likely to be inextricably intertwined with culture than the others. Therefore, we concentrate on it below.

To illustrate the difficulty, we can note that a number of comparisons of ratings of nationality groups have been reported in the literature, generally with the conclusion that some basic similarities in ratings obtain. However, the raters have tended to be of similar upper class status. Thus, we may know that upper class Swedes and Japanese produce similar ratings, but the possible differences between middle-class Swedes and middle-class Japanese, or between lower-class groups in those two countries, remain unknown, as do possible differences between the social-class groups *within* Japan and Sweden. Therefore, concluding that the different cultures generate similar ratings among their members is unwarranted.

The ideal sampling procedure would produce representation of the populations in all the cells of a nationality by social-class matrix. However, the sampling procedures reported in the literature on the ratings of life changes have effectively filled only a portion of the cells (Table 1). A range of social class group ratings has been reported in studies in the United States, but typically only upper class ratings have been reported in non-U.S. studies. In effect, most

TABLE 1

Nationality and Social Class Patterning of Reported Studies.

	Social Class		
Nationality Groups	Upper	Middle	Lower
United States	Yes	Yes	Yes
Japan	Yes	No	No
Belgium	Yes	No	No
Sweden	Yes	No	No
Malaysia	Yes	No	No
Other	Yes	No	No

of the cross-national comparisons reported have been of upper-class respondents. For example, there are upper-class Americans (Holmes and Rahe, 1967) to compare with upper-class Japanese (Masuda and Holmes, 1967), Swedes (Rahe et al., 1971), and Belgians (Harmon et al., 1970). Certain other cells of the matrix may be filled in isolated studies, but systematic comparisons of ratings across the cells is not possible given the current literature.

Askenasy et al. (1977) have pointed out that the major reason for disproportionate upper-class sampling, and for the similar ratings of life events across nations, has been that all previous studies, except for Miller et al.'s (1974), have been on sample of convenience. The only other exceptions of which the current authors are aware are the Askenasy et al. (1977) study and their own (Hough et al., 1979). Askenasy et al. (1977) pointed out that samples of friends, acquaintances, and students of researchers are likely to be more homogeneous and higher in status than representative samples of a community or nation.

An additional problem has characterized comparative studies of subcultural groups within the United States. To be sure, lower and upper class and different subcultural groups have been sampled. However, the empirical fact that subcultural groups tend to occupy distinct positions in the status structure has meant that if no special sampling procedure is used, a cross-racial or cross-subcultural comparison within the United States tends to be, at the same time, a cross-class comparison. Thus, the Komaroff et al. (1968) research on blacks and Mexican-Americans of Los Angeles was a study of lower-class persons and a comparison of that sample with the original Holmes and Rahe (1967) Washington state sample actually involves an ethnic group *and* a class comparison. Consequently, it is difficult to determine whether class or culture—or some form of interaction between them—produces observed differences in the ratings across the two studies.

Instrument Development and Translation—Wording life-change event lists so that the individual items will have the same substantive meaning across all groups in which they are to be used is difficult. Individuals obviously interpret what is meant by the stimulus "event" in light of their own experience and, where the life experience of one group of individuals differs from another, there is always the potential of finding varying event ratings which are, in effect, ratings of different stimuli. For example, when the event "change in living conditions" was given the highest rank in the earthquake city of Huaráz, respondents were obviously attributing a meaning to that "event" that is not common to others who have rated the same item on similar lists. This admittedly extreme case illustrates the problems in making the assumption that ratings mean the same thing in different social settings.

To the degree, then, that cultures provide individuals with varying interpretations of the meaning of life events, cross-cultural ratings of events will not result in incontrovertible conclusions relative to perceptions of the amount of change required by exactly the same event. The only means apparent for controlling for this problem are careful translation procedures. Brislin (1980) provides an excellent description of the literature on procedures currently in use in general cross-cultural psychological research, but little has been written concerning the techniques that should be employed in translating life-change scales or the possible impacts of the difficulties encountered in translating specific events on resulting life-change ratings.

It may also be that, rather than simple translation of event lists, some procedures like those of the Triandis group (Triandis, 1972, 1976; Davidson et al., 1976) may have to be used to identify "emic" items within each culture to represent the more general "etic" concept represented by the original event in the English language. A further extension of this argument suggests that identifying the universe of events significant to a given culture may be more crucial than is acknowledged in most current research. That is, it may be that quite different events are significant indicators of life change in different cultures. If so, revised event lists may have to be used in different cultural settings to measure the same general theoretical construct.

Instrument Comprehension—The magnitude estimation procedure often used to generate life-change event scores is difficult for some respondents to understand. Askenasy et al. (1977) have shown that people low in education find the task more difficult than do the more educated. To the extent that error variance resulting from inability to perform the rating task exists in a set of data, true differences between groups will be obscured and a false appearance of consensus will emerge. The Askenasy study was one of the few to sample deliberately from a range of status levels within ethnic groups, and the authors found the expected evidence that lower-class respondents tended not to understand the ratings task as well as upper-class respondents. This finding implies that there are more cross-class and cross-cultural differences than have been discovered, but it does not necessarily imply the obverse—that the differences that have been found are spurious.

The magnitude estimation procedure required by the SRRS has been criticized for its difficulty explicitly by Hough et al. (1976), implicitly found wanting by Paykel et al. (1971) (who evidently discarded the technique in their search for a scaling procedure), and defended by B. S. Dohrenwend et al. (1978) as usable, given checks on the respondent's ability to perform an admittedly difficult task.

Biased Response Patterns—One of the pervasive problems of comparative studies of life-change ratings has been the tendency of some groups to give higher change values to all the events. In such cases it is not clear whether "significant" differences between groups are to be explained as due to real cultural differences in perceptions of the items or to a general rating bias. There are at least three possible sources of rating bias: (1) when magnitude estimations are used to gather the data, the event against which all other events are compared, marriage, itself may be different in relative importance from group to group; (2) some groups may have a generalized tendency to use larger numbers than do other groups; and (3) some groups may really perceive all events as requiring more adjustment. One way to control for a possible bias is to compare the relative positions of the events, not the scores themselves. Rahe (1969) did this by comparing the ranking of events, not their scores. Another type of control was used by Paykel et al. (1976), who calculated the overall difference in means between the English and the American sample, subtracting half that difference from each English score and adding it to each American score. B. S. Dohrenwend et al. (1978) suggested that Paykel et al.'s correction might have masked and distorted other group differences, and that it did not control for individual biases in ratings. They therefore calculated each subject's mean rating, which they conceputalized as some combination of his or her perception of the comparison event and his or her overall perception of how much change events require. They then analyzed their rating data both with and without this adjustment, and discovered that only with the control were some expected class differences found.

Problems in Interpretation and Theory Construction—Finally there is the combined theoretical and methodological problem of how to understand and explain cultural differences, and how to use information from prior studies to predict data in future studies. Thus far, all comparative rating studies have been exploratory, not predictive, and differences are explained after they are found. For example, Masuda and Holmes (1967) explained the Japanese concern with detention in jail after that concern had been documented. There is a need for systematic summaries of the data gathered thus far, for predictions based on the summaries, and for testing in future studies whatever hypotheses seem plausible. This task is made difficult by an additional methodological problem. Researchers, partly because their research needs differ and partly to reduce some of the problems of the Holmes and Rahe list, have devleoped a plethora of differing event lists. This, along with the methodological problems described above, reduces opportunities for meaningful comparisons.

It is also unfortunate for the sake of parsimony but nonetheless true that cultural differences have a tendency to be specific and unique. We may have to content ourselves with identification of a set of events on which culture A differs from culture B and another set on which culture A differs from culture C, but not be able to explain the differences beyond a circular appeal to culture. By comparison, social-class differences are more likely to be predictable. If we have a number of countries in which upper-class respondents have similar ratings, we might attribute the similarities to class. If we can also show that there are differences across classes within one culture but not across cultures within one social class, we have strong evidence for attributing the difference to class.

Whatever the relative predictive capacity of culture and social class for variations in life-event ratings, future research would be materially improved if it were to focus on testing theoretical predictions about the sources of such variations. The predictions could be in the form of suggesting that some variations in cultural attitudes and beliefs (e.g., the relative importance of preserving traditional religion, family, and work patterns) or in some phenomenon only associated with culture (e.g., degree of material well-being) are associated with variations in the rating of events. We now turn to an example of that sort of analysis. Other possible theoretical predictions are suggested in the concluding section.

Differences Reexamined

While the analysis reported below is in many respects exploratory, it at least suggests the sort of theoretically predictive work that would help clarify the findings of life-change rating research. The theoretical notion we want to explore is one that has occurred to us upon reading the conclusions of several of the studies and that strikes us as a plausible explanation for some of the findings. This theme may be expressed as follows: economically deprived or threatened groups are more concerned with meeting the basic necessities of life (e.g., with work and with financial matters) than are more secure groups whose main concerns revolve around family and interpersonal relationships. We are reminded of Maslow's (1968) contention that there is a hierarchy of needs: "The single holistic principle that binds together the multiplicity of human motives is the tendency for a new and higher need to emerge as the lower need fulfills itself by being sufficiently gratified" (p. 55). Maslow maintains that lower-level needs of safety and security must be met before needs for belongingness and affection become motivators, and that those must be met before desire for respect and self-respect, and ultimately self-actualization, become paramount. This theoretical scheme is consistent with several of the findings reported thus far:

1. Komaroff et al. (1968) found that lower class Mexican-Americans and blacks gave higher scores to issues of work, money, and living conditions than had the original Holmes and Rahe raters (cf. Wyatt, 1977);

2. Rosenberg and B. S. Dohrenwend (1975) reported that relatively advantaged Caucasians gave higher scores to interpersonal items than relatively disadvantaged ethnic groups;

3. Janney et al. (1977) found that bodily necessities were rated relatively high in disadvantaged groups, while personal and interpersonal dynamics were rated relatively low. Their sum-

mary assumes Maslow's position: "The decrease in perception of personal and interpersonal events in the earthquake city of Huaráz probably evolved because emotional needs were superseded by physical needs." (P. 26)

These studies almost exhaust the literature on lower-class raters, and the findings are consistent with what one would predict from Maslow's theory. Hence, we thought that further analysis might be profitable. More specifically, we decided to compile data from the currently published studies to test the hypotheses that social class would be related positively to the ratings of personal, family, and failure events and related negatively to the ratings of financial and work-related events. We also hypothesized that when controlling for culture, social class differences in ratings would persist.

We then attempted to develop appropriate procedures for consolidating information on life-event ratings, social class, and culture from the available published data. In order to compare groups without having to compare methods and item differences at the same time, we limited ourselves to the fourteen studies we could identify that published geometric group means for the Holmes and Rahe events.

We were also concerned with the tendency of some groups to give higher scores than other groups and controlled for this tendency by calculating Z scores within one group's geometric means on the 43 life events. Comparisons were then made by looking at the Z scores for a set of items across the relevant groups. This adjustment had the effect of holding the group mean and standard deviation constant.

We next categorized the items of the Holmes and Rahe list under the rubrics of Family, Financial, Work, Personal, and Failure. The contents of each category are shown in Table 2.

When we examined the studies for social-class information, we found education to be the variable for which data were most frequently available. Consequently, it became our primary indicator of social class. Usually, education information was reported in a frequency distribution by number of years of education. For the studies in which this was the case, we estimated the average education from that information. For some samples, however, no estimation procedures were necessary since all of the respondents were currently in school and therefore had the same number of years of education. Since only broad categories of education were used to describe the Holmes and Rahe (1967) and Harmon et al. (1970) samples, and since no data were available on the education of the

TABLE 2

Contents of Life-Event Categories.

Category 1. Family	*Category 2. Financial*	*Category 4. Personal*
death of spouse	change in financial state	sex difficulties
divorce	mortgage over $10,000	change in personal habits
marital separation	foreclosure of loan or mortgage	change in recreation
death of close family member		change in social activities
marriage	*Category 3. Work*	change in sleep habits
marital reconciliation	fired at work	change in eating habits
change in health of family member	retirement	vacation
pregnancy	business readjustment	
gain of new family member	change in financial state	*Category 5. Failure*
change in number of arguments with spouse	change to different line of work	divorce
son or daughter leaving home	change in responsibilities at work	marital separation
trouble with in-laws	trouble with boss	jail term
wife begins or stops work	change in work hours or conditions	fired at work
change in number of family get/togethers		sex difficulties
		trouble with in-laws
		trouble with boss

Komaroff et al. (1968) respondents, we had to remain satisfied with simply placing groups into low, middle, or upper class categories rather than ranking them in terms of mean years of education as we would have preferred. The creation of the three social class categories met two criteria. First, we wanted those groups with ambiguous educational levels to be placed correctly in terms of relative social class position. Second, we wanted approximately equal numbers in each social class group. Fortunately, the use of the second criterion did not compromise the first. The groups placed in each social class category were as follows:

Lower Class:
  Komaroff et al. (1968), blacks and Mexican-Americans.
  Janney et al. (1977), Salvadorians.
  Harmon et al. (1976), French.
  Miller et al. (1974), North Carolinians.
Middle Class:
  Janney et al. (1977), Peruvian and Spanish.
  Harmon et al. (1970), Swiss.
Upper Class:
  Harmon et al. (1970), Belgians.
  Holmes and Rahe (1967), Washingtonians.
  Moon et al. (1971), Malaysians.
  Rahe et al. (1971), Swedes.
  Masuda and Holmes (1967), Japanese.

These groups are best thought of not as discrete social-class groupings but as groups whose *relative* positions are, respectively, low, middle, and high.

The Hawaiians of Rahe (1969) and the blacks of Wyatt (1977) were given the Holmes and Rahe list, but had to be omitted from the current analysis because geometric means were not published.

Since we wanted to make generalizations about broad cultural groupings rather than dwell on individual cases (the reader is invited to read the conclusions of the studies reviewed here for that emphasis), we created categories of (1) Northern European (Swiss, Belgians, Swedes, and French); (2) Western (the Northern Europeans plus the Holmes and Rahe sample and the North Carolinians); and (3) Latin (Spanish, Peruvians, Mexican-Americans, and Salvadorans). Notice that when social class and culture were cross-tabulated (table 3), there were no upper-class Latins and no lower-class Malaysians and Japanese.

We now turn to the findings. We had predicted that the relative ratings given personal, family, and failure events would be positively

TABLE 3

Z Scores of Life-Event Indexes by Class and Cultural Groups (Rank Across Categories within Parentheses).

Groups	Life Event Index Category				
	Family	Financial	Work	Personal	Failure
Class group					
High	(2) 0.28	(4) −0.12	(3) 0.04	(5) −0.35	(1) 0.42
Middle	(3.5) 0.07	(1.5) 0.25	(3.5) 0.06	(5) −0.30	(1.5) 0.24
Low[a]	(1) 0.18	(2.5) 0.11 (0.09)	(4) 0.01	(5) −0.26 (−0.26)	(2.5) 0.12
Cultural groupings					
Northern European	(2) 0.31	(4) −0.07	(3) 0.06	(5) −0.40	(1) 0.39
Western[a]	(2) 0.31	(4) −0.08 (−0.06)	(3) 0.05	(5) −0.39 (−0.37)	(1) 0.39
Latin	(3.5) 0.04	(1) 0.24	(3.5) 0.04	(5) −0.22	(2) 0.12
Culture by class					
High Western	(2) 0.31	(4) −0.16	(3) 0.05	(5) −0.36	(1) 0.40
Middle Western (Swiss)	(2) 0.27	(3) 0.17	(4) 0.08	(5) −0.42	(1) 0.38
Low Western[a]	(1.5) 0.34	(4) −0.10 (−0.03)	(3) 0.03	(5) −0.46 (−0.35)	(1.5) 0.34
Middle Latin	(3) 0.06	(2) 0.15	(4) 0.00	(5) −0.30	(1) 0.26
Low Latin	(3.5) 0.03	(1) 0.29	(2) 0.07	(5) −0.16	(3.5) 0.03

[a]Four items on the Holmes and Rahe list were excluded from the North Carolina SRRS. These four appeared on the Family, Work, and Failure indexes. The North Carolina data are not represented in the Family, Work, and Failure columns, but are represented in parentheses in the Financial and Personal columns.

associated with social class and that those given financial and work related events would be negatively associated with social class. As noted above, these hypotheses were thought to be at least consonant with Maslow's theory of a hierarchy of needs. Upper-class persons, who are more financially and work secure, should have more time, resources, energy, and motivation to pursue the relatively higher needs in the realms of personal activities, family and personal success (i.e., absence of failure). Obversely, lower-class respondents should find the satisfaction of their more basic financial and work needs less certain and therefore be relatively more concerned with them and less with satisfaction in the interpersonal and family areas. We also hypothesized that, controlling for culture, the social-class differences would remain.

Admittedly, the epistemic fit between the concepts of Maslow's theory and our hypotheses may not be perfect. Social-class differences and ratings of life-change events may not be perfect indicators of what Maslow had in mind when he wrote of motivators and needs. However, the hypotheses suggested above seem consistent with his notions, and they have the potential of bringing some order and clarity to our understanding of rating patterns. To a moderate degree, that potential was realized in the data as they are summarized in table 3.

The data shown in table 3 allowed comparisons of Z scores and of rankings. We first looked at each column of Z scores to allow comparison of the relative importance of the particular life-event index across status and cultural categories. Here we see that there is not clear substantiation for the hypotheses that work and financial items would be of greater importance in lower-class groups. There is little difference in the rating of work across the status groups. High social-class groups do, however, tend to perceive financial events as less important than lower-class groups. However, note that the predicted order of ratings is reversed for middle- and lower-class groups. When culture is controlled, the same patterns obtain for the Western culture groups, but the hypothesized relationships are found in the Latin group.

With respect to the hypothesis that concern with family, personal, and failure events would increase as status increases, the clearest pattern emerges for the failure events. The expected relationship holds when all thirteen samples are considered (the Z's go from 0.12 to 0.24 to 0.42 as status increases) and within both the Western and Latin groups. There is support for the hypothesized relationship of social class with family-event ratings only in the Latin group, and

there the differences are very weak. Contrary to what was hypothesized, there was a tendency for concern with personal items to
decrease in importance as class increases, both across all the class
groups and within the Latin and Western groups.

A second way of examining the data is to compare the ranks
across the groups. This procedure might seem to provide a more
direct test of Maslow's scheme, but the rankings themselves are a
function of both the relative importance accorded the items in a
particular group and of the "intrinsic" importance of the items in a
particular category vis a vis other categories. Thus, the analysis of
the rankings sheds no light on the personal items because they were
so relatively trivial that they were last in importance in all groups.
The analysis of the ranks for other categories of events does tend to
confirm the findings mentioned above. Again, only in the Latin
groups is concern with work and financial matters negatively related
to class, and the ranks of the failure items show their greater
importance in upper-class groups.

We have thus shown that some conclusions concerning perceptions of life events are consistent with a more general theory and
then that the theory is a fairly reasonable predictor of at least
portions of the summary data. However, we should note that our
"predictions" are not predictions in the usual sense since the theory
emerged partially from the data in which the "test" was made.
Therefore, it is not surprising that there is some correspondence. A
more powerful case for the theory could be made if it could be
shown to predict new data.

Finally, it should be noted that cultural differences were found in
the relatively greater importance attached to family matters in the
Western and financial matters in the Latin groups. These conclusions emerge both from the analysis of the Z's themselves and the
analysis of the ranks of the Z's.

Summary and Conclusions

This chapter began as a discussion of cultural differences in perceptions of life events. We reviewed the methodologies typically
employed to detect cultural differences and the findings related to
differences, concluding that methodological problems related to
determining whether variations do occur may well have obscured
the significance of the available findings. Among those methodological problems are the characteristics of the samples typically used.
They have been disproportionately homogeneous upper-class sam-

ples of convenience that would yield similar ratings and minimize
the likelihood of determining whatever real cultural differences in
perception might exist. The failure to sample a range of social
classes within cultures has made it difficult to determine whether
similarities and/or differences found across cultures are due to
cultural or social-class effects. Even in the United States, where
there has been a greater tendency to sample a wider range of social-
class groups, the confounding of subculture and class makes it
difficult to assess their relative impact on ratings.

Another significant methodological problem making it difficult to
interpret findings has been the lack of translation and instrument
construction procedures that can assure us of some reasonable
degree of consistency in meaning across cultural groups. Further,
the difficulty of the rating task probably introduces error variance,
particularly among lower-class groups, which cannot help but result
in a false consensus of ratings. Possible rating biases were discussed
as a final set of problems making the interpretation of findings
difficult.

Finally, we noted that most of the work to this point has been
exploratory and atheoretical. We noted that cultural differences
tend to be specific, confronting the researcher with the task of either
listing innumerable differences or, as we have suggested, of letting
that issue lag in pursuit of more general (and generalizable) goals.
We argued that future studies could achieve greater scientific
parsimony and insight if researchers were to concentrate more on
the testing of theoretical notions of how ratings may vary across
cultures. We suggested that Maslow's hierarchy of needs provides a
theoretical perspective from which it can be reasonably argued that
the level of material need in a group of raters may interact with
culture to produce a consistent set of variations in scoring. That
notion was examined in our re-analysis of the available data and we
discovered some moderate degree of fit.

We would emphasize here, however, that the hierarchy of need
hypothesis was intended to be suggestive and illustrative. There are
innumerable theoretical perspectives from which regularities in
rating across cultures might be predicted. One alternative that we
feel deserves further exploration is the "frequency" hypothesis
which predicts that rare or unfamiliar events are ranked higher than
common familiar events. Mirowsky (1979), in a yet unfinished
analysis, has found some evidence supporting that hypothesis using
the Hough et al. (1979) El Paso–Ciudad Juarez data. Miller and his
associates' (1974) conclusion that taking out a large mortgage ranks

higher in the North Carolina sample because it is antithetical to and relatively uncommon in a rural Southern way of life reflects the same hypothesis as does Askenasy et al.'s (1977) suggestion that divorce ranked lower in their samples of disadvantaged groups because it is a more common occurrence there. There is, however, similar anecdotal negative evidence, evidence which happens to support the hierarchy of needs hypothesis. For example, Janney et al. (1977) described the following differences between Arequipa and Huaráz ratings:

The earthquake victims placed relatively more importance upon events of an economic nature than did the Arequipa group. They ranked "foreclosure of a loan or mortgage," "change of responsibilities at work," and "trouble with the boss" considerably higher than did Arequipenos. Items indicative of interpersonal dynamics, in contrast, were ranked lower by Huaráz subjects. "Marriage," for example, was placed 11 ranks lower in Huaráz than in Arequipa. In addition, the people of Huaráz ranked "divorce," "marital reconciliation," "outstanding personal achievement," and "pregnancy" clearly lower than all three other countries (El Salvador, Spain and the United States) as well as Arequipa. (P. 26)

It seems unlikely to us that those particular work and financial events occurred with more frequency in Huaráz and that the interpersonal events happened with less frequency there. However, the frequency hypothesis deserves more systematic testing.

Other possible hypotheses might concentrate on fits between what is regarded as important or particularly threatening in different *types* of cultures and what is rated as important in terms of life change. To name just a few, cross-cultural comparisons could be done by geographical region, mode of production, type of religion, or heterogeneity.

Whatever the theoretical perspective adopted, it is our feeling that more significant progress in the cross-cultural study of life event ratings is contingent upon the development of predictive studies which overcome at least some of the methodological problems we have discussed above.

References

Askenasy, A. R., Dohrenwend, B. P., & Dohrenwend, B. S. (1977), Some effects of social class and ethnic group membership on judgments of the magnitude of stressful life events: a research note. *J. Hlth Soc. Behav.* 18:432–439.

Brislin, R. W. (1980), Translation and content analysis of oral and written materials, In: *Handbook of Cross Cultural Psychology.* vol. 2, *Methodology*, ed. H. C. Triandis & J. W. Berry. Boston: Allyn and Bacon, pp. 389–444.

Davidson, A. R., Jaccard, J. C., Triandis, H. C., Morales, A. M., & Diaz-Guerrero (1976), Cross-cultural model testing: toward a solution of the emic-etic dilemma. *Int. J. Psych.*, 11:1–13.

Dohrenwend, B. S. Krasnoff, L., Askenasy, A. R., & Dohrenwend, B. P. (1978), Exemplification of a method for scaling life events: the PERI life events scale. *J. Hlth Soc. Behav.*, 19:205–229.

Fairbank, D. T. (1977), Latent trait analysis: working paper 2. Los Angeles: Life Change and Illness Research Project, Brentwood VA Medical Center.

Harmon, D. K., Masuda, M., & Holmes, T. H. (1970), The Social Readjustment Rating Scale: a cross-cultural study of western Europeans and Americans. *J. Psychosom. Res.*, 14:391–400.

Holmes, T. H. & Rahe, R. H. (1967), The Social Readjustment Rating Scale. *J. Psychosom. Res.*, 11:213–218.

Hough, R. L., Burnam, M. A., Fairbank, D. T., & Wainer, H. (1979), The scaling of life change impacts across culturally heterogeneous groups: working paper 17. Los Angeles: Life Change and Illness Research Project, Brentwood VA Medical Center.

Hough, R. L., Fairbank, D. T., & Garcia, A. M. (1976), Problems in the ratio measurement of life stress. *J. Hlth Soc. Behav.*, 17:70–82.

Janney, J. G., Masuda, M., & Holmes, T. H. (1977), Impact of a natural catastrophe on life events. *J. Hum. Stress*, 3:22–34, 47.

Komaroff, A. L., Masuda, M., & Holmes, T. H. (1968), The Social Readjustment Rating Scale: a comparative study of Negro, Mexican and white Americans. *J. Psychosom. Res.*, 12:121–128.

Maslow, A. (1968), *Toward a Psychology of Being*, 2nd ed. New York: Van Nostrand Reinhold.

Masuda, M. & Holmes, T. H. (1967), The Social Readjustment Rating Scale: a cross-cultural study of Japanese and Americans. *J. Psychosom. Res.*, 11:227–237.

Miller, F. T., Bentz, W. K., Aponte, J. F., & Brogan, D. R. (1974), Perception of life crisis events: comparative study of rural and urban samples. In: *Stressful Life Events: Their Nature and Effects*, ed. B. S. Dohrenwend & B. P. Dohrenwend. pp. 259–273.

Mirowsky, John II (1979), Personal communication.

Mirowsky, John II & Wheaton, B., (1978), A comparison of factor structures for a sample of life change events in four populations: working paper 9. Los Angeles: Life Change and Illness Research Project, Brentwood VA Medical Center.

Myjer, D'A., Mirowsky, J. II, & Wheaton, B. (1979), A comparative confirmatory factor analysis of life event rating data in a Mexican-American population: working paper no. 29. Los Angeles: Life Change and Illness Research Project, Brentwood VA Medical Center.

Paykel, E. S., McGuiness, B., & Gomez, J. (1976), An Anglo-American comparison of the scaling of life events. *Brit. J. Med. Psychol.*, 49:237–247.

Paykel, E. S., Prusoff, B. A., & Uhlenhuth, E. H. (1971), Scaling of life events. *Arch. Gen. Psychiat.*, 25:340–347.

Rahe, R. H. (1969), Multi-cultural correlations of life change scaling: America, Japan, Denmark and Sweden. *J. Psychosom. Res.*, 13:191–195.

Rahe, R. H., Lundberg, U., Bennett, L., & Theorell, T. (1971), The Social Readjustment Rating Scale: a comparative study of Swedes and Americans. *J. Psychosom. Res.*, 15:241–249.

Rahe, R. H. & Romo, M. (1974), Recent life changes and the onset of myocardial infarction and coronary death in Helsinki. In: *Life Stresses and Illness*, ed. E. K. E. Gunderson and R. H. Rahe. Springfield, Ill.: Charles C Thomas, pp. 105–120.

Rosenberg, E. J. & Dohrenwend, B. S. (1975), Effects of experience and ethnicity on ratings of life events as stressors. *J. Hlth Soc. Behav.*, 16:127–129.

Triandis, H. (1972), *The Analysis of Subjective Culture*. New York: Wiley.

Triandis, H. (1976), Approaches toward minimizing translation problems. *Translation: Applications and Research*, ed. R. Brislin. New York: Wiley/Halsted, pp. 229–243.

Wainer, H., Fairbank, D. T., & Hough, R. L. (1978), Predicting the impact of simple and compound life change events. *Appl. Psych. Meas.*, 2:311–320.

Woon, T. H., Masuda, M., Wagner, N. N., & Holmes, T. H. (1971), The Social Readjustment Rating Scale: a cross-cultural study of Malaysians and Americans. *J. Cross-Cultural. Psychol.*, 2:373–86.

Wyatt, G. E., (1977), A comparison of the scaling of Afro-Americans' life-change events. *J. Hum. Stress*, 3:13–18.

The Reliability of Life-Event Reports

RICHARD NEUGEBAUER

In the past 15 years numerous studies have implicated stressful life events in the etiology or exacerbation of various diseases and disorders. Although disparate in medical subject matter and design, these investigations have frequently relied on the same type of instrument to measure stressors: a life-event checklist. Research on the measurement properties of these checklists has struggled to keep pace with substantive studies. While scaling issues have received some, increasingly controversial, attention, investigations of reliability remain rare. We have located only 9 papers reporting the results of 11 studies. Since instrument reliability is generally regarded as a precondition for validity, it is puzzling that this relative neglect has not occasioned more surprise in the literature and provoked more prompt remedial action.

This chapter brings together the findings of reliability studies conducted to date. After reviewing their results, I will assess the logic of their approach to the measurement of checklist reliability and the appropriateness of their study designs and statistics. Finally, I will summarize the findings from these studies concerning possible sources of unreliability.

Summary of Study Designs and Findings

Reliability is the ratio of the true-score variance in a measure to the observed-score variance of the measure. This formulation from classic measurement theory enjoys a cheery simplicity. Unfortunately, the principles for selecting study designs and reliability statistics compatible with the nature of the measure and with research theory can be complex, tortuous, and often obscure. The reliability of life-event measures has been evaluated in two ways: with a "test-retest" and with a "paired-subjects" design. In the test-retest situation, a group of individuals complete a life-event inventory at two points in time in which they report on events occurring in the same period of calendar time. In the paired-subjects setting, two subjects are interviewed separately, but at the same point in time, concerning life events experienced during a specified period by one member of the pair. The two sets of life-event scores or reports

are then examined for their degree of consistency or agreement over
time or between subjects.

Test-Retest Studies of Reliability—Four groups of investigators
have conducted test-retest studies of the reliability of life-event
inventories. In all cases, the inventory was self-administered usually
as a paper and pencil questionnaire, rather than presented by means
of an interview. At the first administration (time 1) a group of
subjects, all drawn from the same industry or occupation, completed the questionnaire, either individually or at a group session.
Time periods covered by the questionnaire at time 1 have ranged
from 24 months to 8½ years. The second administration of the
questionnaire (time 2) is scheduled anywhere from 2 weeks to 2
years after time 1. While the time 2 questionnaire inquires about
immediately preceding events, it also extends sufficiently far back in
time to overlap partially or completely with the period covered at
time 1. The reliability of subjects' scores is then assessed with a
correlation coefficient (Pearson's *r*) for the entire overlapping period
or for certain subperiods. Several studies also compute separate
reliability coefficients for subgroups of checklist items. The design
and findings of these investigations are arrayed in table 1.

In a 1964 Seattle study by Casey et al. (1967) 88 physicians in
residency training completed Holmes and Rahe's Schedule of
Recent Experiences (Holmes and Rahe, 1967) in questionnaire
format (SRE) on two occasions 9 months apart. At time 1, subjects
recorded events for each of 8 preceding calendar years, as well as for
the year in progress. At time 2, subjects recorded events for the same
calendar period as at time 1, and for the period between administrations. Fifty-four subjects completed the questionnaire at time 2.
Correlation coefficients were calculated on the weighted Life
Change Unit scores (LCU) for the seventh, the fourth, and the most
recent year for which both time 1 and time 2 reports were available.
The coefficient for each year was 0.67, 0.64, and 0.74 respectively.

McDonald et al. (1972) investigated retest reliability in a sample
of 633 U.S. Navy enlisted men aboard a carrier. Subjects represented all major occupational groups on board, had an average of
11.6 years of education, and a mean age of 22 years. While at sea,
they completed a military version of the SRE at time 1 for the
preceding 30-month period, divided into five, 6-month intervals.
The time 2 questionnaire, scheduled 6 months later, also covered the
preceding 30 months, thereby creating a time 1-time 2 overlap of
four, 6-month periods. Apparently there was no subject attrition.

Starting with the most recent overlapping 6-month interval, the test-retest (weighted?) score correlations were 0.48, 0.54, 0.60, and 0.57. For the more recent overlapping year as a whole, the correlation was 0.61 as compared to 0.52 for the preceding year.

It is noteworthy that neither this study nor the study by Casey et at. (1967) provides a reliability coefficient for the entire time 1-time 2 overlapping period. Since reliability for subperiods of an inventory may depart markedly from the reliability of the instrument as a whole, the published results of these two studies remain incomplete. The report of another study, conducted by Rahe et al. (1974) and discussed later, suffers from the same shortcoming.

In two studies conducted by Thurlow (1971), time 1 and time 2 test administrations of the SRE were scheduled 24 months and 2 weeks apart respectively. In the first study, initial subjects were 165 employees of an Ontario brewery with a mean age of 46 (87% male; 88% married; 40% paid on an hourly basis; 35% salaried, nonsupervisory personnel; and 25% salaried supervisors). Subject attrition did not significantly affect this sociodemographic distribution. At time 1 and time 2 subjects recorded events for each of the 5 immediately preceding years. However, full comparability of test situations was compromised by the introduction of additional measures at time 2. Starting with the most recent overlapping year, LCU score correlations were 0.34, 0.07, and 0.14 respectively. The correlation for the entire 3-year period was 0.26. The second study utilized the same life-event measure and time period for life-event reporting. Subjects were 21 college psychology students (57% female) presumably in an Ontario school, with an average age of 27. LCU score correlation, calculated for all 5 years combined, was 0.78.

More recently, Jenkins et al. (1979) reported on the retest reliability of the 103-item Review of Life Experience (ROLE) inventory, which contains 39 items from the Holmes and Rahe questionnaire and 52 from the Paykel et al. (1971) checklist. The ROLE has a branching format to avoid asking subjects nonapplicable questions and is administered through an interactive computer system with video terminals (Hurst et al., 1978). An all-male sample of 416 air traffic controllers working in New England and New York completed the ROLE at time 1. Subjects were asked to record events that had occurred in the immediately preceding 6-month period or in months 7 through 24 prior to the administration date. Time 1 subjects had a mean age of 36 years; 96% had completed high school and 60% had some higher education as well. At time 2, scheduled

TABLE 1

Studies of Test-Retest Reliability of Self-administered Life-Event Questionnaires.

Study	Sample Size, Time 1/ Time 2	Subject Sociodemographic Characteristics, Time 1	Questionnaire	Time period covered by Time 1 Questionnaire	Interval between Time 1 and Time 2	Duration of Question- naire Overlap	Type of Score	Correlation Coefficient[a] (Pearson's r)
Casey et al., 1967	88/54	physicians in residency training program.	SRE: 40 items	8½ yr	9 mos	8½ yr	weighted score (LCU)	1st yr: 0.67 4th yr: 0.64 7th yr: 0.74
McDonald et al., 1972	663/663	all major occupational groups on board a U.S. Navy carrier. Mean age: 22. Mean yr of education: 11.6.	SRE: 42-item military version	30 mos	6 mos	24 mos, divided into 4 6-mo periods	not stated	1st 6 mos: 0.48 2nd 6 mos: 0.54 3rd 6 mos: 0.60 4th 6 mos: 0.57 1st yr: 0.61 2nd yr: 0.52
Thurlow, 1971	165/111	all personnel levels in brewery: 40% hourly wage; 35% salaried non-supervisory; 25% salaried supervisory. Mean age: 46.	SRE: 38 items	5 yr	2 yr	3 yr	weighted score (LCU)	0.26 1st yr: 0.34 2nd yr: 0.07 3rd yr: 0.14

21/21[b]	Males: 87%. Married: 88%. psychology class. Mean age: 27. Males: 9.	SRE: 38 items	5 yr	2 wk	4 yr, 50 wk[c]	weighted score (LCU)	0.78
Jenkins et al., 1979 416/382	air traffic controllers.[d] Mean age: 36. HSG: 96%. HSG+: 60%.	ROLE: SRE (39 items) PUP (52 items) "Distress"[e] ratings	24 mos	9 mos	6 mos	weighted score (LCU) (LCW) ("Distress")	0.38 0.40 0.45

[a] Time periods are listed in order of recency.
[b] Any explicit statement regarding possible subject attrition omitted.
[c] Though life-event reports overlapped for 258-week period author's account of data analysis gives the impression that each set of scores at time 1 and 2 were calculated for a 260-week period.
[d] No indication whether subject attrition at time 2 significantly altered sociodemographic characteristics of sample.
[e] Computer storage failures reduced the sample size for analysis of "distress" scores to 341 subjects.

approximately 9 months later, subjects reported events happening in the prior 15 months. Owing to geographical transfers and promotions, only 382 men participated at time 2. Jenkins et al. calculated a Holmes and Rahe (HR) weighted score (LCU) and a Paykel et al. (PUP) weighted score (LCW). In addition, at both administrations, subjects assigned "distress" ratings to each of the 103 events which they had personally experienced. The correlation coefficients for each type of score for the 6-month period of overlap were 0.38 (HR), 0.40 (PUP), and 0.45 ("distress").

In addition to assessing consistency of scores over time as measured by a correlation coefficient, Casey et al. (1967) and Jenkins et al. (1979) also investigated agreement (as distinct from consistency) in the magnitude of subjects' scores. Casey et al. assessed score agreement in two ways. First, they explored the extent to which the sample's mean LCU score differed in the 3 years examined in detail. The sample's fourth-year mean was 35% lower than the most recent year's mean, the seventh year mean was 50% lower. (This analysis required data from only a single administration of the checklist; the authors did not clarify whether the time 1 or time 2 results were used in this calculation of means.) Second, adopting a peculiar statistical approach, Casey et al. utilized the variance of the mean of individual score differences to assess score agreement. The standard deviation (40 LCUs) of the mean LCU score difference between time 1 and time 2 was adopted as the cut-off point for scores considered to be in agreement. Any subject whose time 1-time 2 scores for a given year differed by at least 40 LCUs was classified as a discrepant case for that year. With this criterion point, 81% of the subjects had discrepant scores for at least 1 of the 3 years investigated. Unfortunately, the use of the standard deviation of the *mean* score difference rather than simply of the score differences makes these results uninterpretable.

Jenkins et al. (1979) assessed score agreement by examining decline in sample mean score from time 1 to time 2 and by reference to the variance of difference scores. The sample's mean score in different scoring metrics declined from time 1 to time 2 by 46% (HR), 40% (PUP), and 34% ("distress" scores). Agreement of HR scores was explored in greater detail by calculating the number of subjects whose HR scores between time 1 and time 2 differed by more than one standard error of measurement for the distribution of difference scores. Seventy-four percent of the subjects fell in this category (although of this group, 15% reported higher scores at time

2). The authors noted that a similar pattern emerged for PUP and "distress" scores.

Paired-Subjects Studies of Reliability—A number of investigators have examined the reliability of life-event instruments by interviewing the study subject proper and one or more close relatives or friends at one point in time regarding recent life events experienced by the subject. In these studies, instrument reliability is measured either in terms of intrapair agreement or score consistency. With a single exception (Rahe et al., 1974), the paired-subjects design has been adopted exclusively by researchers concerned with the relationship of stressful life events to psychiatric disorders. The general results of these investigations are summarized in table 2.

Hudgens et al. (1970) were the first researchers to use intrapair agreement to measure the reliability of life-event recall. Study patients were 80 diagnostically heterogenous admissions to a psychiatric hospital in St. Louis, Missouri. The majority (56%) suffered from an affective disorder, in most cases depression. The patients had a mean age of 45 years; 34% male; 73% currently married. Patients were interviewed at admission, and informants, totaling 103, were recruited from among accompanying persons. (Twenty-one "pairs" were comprised of one patient and two informants; one "pair" of one patient and three informants.) All informants were relatives of the patients; in 69% of the pairs, an informant was the spouse. Overall, 88% of the patients had a household member as at least one of the informants. Patients and coinformants were interviewed separately but close in time regarding life events experienced by the patient in the year prior to admission. (Positive responses of multiple informants were aggregated.)

Intrapair agreement for the inventory as a whole was measured by means of a complex rate which relied upon the division of the checklist into 11 topical categories or "stress areas," such as "sickness of relative, friend, or spouse," "medical disease in patient," "financial difficulties," and so forth. The numerator of the rate consisted of the number of patient-coinformant pairs agreeing that an event (but not necessarily the same event) had occurred in a given stress area. The denominator represented the total number of events reported by at least one member of the pair. Overall intrapair agreement, based on this index, was 57%.

Brown and Birley (1968) and Brown et al. (1973) adopted a similar study design to measure instrument reliability while investi-

TABLE 2

Studies of Paired-Subjects Reliability of Life-Event Interviews.

Study	Sample Size	Patient Sociodemographic Characteristics	Interview	Time Period Covered	Diagnosis & Patient Status	Measure of Reliability	Reliability
Hudgens et al., 1970	80	Mean age: 45 Males: 27 Married: 58	as described in study	1 yr	Heterogeneous psychiatric inpatients, plurality (39) depressed	intrapair agreement on general stress areas	0.57
Brown & Birley, 1968; Brown et al., 1973	50	Mean age: 34 Males: 24 Never married: 31 Left school before 16: 31	as described in study	13 wk[a]	schizophrenic inpatients	intrapair agreement on individual events	0.81
Brown et al., 1973	50	Mean age: 43[b] Females: 50	as described in study	1 yr	depression (41 inpatients, 73 outpatients[b])	intrapair agreement on individual events	0.79
Schless and Mendels, 1979	62	Mean age: 37[c] Males: 47%[c]	IDE	not specified	depression, all outpatients	intrapair agreement on individual events (restricted to 22 most frequent items)	0.43
	35		PERI	not specified, probably 1 yr			0.43[d]

Study	N	Sample characteristics	Instrument	Test-retest interval	Outcome	Statistic	Results
Rahe et al., 1974	116	Mean age: 55, [b] all <65 yr; Males: 78% [b]; Married: 74% [b]; skilled and un-skilled occupations overrepresented	SRE: 42 items	2 yr	acute myocardial infarctions	correlation co-efficient of weighted (LCU) scores	Pairs with recently ill patient 1st yr: 0.75[e]; 2nd yr: 0.51; 1st 6 mos: 0.67; 3rd 6 mos: 0.56; 2nd 6 mos: 0.65; 4th 6 mos: 0.55. Pairs without recent illness: 1st yr: 0.7[e]; 2nd yr: 0.49; 1st 6 mos: 0.28; 3rd 6 mos: 0.47; 2nd 6 mos: −0.13; 4th 6 mos: 0.50

[a] The author did not state whether the agreement statistics applied only to life-event reports for the 13 weeks prior to onset or included reports for the weeks between onset and admission.

[b] This statistic refers to the larger patient sample from which subjects for the reliability study were drawn. The author did not specify whether the distribution of the subjects in the reliability investigation departed significantly from the larger sample with regard to this variable.

[c] This figure refers to an original group of 117 patients. There is a discrepancy whereby 20 patients are unaccounted for.

[d] This figure is meant to be indicative not exact. The authors do not provide a specific rate of intrapair agreement for the PERI interview, but state that the results were similar to those for the IDE.

[e] Time periods are listed in order of recency.

gating the role of life events in schizophrenia and depression. In the first study, 50 hospitalized schizophrenics (19 experiencing their first psychotic break) were interviewed within 9 weeks of illness onset (median, 1 week) regarding life events in the period between onset and admission and in the 13 weeks prior to onset. Mean age of patients was 34; 62% had left school before the age of 16; 62% had never been married; half were women. A relative of each patient was seen separately by another interviewer blind to the results of the patient interview. The relative was asked about the patient's life events over the same time period. Brown and Birley (1968) reported 81% intrapair agreement between patients and relatives. (It is unclear whether this figure refers to the entire period covered by the interview or to the more restricted 13-week period prior to onset.) Brown and Birley's statistic represents pair agreement over the occurrence of individual events whereas Hudgens et al. (1970) found agreement merely over the occurrence of *any* event in a general event category.

Brown et al. (1973) also investigated the reliability of life-event reports of the first 50 patients to enter a study of depressive illness among women residing in a south London borough. The entire sample consisted of 114 women with a primary diagnosis of depression, who had experienced on onset or clear exacerbation of symptoms within the 12 months prior to hospital admission (73 were inpatients) or initial outpatient contact. The mean age was 43. (The specific sociodemographic and treatment status of the 50 patients included in the reliability study were not reported.) In the reliability study, each patient and a close relative were interviewed regarding the patient's life events in the year prior to admission or first outpatient contact. Overall intrapair agreement was 79%.

In a study examining the contribution to patient life-event reports of separate interviews with relatives, Schless and Mendels (1978) present data that can be reinterpreted in terms of intrapair agreement. Schless and Mendels conducted three small-scale studies utilizing two different life-event instruments. The patients in the three studies were 117 outpatient depressives with a mean age of 37. Half of the subjects were female. Except for 20 friends, all coinformants were patients' relatives. Thirty-one pairs were interviewed using a 164-item version of the Inventory of Discrete Events (IDE), an instrument derived by the authors from modifications of the SRE and with additions suggested by other investigators. Another 31 pairs were interviewed with a 184-item IDE and the remaining group, 35 pairs, with a 102 item life event interview developed by the

Dohrenwends (B. S. Dohrenwend et al., 1978). (Twenty pairs are unaccounted for in this report).

Schless and Mendels aggregated the data from the two IDE studies. The estimate of intrapair agreement, extrapolated from their data, refers to agreement on individual events. It was calculated by dividing the total number of agreed-upon events by the number of events reported by at least one member of a pair. Unfortunately, Schless and Mendels presented data only for the 22 most frequently reported items on the IDE inventory. Overall intrapair agreement on the IDE for these 22 items was 43%. The PERI results were said to be similar.

In marked contrast to the four preceding investigations, Rahe et al. (1974) assessed paired-subjects reliability in terms of score consistency. The patients were 116 Finnish survivors of acute myocardial infarctions under 65 years of age. Spouses served as the coinformants in all instances but one. Cases were drawn from a larger sample (279) of myocardial infarction patients (mean age 55, 22% female, 74% married). Each member of a pair was seen separately by a nurse-interviewer. The interview, based on a translation of the SRE, covered events in the preceding two years. In the analysis, patients were divided into those who had experienced illnesses (other than the recent myocardial infarction) in the preceding two years (48) and those who had not (68). LCU scores for subjects were calculated separately for each year and for each half-year, and the correlations between paired subjects' scores computed accordingly. (Score correlations for quarter-year periods were also calculated, but are not reported here.) For pairs in which the patient had undergone a recent illness, the score correlations were 0.75 and 0.51 for the first (earlier) and second years respectively; for the half years the parallel correlations were 0.67, 0.65, 0.56, and 0.55. For pairs in which the patient had not had a recent illness, the corresponding correlations were 0.07 and 0.49 for the year periods and 0.28, –0.13, 0.47, and 0.50 for the half-year periods.

Appropriateness of Study Designs and Statistics—These investigators do not explain their choice of a reliability design, nor provide an explicit measurement model or framework for interpreting their data on measurement error. Consequently, some reading between the lines becomes necessary if we are to evaluate this research area. Two different and opposing measurement concepts may be discerned in these studies: a notion of checklists as direct measures of an internal, subject characteristic (stress) and an idea of checklists as measures that ask subjects to rate external objects (events) as to their occurrence.

Measurement error in tests of subject characteristics is often understood in terms of a domain-sampling model. This model postulates that any given test of an attribute is comprised of a random sample of items drawn from the universe or domain of all possible items measuring that attribute. Test reliability represents the correlation of subjects' scores on a given sample of items with their true scores. Classically, this correlation is estimated by item-score intercorrelations on a given measure, but estimation by means of score correlations on parallel tests is easily comprehended within this model (Nunnally, 1967), and, to a lesser extent, so too is score correlations on two administrations of the same test. In the domain-sampling model, item responses are summed to form an aggregate score for each subject because items drawn from the same domain measure the same attribute.

The selection of a test-retest design to measure life-event reliability, combined with the use of a correlation coefficient to assess the consistency of aggregated scores, invokes just such a measurement model. It is overstating the case only slightly to say that these investigators view checklists, not as instruments measuring the number and magnitude of stressors to which the respondent has been exposed, but as direct measures of an individual's level of stress seen as a unidimensional subject characteristic. While test-retest designs and Pearson's r are appropriate for measures of personality, intelligence, or other subject attributes (although a parallel rather than identical test would be preferable at time 2), they are less satisfactory for life-event checklists on both substantive and statistical grounds.

The method chosen to measure instrument reliability must be consistent with the theory and findings of substantive research. But the assumption that the stress presumably measured by these checklists is unidimensional and a simple linear function of item weights, irrespective of the type of stressor, is widely disputed (B. S. Dohrenwend, 1973; Ross and Mirowsky, 1979) and certainly not justified for psychiatric disorders (Paykel et al., 1969; Brown et al., 1973; Jacobs and Myers, 1976). Consequently, at present, the value and meaning of the reliability coefficients for aggregated LCU scores remain uncertain. The statistical problems concern the use of correlation coefficients to assess score consistency on two parallel or identical tests. These correlations are distinctly improper and misleading where a group's mean score and the standard deviation of the scores are not approximately equal on both test administrations. Yet with two administrations of a life-event checklist, such departures might be expected and, with regard to differences in the mean, were anticipated and documented by some of these studies (e.g., Casey et al. (1967); Jenkins et al., 1979).

In addition to providing estimates of score inconsistency, two test-retest studies also report a serious decrement in subject recall over a nine month passage of time. It is of interest, therefore, to determine whether these results, generated from test-retest studies, can be extrapolated with confidence to recall in time periods progressively more distant from a single test date. Certainly such decrements would be expected on common-sense grounds alone and, more importantly, several validity studies of subject recall of medical care, illness episodes, and hospitalizations also indicate substantial (*Reporting of Hospitalization in the Health Interview Survey*, 1965), progressive (Mooney, 1962), and sometimes surprisingly prompt (*Health Interview Responses Compared with Medical Records*, 1965) forgetting. Furthermore, two groups of investigators, Nelson et al. (1972) and Uhlenhuth et al. (1977), who administered life-event questionnaires to subjects on only one occasion, reported a strong direct relationship between recency of time period and magnitude of subject recall for that period. On the other hand, two major, carefully conducted investigations employing life-event interviews with community residents reported no significant decrements in recall for the year period covered by the instrument (Paykel et al., 1969; Brown et al., 1973). No explanation has been advanced to account for these diametrically opposed results on what appears to be a comparatively simple research question.

The failure of score decrement findings to be replicated consistently in analyses of single-test data may have important implications for test-retest findings regarding score consistency and checklist reliability generally. The low correlation coefficients reported in test-retest studies are considered relevant to the issue of checklist reliability because it is assumed legitimate to apply these results directly to single test administration situations. The contradictory findings in the area of score decrement indicate that this automatic transfer of test-retest results may be improper. (The reliability of life-event scores for the tenth month prior to the date of a time 1 administration may be different, for example, from that of the month preceding time 1 recalled 9 months later at time 2.) There is the further suggestion, in the paradoxical results concerning score decrements, that score inconsistency and decrement may be less a function of passage of time than a consequence of other factors affecting checklist responses, such as method of administration or subject characteristics.

If the domain-sampling model encounters statistical obstacles when applied to the life-event checklist situation, it also lacks logical coherence. In the first place, it is difficult to see many items on the inventories, such as "death of spouse" or "birth of child," as a sample of items drawn from some larger domain. In addition, by definition, the inventory measures subject report of external events, not subject attributes. Clearly, viewing checklist completion as a process similar to that of an observer rating an object (here, an event) on the binary, categorical scale "occurred," "did not occur," is a closer approximation to the actual measurement task. Although they never state so explicitly, investigators using paired-subjects designs appear to have this framework in mind. These paired-subjects' reliability studies represent, therefore, the analogue in life-event research of the interrater design commonly used for assessing of categorical scale agreement (Cohen, 1960; Fleiss, 1971; Fleiss, 1975).

This analogy with the interrater model helps to illuminate several conceptual and statistical shortcomings in the paired-subjects design. First, the interrater model assumes that the raters are independent and that the number of targets is specifiable and, in any given test situation, specified. Neither condition obtains for paired-subjects reliability studies using life-event checklists. For one thing, the two raters are not independent. While members of the same pair are interviewed separately, their ratings on the occurrence or nonoccurrence of events in the patient's life are, of course, influenced by prior communication. The raters also occupy an asymmetric relationship to the rated events. Secondly, in life-event inventories the number of targets is unknown. Whereas each inventory has a fixed number of items, a given item may prompt recall of more than one event. The strategy adopted to deal with this problem in life-event reliability studies has been to consider the total number of events reported by either member of the pair as specifying the total number (N) of rated events. While handily permitting a mathematical calculation of percent agreement, this device imputes an undeserved validity to patient and coinformant reports, and prevents their agreement over "nonoccurrent" events from being reflected in the agreement statistic. Furthermore, the literature on categorical scale agreement makes clear that a statistic that does not summarize the extent of interrater agreement only after discounting for chance concordance is incorrect in theory and can be misleading in practice. Yet the approach taken in the paired-subjects studies of measuring interrater agreement by dividing the number of targets receiving agreed-upon rating by the number of N targets does indeed fail to discount for chance agreement at the same time that it fails to count agreements on nonoccurrent targets. Thus, the task of completing the life-event checklist, while superficially resembling the rater-target situation, departs from it in fundamental respects. In short, conceptualization of an appropriate measurement model for interpreting life-event reliability, the design of reliability studies corresponding to this model and the development of suitable statistics must be placed on the agenda for future research.

Sources of Unreliability

The foregoing discussion emphasized the limited value of available reliability estimates because of currently unresolved theoretical and statistical issues. Despite these problems, this section will accept the reported coefficients at face value to permit an exploratory identification of factors influencing reliability.

The enormous range of reliability coefficients reported in each of the two sets of studies (from 0.07 to 0.78 for retest studies and from 0.07, or even -0.13, to 0.81, for paired-subjects) covers the entire spectrum from unacceptably low (below 0.50) to high (above 0.60, assuming the measure were still in the development stage, otherwise above, say, 0.70) reliability. However, 70% of these coefficients were 0.60 or less. Exploration of factors contributing to this variability confronts considerable obstacles since the paucity of investigations is matched by the confounding within studies of possible sources of unreliability. In addition, significance tests on r values and on percent of intrapair agreement have little meaning given the former's vulnerability to departures from bivariate normality and the limited appropriateness, for reasons just discussed, of both statistics. Consequently, the inferences drawn from the following collation of study findings and examination of trends across studies, must be considered preliminary at best.

Life-event checklist reliability is likely to be influenced by five factors or types of factors: method of test administration, test length, event characteristics, item wording, and subject characteristics. It would be of great interest to know whether self-administered checklists are more reliable than interviews. Unfortunately, all paired-subjects studies employ interviews and all test-retest research untilized self-administered questionnaires. Consequently, we are unable to explore the effect of administrative method on reliability. However, the remaining factors will be examined in turn.

Test Length—In psychometric theory, increasing test length with items drawn from the common domain is understood to improve test reliability, other factors remaining constant. This relationship derives from the intercorrelation of items drawn from the same domain. Although life-event theory does not posit intercorrelation among checklist items, some degree of intercorrelation has been reported (Pugh et al., 1971; Rahe et al., 1971). It is possible, therefore, that test length influences life-event reliability.

For life-event inventories, "test length" has two components: number of checklist items and duration of time period to which these items are applied. Jenkins et al.'s (1979) "distress" scale (103 items) had a higher retest correlation coefficient than the two other scales, PUP (52 items) or HR (39 items) of which it was partially comprised. On the other hand, reliabilities for 6-month subperiods were not strinkingly different from reliabilities for 1-year periods in the studies by McDonald et al. (1972) and Rahe et al. (1971). However, the research question would have been better addressed by examining the impact of test length on reliability by study design, rather than by data manipulation. In the future separate administrations of checklists of varying lengths and covering varying time periods should be conducted. At present, these findings regarding test length are inconclusive.

Event Characteristics—Among factors likely to effect reliability, event characteristics have received most attention. The contribution to reliability of the following four event qualities have been examined within studies: saliency (event weight), recency, areas of life experience entailed, (e.g., marital, health, legal), and objectivity.

Saliency or score weight is by definition considered a direct indicator of an event's importance, and recency might also be considered to relate to event importance. On common-sense grounds we would expect that event importance would be correlated positively with reliability of recall and both Casey et al. (1967) and Brown et al. (1968, 1973) did find greater recall reliability for more salient experiences. These data are bolstered by results from studies of recall validity of illness episodes. In general, these studies report more accurate recall for illnesses of greater salience (Mechanic and

Newton, 1965). But despite this consensus across several types of studies, certain life-event item analyses have produced unsettling results. For example, at time 1 in the Jenkins et al. (1979) study, 16 subjects reported the death of a relative or close friend, yet at time 2, only one of these subjects reported such an event. On the Schless and Mendels' (1978) IDE inventory, the event "death of relative" was reported 17 times either by the patient or by the coinformant, but the event was reported in eight instances only by the patient and in five only by the coinformant. Finally, the overall intrapair agreement level of 57% reported by Hudgens et al. (1970) was raised merely to 63% when intrapair recall was restricted to the stress area "death of spouse, relative, or friend." These findings should delay our bringing premature closure to the question of the relationship between saliency and recall.

The evidence regarding recency and recall is also ambiguous. While magnitude of recall may be influenced by recency, the consistency of recall shows no such obvious relationship. The correlation coefficients reported by McDonald et al. (1972) and by Thurlow (1971) (the brewery study) for time periods progressively more distant from time 1 suggest only a meager association between recency and recall consistency. Rahe et al.'s (1974) data for pairs containing recently ill patients appear to show a direct association between recency and consistency, but the data from pairs with patients who were not recently ill does not confirm this finding. In short, the effects on recall of recency as well as saliency remain open research issues.

Six investigators compared the reliability of items grouped into topical or conceptual categories. However, the analysis and interpretation of these cross-study trends is greatly complicated by the heterogeneity of methods used to calculate the reliability of item subgroups, even among studies that employ the same overall reliability design. In addition, the four investigations of topical reliabilities (McDonald et al. (1972); Jenkins et al. (1979); Hudgens et al. (1970); and Schless and Mendels (1978) did not adopt uniform event subgroups. For example, McDonald and his colleagues used four relatively broad categories: "disciplinary," "marital," "work," and "personal and social" derived from a cluster analysis performed on similar data by Rahe et al. (1971) and Pugh et al. (1971). In contrast, Hudgens and his co-workers' 11 topics are naturally much more specific, e.g., "friction with spouse or lover," "friction with parent, sibling, or child," "problems with alcohol," and so forth.

Only six topics appear to be comparable or can be made (by

collapsing two or three distinct categories) to approach comparability across studies: "work," "legal," "health," "marital," "personal
and social," and "death." To facilitate identification of cross-study
trends, the reliability of a given rubric within a study will be
characterized by its relationship to the median topical reliability
value of that study, irrespective of whether the median represents a
high or low reliability value per se. On this basis, "work," reported
as a distinct category in three studies, shows consistently low
reliability; "legal," considered in two studies, is high in both;
"health," presented in two studies as a single category and, in a
third, as two separate topics, has a reliability close median value
in two studies and the highest reliability in the third. "Personal and
social," presented as a linked category in two studies and discernible
as three separate topics in a third, is characterized in general by
relatively low reliability. "Death," as a specific type of loss, is
addressed in two studies only. In one of these it constitutes the
median value; in the other, it is the least reliable topic.

These findings for topical reliabilities may cause some surprise.
Several researchers have attributed the results in part to statistical
artifact, stemming from the relative rarity of events reported under
some rubrics as compared to those reported under others. However,
the reasons for expecting topical differences, except insofar as topics
are correlated with saliency, are nowhere spelled out and are
certainly not self-evident. Apart from some post hoc interpretations,
none of these investigators advanced a theory or any logical grounds
for anticipating topical variability. Consequently, in the absence of
a theoretical framework for evaluating these results had given the
limited number of studies, together with the limits on their comparability, these data remain unconvincing.

Hudgens et al. (1970) and Thurlow (1971) classified inventory
items dichotomously as either objective or subjective. "Objective"
items, such as "death of relative," or "legal trouble," concerned
events which were externally verifiable and whose reporting appeared to depend largely on subject recall. Respondents' judgment
and emotions were more involved in "subjective" items, for example, "friction with spouse" and "problems with alcohol." In the
Hudgens et al. study, objective items enjoyed higher reliability than
subjective ones, although the difference was not particularly size-
able. In the Thurlow study the results from brewery workers and
psychology students were more equivocal, although tending to
suggest greater consistency in reporting of objective items.

Jenkins et al. (1979) applied a similar distinction to their topical grouping of items in a post hoc analysis and reported parallel results. Twenty of Schless and Mendels' (1978) 22 items may be classified similarly and, again, objective items show somewhat greater reliability. The broad consistency of these results employing both types of reliability designs lends them some authority.

Only Thurlow (1971) examined reliability at the meticulous level of item language. Items employing the evaluative word "substantial" or containing double statements, such as whether subjects were eating a lot more or a lot less, had test-retest reliabilities below this study's median item correlation coefficient. The greater emphasis on respondents' subjective judgment as distinct from simple recall in items using "substantial" was adduced to explain their lower reliability.

Subject Characteristics—Since cognitive abilities, judgment, and emotions are involved in life-event reporting it is of considerable interest to assess whether these checklists are grossly unreliable for certain types of subjects. The possible effects on reliability of age, sex, severity of symptomatology specifically, psychiatric symptomatology, degree of stress at time of administration, and characteristics of the pair relationship, have each been investigated in one study. The influence of socioeconomic status and diagnosis have not been examined within studies. However, given their importance, we will conduct certain cross-study comparisons despite the methodological impropriety.

With patients ranging in age from 17 to 72, Hudgens et al. (1970) found no relationship between age and reliability. However, they did report that pairs with female patients had significantly lower levels of intrapair agreement.

We might expect reliable recall and conscientious event reporting to be related directly to socioeconomic status, specifically to levels of education and professional status. These expectations are broadly confirmed by uncontrolled comparisons across the four test-retest studies. Groups at the upper end of the social and professional spectrum—the physicians and psychology students—provided reasonably consistent life-event reports, while brewery workers, at the lower end, gave markedly inconsistent accounts. Air traffic controllers and a heterogenous group of navy personnel, both occupying a middle position in terms of education, produced only moderately consistent reports.

Reliability levels associated with different diagnostic groups are extremely intriguing because of their apparent implausibility.

Brown and Birley (1968) reported exceptionally good reliability with schizophrenic inpatients. This result is surprising in its own right and even more so, perhaps, when compared to Schless and Mendels' (1978) finding of low reliability for depressed outpatients. Due to confounding of interview methods and patient type, the explanation for these differences remains uncertain. However, the within-study failure by Brown et al. (1973) to uncover an association between severity of depression and agreement level underscores this apparent lack of a strong, expectedly direct relationship between clinical status and reliability. Hudgens et al. (1970) also reported that agreement levels for affective patient-pairs did not differ significantly from the level for the remaining pairs, but this finding is uninterpretable because of the extreme diagnostic heterogeneity of the latter group.

No study broached the issue of ethnic differences in reliability and the omission by all authors of data on subjects' ethnic status precludes even uncontrolled explorations of this question.

With regard to the effect of subjects' exposure to stress on their reliability, Hudgens et al. (1970) reported an inverse relationship between the amount of reported stress and reliability. The influence of stress on recall decrement was examined by Casey et al. (1967) and Jenkins et al. (1979). The former found no association between subjects' current level of stress and the magnitude of recall for an earlier period, whereas the latter observed that the magnitude score difference between time 1 and time 2 was positively correlated with the score at time 1.

The effect of certain pair characteristics on intrapair agreement has also received some brief, if unrewarding, attention. Hudgens et al. (1970) and Brown et al. (1973) did not find a significant difference in intrapair agreement levels when paired members of the same household were contrasted with paired individuals not living together. A similar analysis by Brown and his team, comparing pairs where the informant was and was not indicated to be a close confidant, also failed to show a difference in agreement levels.

Conclusion

In the field of life-events research, reliability questions have not received sustained theoretical attention or rigorous empirical investigation. No concept of the measurement characteristics of checklists has been explicitly elaborated. For this reason, it is uncertain whether the estimates obtained by test-retest or paired-subjects studies are appropriate indices of checklist reliability. Furthermore, the amount of interpretable data available from reliability investigations is severely limited because their study designs, frequently hobbled by the confounding of factors of interest, preclude extensive anatomization of measurement error.

In general, the reliability estimates reported in these studies are low to moderate. However, unreliability attenuates the observed strength of associations between variables. Therefore, if we were to accept these reliability values as legitimate, the general inference would be that stressful life events (or whatever is measured by such checklists) play a more important role in illness onset or exacerbation than is currently appreciated. Certainly, this is a defensible implication for controlled studies of life events and illness. Yet it is worth noting that test-retest findings, usually based on time 1-time 2 intervals of at least 6-months' duration, may have little applicability to life-event checklists covering much shorter time periods. The reliability of such checklists, which will probably be used increasingly in prospective designs, remains to be established.

In contrast to these reliability results proper, the findings on time 1-time 2 decrements in score magnitude would, if accepted, challenge the conclusions of life event studies which rely upon data from clinical series. Measuring life-event frequencies in patients only, these studies report excess stressors in time periods closest to illness onset. Data on score decrements from test-retest studies suggest clearly that such excess is readily explained as mere artifact of declining recall in time intervals progressively more distant from the date of the single checklist administration. However, the failure of two leading studies to document these decrements with data obtained at a single checklist administration should delay the outright rejection of these result from clinical series, at least on this basis.

Research on checklist reliability should provide not merely overall estimates of measurement error but information on the specific sources of that error. These investigators conducted limited efforts to dissect their general reliability findings and in just a few instances could the dissection generate interpretable data. Of the various factors that might influence reliability, credible and generally consistent results were produced only for the division of the checklist into objective and subjective items, with the former enjoying slightly better reliability in test-retest and paired-subjects situations.

Future substantive research could benefit greatly from a knowledge of the reliability of checklist interviews as compared with self-administered questionnaires. Information on the possible inappropriateness of the checklist format generally for certain types of subjects would also be of interest and importance. Neither question has been explored in a controlled manner. Thus, while studies of stressful life events and illness using event checklists continue apace, major questions concerning the reliability of the basic research instrument remain uninvestigated.

References

Brown, G. W. & Birley, J. L. T. (1968), Crisis and life changes and the onset of schizophrenia. *J. Hlth Soc. Behav.*, 9:203–14.
Brown, G. W., Sklair F., Harris, T. O., & Birley, J. L. T. (1973), Life-events and psychiatric disorders. Part 1: some methodological issues. *Psychosom. Med.*, 3:74–87.
Casey, R. L., Masuda, M., & Holmes, T. H. (1967), Quantitative study of recall of life events. *J. Psychosom. Res.*, 11:239–247.
Cohen, J. (1960), A coefficient of agreement for nominal scales. *Educ. Psychol. Meas.*, 20:37–46.
Dohrenwend, B. S. (1973), Life events as stressors: a methodological inquiry. *J. Hlth Soc. Behav.*, 14:167–175.
Dohrenwend, B. S., Krasnoff, L., Askenasy, A. R., & Dohrenwend, B. P. (1978), Exemplification of a method for scaling life events: the PERI Life Event Scale. *J. Hlth Soc. Behav.*, 19:205–229.
Fleiss, J. L. (1971), Measuring nominal scale agreement among many raters. *Psychol. Bull.*, 76:378–382.
Fleiss, J. L. (1975), Measuring agreement between two judges on the presence or absence of a trait. *Biometrics*, 31:651–659.
Health Interview Responses Compared with Medical Records. Vital Health Stat (1965), Public Health Service Publication No. 1000, Series 2, No. 7. Washington, D.C., U.S. Department of Health, Education and Welfare.
Holmes, T. H. & Rahe, R. M. (1967), The social readjustment rating scale. *J. Psychosom. Res.*, 11:213–218.
Hudgens, R. W., Robins, E., & Delong, W. B. (1970), The reporting of recent stress in the lives of psychiatric patients. *Brit. J. Psychiat.*, 117:635–643.
Hurst, M. W., Jenkins, C. D., & Rose, R. M. (1978), The assessment of life change stress: a comparative and methodological study. *Psychosom. Med.*, 40:126–141.
Jacobs, S. & Myers, J. (1976), Recent life events and acute schizophrenic psychosis: a controlled study. *J. Nerv. Ment. Dis.*, 162:75–87.
Jenkins, C. D., Hurst, M. W., & Rose, R. M. (1979), Life changes: do people really remember? *Arch. Gen. Psychiat.*, 36:379–384.
McDonald, B. W., Pugh, W. M., Gunderson, E. K. E., & Rahe, R. H. (1972), Reliability of life change cluster scores. *Brit. J. Soc. Clin. Psychol.*, 11:407–409.
Mechanic, D. & Newton, M. (1965), Some problems in the analysis of morbidity data. *J. Chron. Dis.*, 18:569–580.
Mooney, H. W. (1962), *Methodology in Two California Health Surveys. Public Health Monog.* No. 70. U.S. Department of Health, Education and Welfare Publication No. 942. Washington, D.C., Public Health Service.

Nelson, P., Mensh, I. N., Hecht, E., & Schwartz, A. (1972), Variables in the reporting of recent life changes. *J. Psychosom. Res.*, 16:465–471.
Nunnally, J. C. (1967), *Psychometric Theory.* New York, McGraw-Hill.
Paykel, E. S., Myers, J. K., Dienelt, M. N., Klerman, G. L., Lindental, J. J., & Pepper, M. P. (1969), Life events and depression: a controlled study. *Arch. Gen. Psychiat.*, 21:753–760.
Paykel, E. S., Prusoff, B. A., & Uhlenhuth, E. H. (1971), Scaling of life events. *Arch. Gen. Psychiat.*, 25:340–347.
Pugh, W., Erickson, J. M., Rubin, R. T., Gunderson, E. K. E., & Rahe, R. H. (1971), Cluster analyses of life changes. II. Method and replication in Navy subpopulations. *Arch. Gen. Psychiat.*, 25:333–339.
Rahe, R. H., Pugh, W., Erickson, J. M., Gunderson, E. K. E., & Rubin, R. T. (1971), Cluster analyses of life changes. I. Consistency of clusters across large Navy samples. *Arch. Gen. Psychiat.*, 25:330–332.
Rahe, R. H., Romo, M., Bennett, L., & Siltanen, P. (1974), Recent life changes, myocardial infarction, and abrupt coronary death. *Intern. Med.*, 133:221–228.
Reporting of Hospitalization in the Health Interview Survey. Vital Health Stat. (1965), Public Health Service Publication No. 1000, Series 2, No. 6. Washington, D.C., U.S. Department of Health, Education and Welfare.
Ross, E. E. & Mirowsky, J. (1979), A comparison of life-event weighting schemes: change, undesirability, and effect-proportional indices. *J. Hlth Soc. Behav.*, 20:166–177.
Schless, A. P. & Mendels, J. (1978), The value of interviewing family and friends in assessing life stressors. *Arch. Gen. Psychiat.*, 35:565–567.
Thurlow, H. J. (1971), Illness in relation to life situation and sick role tendency. *J. Psychosom. Res.*, 15:73–88.
Uhlenhuth, E. H., Haberman, S. J., Balter, M. D., & Lipman, R. S. (1977), Remembering life events. In: *The Origins and Course of Psychopathology: Methods of Longitudinal Research*, ed. J. S. Strauss, H. M. Babigian, & M. Roff. New York, Plenum Press, pp. 117–132.

Methodological Issues in the Interpretations of the Consequences of Extreme Situations

JOHN E. HELZER, M.D.

Studies of the contribution of stressful life events to the development of psychiatric disorder have been criticized on substantive and methodological grounds. Theoretically, some of the frequently mentioned difficulties should be minimized when extreme rather than more-common events are studied. For example, Rabkin and Struening (1976) question the size and practical significance of the demonstrated associations between events and later illness in most studies. They point out that when correlation coefficients between event and outcome are reported, they are generally low, suggesting that the events studied account for only a small proportion of the total illness variance. However, if stress is a significant contributor to illness, extreme events and the resulting extreme stress should show a stronger association with later outcome. Extreme events should maximize the amount of variance explained in subsequent illness.

Mechanic (1974) has suggested that life events may be more closely associated with care-seeking behavior than illness per se. He points out that the dependent variable in many life-events studies is mild illness as reported in work or health records. Individuals may be more likely to seek consultation when under stress. Thus, perhaps what is being measured is the tendency to consult for illness rather than its development. Here again, the study of extreme situations often avoids this selectivity because such studies are usually event-focused rather than illness-focused. In an event-focused study, a common approach is to interview a series of respondents who have experienced a given event and inquire about the occurrence of subsequent disorder regardless of whether care was sought. Clayton et al. (1972), for example, found that women whose husbands had recently died had enough depressive symptoms during the bereavement period to meet criteria for a diagnosis of depressive disorder, but the rate of consultation with a mental health professional was very low. A personal interview, event-focused study does not render Mechanic's criticism moot because even extreme events may be more memorable if consultation was sought for resulting problems. But, if disorder is rated independently of consultation, the difficulty of interpreting whether stressful events led to increased illness or increased help-seeking behavior is minimized.

Hudgens (1974) is critical of the fact that most life-events studies are retrospective, making it difficult to date occurrences accurately and therefore difficult to temporally order antecedents and outcomes. Temporal ordering is particularly hard when the independent variable includes trivial or common events and the dependent variable includes mild illness. But, the study of extreme events also helps to overcome some of these difficulties. First, extreme events can be dated more accurately. Second, since an extreme event is so memorable, it may be easier for a respondent to recall whether other occurrences and/or symptoms antedated or postdated the event. In fact, a technique often used in any kind of retrospective study is to have respondents focus on memorable and datable events, such as high school graduation, marriage, or the death of a prominent person, as a means of dating less memorable details of their personal lives.

All life-events studies, but particularly retrospective ones, are especially difficult to interpret when events and symptoms of illness are confounded. Consider, for example, a life-events study in which separations from a spouse is an event and depressive disorder is one of the possible outcomes. The event in this case is a likely concomitant of the outcome since one of the frequent early symptoms of depression is irritability which in turn can lead to increased interpersonal difficulties with significant persons. Thus, what is being conceptualized as an antecedent event predicting a psychiatric outcome may actually be part of the early symptomatology of a depressive syndrome already underway. Hudgens (1974) cites one popular life-events scale in which 29 of the 43 events inquired about are frequently symptoms or consequences of psychiatric disorder. B. P. Dohrenwend (1974) emphasizes this point by suggesting that it is particularly difficult to distingusih antecedents from consequences when the events studied are within the individual's control.

Here again, the study of extreme events should minimize such difficulties. First, because they are extreme, such events are unlikely to be confused with symptoms or consequences of illness. Second, while the probability of extreme events occurring may be influenced by the individual's personal characteristics, as we will discuss in more detail below, their actual occurrence is likely to be outside the control of the individual.

Retrospective studies also increase what Brown (1974) calls direct contamination, the tendency by a respondent to retrospectively overreport life events prior to the onset of illness so as to justify or "make sense" of his illness. Again, while this difficulty would not be eliminated altogether, it should be minimized in studies of extreme situations. Since extreme events are likely to be memorable regardless of the state of subsequent health, there is less likely to be differential overreporting of them in ill versus well populations.

Life-events research has been criticized because of a lack of specificity in defining the event, the outcome, and the conditions under which the two are linked. Mechanic, for example, points out that it is of interest, but not especially helpful, to know that stress precedes illness more frequently than chance expectation. Since illness often occurs without significant antecedent stress and since even severe stress can be weathered without development of illness, the conditions under which stress and illness are associated need to be defined (Mechanic, 1974). Other authors have also called for life-events studies which focus on particular kinds of events, definable mediating factors such as social supports, and specific dependent variables such as particular types of illness (Rabkin and Struening, 1976; B. P. Dohrenwend, 1974). Since they are event-oriented, extreme-events studies do narrow the focus of research. By concentrating on a specific, dramatic, and datable event, the study of extreme situations addresses at least one of these areas, i.e., specifying the event.

This chapter will focus on the problem of separating the contribution of predisposition to outcome from the contribution of the event itself. These two elements are usually confounded because predisposition is one of the factors influencing the occurrence of events to which one might be exposed. In studies of extreme events, the influence of predisposition on later outcome might be minimized, thus making the association between events and outcome less subject to predispositional variation. This minimization could operate in two ways.

First, it seems logical to assume that predisposition will have relatively less influence on who will experience extreme events than on who will experience more common types of events. For example, widespread disasters often affect a populace without respect to social class or position, thus minimizing the importance of predisposition. Some caution is necessary because predisposition may play a greater role than is immediately apparent. For example, an extreme event over which most individuals have little influence is the death of a spouse. But, just because death is relatively capricious does not mean that the predispositions of the bereaved are irrelevant. Assortative mating can confound the interpretation of the impact of a spouse's death. Predisposition can obviously influence the selection of a mate with a high risk of early death as well as influence the type of emotional response when the mate dies, thus complicating the separation of predisposition and outcome. A similar problem occurs in interpreting the contribution of death of a parent to later problems in children. Genetic factors increasing the parent's risk of early death might be passed on to children and predispose the child to have problems. Attributing later problems in the child to early death of the parent without considering the contribution of the child's own genetic predisposition would be a mistake. Even in the case of natural disasters such as floods and tornados, personal variables that are predictive of later outcome, such as low educational achievement or early use of alcohol, might also influence the likelihood of injury from such disasters because of association with location or sturdiness of the dwelling in which the individual resides.

There is a second way in which extreme events may minimize the influence of predisposition. Assuming that extreme events have a large emotional impact, such occurrences might simply overwhelm the effect of more distant antecedents like predisposition. B. P. Dohrenwend and B. S. Dohrenwend (1978) have pointed out, for example, that extreme stress might override mediating factors such as prior psychopathology in the development of subsequent illness. If that is true, measurement of the contribution of extreme events to later outcome is made easier.

Some authors have assumed that extreme situations do indeed overwhelm the influence of prior antecedents. For example, Hocking (1970) has said:

Constitutional factors and pattern of childhood rearing are of undoubted importance in the reactions of individuals to the stress and strains of everyday life . . . [but] when the duration and degree of stress are severe, preexisting personality characteristics do little more than determine how long an individual can tolerate the situation before the onset of neurotic symptoms. (P. 542)

It seems logical to assume that the relative contribution of predisposition to outcome diminishes with the extremity of life events. But there have been few attempts to measure whether this is true.

Much of what we know about the outcome of extreme events comes from the literature dealing with wartime stress. In this literature, there is often no specific recognition of and even less frequently an attempt to measure the impact of predisposition. For example, in a recent collection of papers on the effects of extreme stress in Vietnam veterans (Figley, 1978), only one author attempted to compare the influence of predisposition to that of wartime stress on later emotional disability (Worthington, 1978). This tendency to overlook the influence of predisposition in reactions to the stress of war is not confined to studies of Vietnam veterans. Beebe (1975), for example, discusses the excess psychological and psychiatric disability among inmates of World War II Japanese, Korean, and European POW camps. Little consideration is given to the influence of variables which antedate the POW experience in assessing outcome.

Even when mentioned specifically, antecedent variables sometimes tend to be dismissed. DeFazio (1978) suggests that men who were sociopathic before going to Vietnam and continued to exhibit antisocial behavior after return might not have had these problems if they had not been in combat.

On the other hand, some authors have examined predisposition in the context of assessing the effect of extreme stress. Brill and Beebe (1955) in their five-year follow-up of World War II veterans, found that combatants with preservice personality disorders were six times more likely to be psychiatrically disabled at follow-up than those without antecedent personality problems. Hunter (1978) found a direct association between the length of captivity of American POW's in Vietnam and the likelihood of a psychiatric diagnosis two years postrelease. However, she also found that men who had predisposing factors in their history were far more likely to receive a psychiatric diagnosis than those who did not. Based on his study of 147 army veterans, Worthington (1978) concluded that preservice variables may be more powerful than inservice variables as predictors of postwar adjustment. Finally, Yager (1976) found that soldiers with postcombat violence more frequently had a history of fighting in childhood or adolescence than those without postcombat violence. He concluded that the first group may be more violence prone both before and after combat, but points out that there are few studies of the effect of wartime stress on later adjustment in which the influence of predisposition is taken into account.

Recognition that predisposition may be an important variable in predicting outcome even in situations of extreme stress is important. However, we are not aware of any studies that have attempted to quantify the relative contribution of predisposition under varying levels of stress. We have recently reported on the long-term emotional effect of combat among U.S. servicemen stationed in Vietnam (Helzer et al., 1978, 1979). This data set provides an opportunity to address the question of the importance of predisposition when stress is moderate or extreme because we are able to quantify the interaction between predisposition (characteristics present before entering the military) and the stress of military combat in the later development of a specific outcome, depression. Based on previous work, our hypothesis was that certain pre-Vietnam characteristics (predispositions) would predict depression in Vietnam returnees, but that predisposition would be a more powerful predictor in men who had seen little combat in Vietnam than in men who had experienced more extreme combat stress.

Methods

Sample—The sample reported in this investigation was drawn from the approximately 13,760 U.S. Army enlisted men who returned to the United States from Vietnam in September 1971. Men were eligible regardless of whether they were draftees or volunteers, whether they had been released from service or were still on active duty. From the names of all eligible men contained in the appropriate Army active duty files, we selected a random sample of 943 men. The sample was divided about evenly into two groups: (1) a general sample of 470 subjects randomly chosen from all returnees; and (2) a "drug positive" sample of 495 subjects randomly selected from a group of men who had been identified as illicit drug users on the basis of a urine screening test at the time of departure from Vietnam. There was an overlap of 22 men in the two samples.

Between May and September 1972, an attempt was made to locate and interview all 943 returnees. No limit was set on the number of attempts that could be made to contact a respondent, and interviews were completed with 94% of the total sample. Interviews were obtained for 90% or more of every subgroup defined by race, age, rank, or type of discharge. Examinations were done by trained interviewers using a structured instrument covering demographic variables and events which occurred prior to going into the service, events occurring in Vietnam, and events (as well as deviant behavior, emotional adjustment, and social status) since return. In addition to interviews, army records were obtained for 99% of the sample, and VA hospital records were available for all of those who had obtained VA treatment since discharge from the military.

At the time of the first follow-up, returnees were scattered across the continental United States, Hawaii, Puerto Rico, and the Virgin Islands. Two years after the first examination, the veterans were again located and interviewed. The original sample of 943 was reduced to 605 by eliminating men living outside of the continental United States, those residing in the least populous states, and those inducted before 1969. This limitation enabled us to select and examine a matched nonveteran control group. With the help of the selective service system, we identified 302 men who were matched to the general sample veterans on the basis of draft eligibility, size and location of predraft residential area, age, and education at the time of the veteran's entry into the military. The nonveterans were eligible to serve in the military but did not either because their lottery numbers were not drawn or because they obtained deferments. We located and interviewed 284 (94%) of the controls. For the veterans, the second interview covered years 2 and 3 since return from Vietnam. For comparability of data, each nonveteran was asked about events occurring during this same 2-year period but was also asked about periods which corresponded to specific calendar periods representing the time before the matched veteran had gone into the military and the time of the matched veteran's tour of service.

We were able to locate and examine 571 (95%) of the 605 veterans selected for the second follow-up. The present analysis is confined to the two veterans samples (general and drug-positive) which were combined. To avoid biasing the random sample of all Vietnam returnees with large numbers of men who used illicit drugs heavily in Vietnam, we weighted the drug-positive sample to represent its true proportion in the general sample (Wish et al., 1980).

Variables Studied—We inquired about two types of extreme stress during Vietnam: exposure to combat and being wounded. During the first follow-up examination, we had asked three questions regarding combat experiences:

1. Did you go on combat patrols or have other very dangerous duty?
2. Were you ever under enemy fire?

3. Were you ever surrounded by the enemy?

Because of the small number of men reporting all three combat events, we defined the most extreme combat exposure as a positive response to at least two of our three combat questions. In addition, we asked veterans at first follow-up if they had been wounded during their Vietnam tours. The combat variable allows us to examine the influence of predisposition under varying levels of stress. We also examined being wounded for two reasons. First, it is probably the most extreme stress variable we had available to us. Second, it is a less confounded variable for our analysis because it is not correlated with as many of the predispositions as is combat.

Both combat and being wounded were subjective rather than objective events in this sample since we did not have reliable information available to us with which to confirm the veterans' reports. Although it would seem that combat exposure could be obtained from the military record, assignment to a combat unit as reflected in that record did not necessarily mean assignment to a post within a combat unit that would lead directly to combat involvement. In order to test the validity of our measure of extreme combat stress, we examined two of its correlates. Veterans who reported two or more combat events were 50 times more likely than others to have had friends killed in combat and 90 times more likely to have themselves been wounded while in Vietnam. We had no measure of the intensity of each combat event individually, but exposure to two or more types of combat events was a better predictor of depression than either frequency or duration of individual events.

The outcome variable we focused on for both first and second follow-up is a depressive syndrome. This was defined slightly differently in the two follow-up periods. At the first follow-up, we had inquired about depressive symptoms occurring at any time during the 8 to 12 months since return to the States. We did not investigate whether the symptoms occurred simultaneously because the time interval under investigation was fairly brief. Therefore, at first follow-up a depressive syndrome was defined as a dysphoric mood (depressed, blue, or down in the dumps) for a period of at least 1 month, plus three or more depressive symptoms. The second follow-up interview covered a 2-year period so that we felt it necessary to assess whether the dysphoria and any reported depressive symptoms occurred together. Therefore, the definition of a depressive syndrome at second follow-up was dysphoria for at least

1 month at any time during the 2-year period and three or more depressive symptoms occurring simultaneously with the dysphoria. The depressive symptoms inquired about were the following:

1. Trouble sleeping over a period of several weeks.
2. Anorexia with a greater than eight-pound weight loss.
3. Loss of energy for several weeks.
4. Thoughts of death or self-harm.
5. Worry about insanity.
6. A period of crying spells.
7. Several weeks of difficulty concentrating.
8. A several-week period of feeling worthless or sinful.
9. A several-week period of loss of interest in things that the respondent normally found interesting.

In the first interview, we inquired about the veterans' demographic and personal histories prior to military service. In preliminary analyses, we looked for variables antecedent to military service that predicted depression at the first or second follow-up. Several predictors were found:

1. Childhood or adolescent social deviance defined as a score of five points or more on a scale describing antisocial behavior prior to entering service. The scale was composed of five problem areas: school departure via dropout or expulsion; truancy; fighting; arrests; and a history of early drunkenness. An individual could receive a maximum of two points in each problem area.
2. Drug use defined as any illicit drugs prior to entering the military including marijuana, amphetamines, barbiturates, or narcotics.
3. Failure to graduate from high school.
4. Alcohol problems defined as a report of regular and heavy consumption of alcohol (seven drinks in an evening at least weekly) plus either medical treatment for a drinking problem or one or more of the following symptoms: morning drinking; binge drinking or alcoholic benders; the individual thinking he drinks too much; accidents secondary to drinking; alcohol-related arrests; a blackout from drinking.
5. Parental arrest defined as a report by the respondent that one or both of his parents had been arrested prior to his entry into the military.
6. Parental psychiatric problem defined as a report by the veteran that one or both of his parents had had nervous illness,

breakdown, or mental troubles for which they saw a doctor or were hospitalized.

Results

Depression After Return from Vietnam—The proportions of men reporting a depressive syndrome at first and second follow-up were 8% and 16% respectively. The higher figure for the second follow-up period is not surprising since these percents are period-prevalence figures and the period of time covered by the second interview was about twice as long as that covered by the first. The depressive syndromes the veterans reported were not trivial. For example, at second follow-up about half of the depressed men reported anorexia with an eight-pound weight loss, about one third had thoughts of death or self-harm, and about one quarter had to take time off from their regular activities because of depressive symptoms.

Vietnam Stress and Later Depression—We have previously shown that Vietnam combat predicted later depression in veterans (Helzer et al., 1978, 1979). For both follow-up periods, we found a linear relationship between the number of combat events and the proportion who experienced depression. It has been suggested that illness or injury, especially in the context of a disruption of one's usual social supports (such as that presumably occuring in wartime) is particularly likely to lead to psychopathology (B. P. Dohrenwend and B. S. Dohrenwend, 1978). That was certainly true of this sample. Being wounded was an even stronger predictor of depression at first and second follow-up than was combat. Figure 1 shows the proportion who suffered depression during the second follow-up among nonveterans and three groups of veterans: those who were neither wounded nor exposed to the highest level of combat stress, nonwounded men exposed to at least two combat events, and the wounded. A similar relationship was seen for first follow-up depression in wounded veterans.

Relationship Between Predisposition, Vietnam Stress, and Depression—The six preservice variables defined above predicted later depression, but not all of them did so in both follow-up periods. Parental psychiatric problems failed to predict a depressive syndrome at first follow-up, and alcohol problems and parental arrest were not predictors at second follow-up. Each antecedent

FIGURE 1

Prevalence of Depressive Syndromes in Non-
Veterans and Three Groups of Veterans

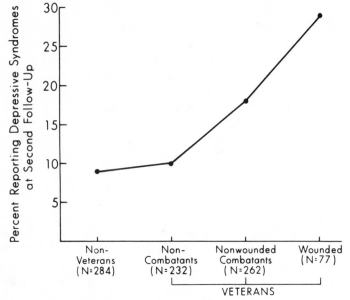

which predicted depression did so at a p level of less than 0.01 or better (X^2, 1 df).

Three of the antecedent variables (deviance, drug use, and high school graduation) also predicted who would see combat. Deviance and drug use were strong predictors of combat ($p < 0.001$ and $p < 0.01$ respectively), and high school graduation was a significant but weak predictor ($p < 0.05$). Being wounded in Vietnam was predicted by only one of the antecedent variables, parental psychiatric problems ($p < 0.01$).

Figure 2 illustrates the association between level of combat in Vietnam and depression at first follow-up in men who did and did not graduate from high school. Clearly, the discovered relationship mostly contradicts our hypothesis. Although the figure shows that the proportion of depression increased with the number of combat events, the influence of the antecedent variable on outcome was greater at higher levels of combat stress, and this contrary to our speculation. At low levels of stress (no or one combat event), there was not a significant difference in prevalence of depressive syndromes between those with and without the predisposing factor,

FIGURE 2

Relationship of Preservice Education to Post-
Vietnam Depression Under Varying Levels
of Combat Stress.

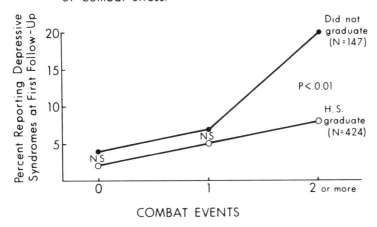

COMBAT EVENTS

whereas at high levels of combat stress, this difference was significant ($p < 0.01$).

Table 1 illustrates the interaction of predisposition and number of
combat events for all of the antecedent variables that predicted first
follow-up depression. At each level of combat, a pair of percentage
figures illustrates the prevalence of depression among men with and
without each antecedent. An attributable risk figure is calculated
from each pair by subtraction. This latter number indicates the
relative contribution of the predisposing variable to later depression
at a given level of combat stress. In addition, we have noted the level
of statistical significance for differences in depression between those
with and without the antecedent. In no case is the contribution of
predisposition higher either in terms of percent attributable risk or
in terms of statistical significance for men without any combat
events than it is for men with some level of combat. Thus, for none
of the antecedents is our hypothesis supported. Because of the
difference in number of men exposed to each level of combat, the
chi-square statistic reported in the table may be misleading. Therefore, we calculated a phi coefficient to indicate the strength of

TABLE 1

Attributable Influence of Preservice Predisposition on Depressive
Syndromes at First Follow-up at Varying Levels of Combat Stress.

	Percent Depressed if Number of Combat Events equals		
Preservice Predisposition	None (N = 103)	One (N = 131)	Two or More (N = 337)
Education			
Did not graduate (N = 146)	4%	7%	20%
High school graduate (N = 425)	2	5	8[a]
Attributable risk	2	2	12
Drug use			
Used drugs (N = 237)	8	12	12
No drug use (N = 334)	1[b]	2[a]	10
Attributable risk	7	10	2
Childhood deviance			
High (N = 211)	11	15	18
Low (N = 360)	0[a]	2[a]	6[c]
Attributable risk	11	13	12
Alcohol use			
Problem use (N = 158)	10	14	24
No problem use (N = 419)	2[a]	4[b]	6[c]
Attributable risk	8	10	18
Parental arrest			
Parent arrested (N = 56)	4	24	28
No parent arrested (N = 515)	2	4[b]	9[a]
Attributable risk	2	20	19

Significance level (x^2, df= 1): [a]$p < 0.01$; [b]$p < 0.05$; [c]$p < 0.01$.

association between each predisposition and later depression for
each level of combat. These findings were consistent with the above;
that is, for none of the predisposing variables was the phi coefficient
higher in men who had not experienced combat than it was for men
experiencing some level of combat.

It is possible that for some of the veterans, depression ascertained
during the first follow-up period actually began prior to their
exposure to the stress variables we studied. The period of exposure

to stress and the first follow-up period were temporally adjacent. If a veteran was first exposed to combat or was wounded late in his Vietnam tour, it is possible that the depressive syndrome he reported at the first follow-up interview was actually present before the extreme stress occurred. However, this applies to first follow-up depressions only. There was little carry-over of depression from the first to the second follow-up (Helzer et al., 1979), and thus depression ascertained at second interview is very unlikely to have preceded exposure to the stress variables we studied.

We therefore examined the relative influence of predisposition and combat stress on depressive syndromes at second follow-up. Figure 3 illustrates the interaction between preservice drug use and level of combat stress in predicting depressive disorder in the second follow-up period. Table 2 documents this interaction for each of the relevant predispositions. Again, the findings are inconsistent with the hypothesis that antecedents have a lesser predictive effect under conditions of extreme stress. In each case, the attributable risk figure for antecedents is greater for men involved in some level of combat. For two variables, drug use and education, attributable risk is highest for men who reported the highest level of combat stress.

FIGURE 3

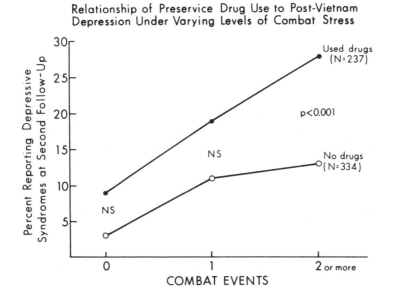

Relationship of Preservice Drug Use to Post-Vietnam Depression Under Varying Levels of Combat Stress

TABLE 2

Attributable Influence of Preservice Predisposition on Depressive
Syndromes at Second Follow-Up at Varying Levels of Combat Stress.

	Percent Depressed if Number of Combat Events equals		
Preservice predisposition	None (N = 103)	One (N = 131)	Two or More (N = 337)
Drug use			
Used drugs (N = 237)	9%	19%	28%
No drug use (N = 334)	3	11	13[a]
Attributable risk	6	8	15
Childhood deviance			
High (N = 211)	3	21	16
Low (N = 360)	5	10	26[b]
Attributable risk	-2	11	10
Education			
Did not graduate (N = 146)	2	23	31
High school graduate (N = 425)	5	10	16[c]
Attributable risk	-3	13	15
Parental psychiatric problems			
Parental problem (N = 137)	0	38	29
No parental problem (N = 434)	6	8[a]	16[b]
Attributable risk	-6	30	13

Significance level (x^2, df= 1): [a]$p < 0.001$; [b]$p < 0.05$; [c]$p < 0.01$.

The other measure of stress we used is having been wounded in
Vietnam. We compared wounded men to all other veterans to see if
this type of extreme stress would reduce the influence of predisposition. Table 3 shows the interaction between the relevant predispositions and being wounded in the prediction of depression at first
follow-up. As was true for combat, the results shown here directly
contradict the hypothesis that the influence of predisposition on
later depression is less at a higher level of stress. The attributable
risk for every predispositional variable is greater in the wounded
men than in the nonwounded. Because of the large difference in the
number of nonwounded versus wounded men, we have reported phi

coefficients showing the degree of association between predisposition and outcome rather than significance levels. In every case, the phi coefficient is greater in wounded men than in nonwounded and for two variables, education and parental arrest, the phi coefficients are several times greater.

Figure 4 graphically illustrates the interaction of preservice drug use and being wounded in predicting depression at second follow-up, and table 4 illustrates this same interaction for all of the predispositional variables which were predictive of depression at second follow-up. Again, for all but one of the variables (parental psychiatric problems), the attributable risk figures and the phi coefficients are greater in veterans who were wounded than in the nonwounded.

TABLE 3

Attributable Influence of Preservice Predisposition on Depressive Syndromes at First Follow-Up Among Wounded and Nonwounded Veterans.

Preservice Predisposition	Percent Depressed Among	
	Nonwounded (N = 494)	Wounded (N = 77)
Drug use		
Used drugs (N = 237)	9%	30%
No drug use (N = 334)	4 (0.10)[a]	19 (0.12)
Attributable risk	5	21
Childhood deviance		
High (N = 211)	12	41
Low (N = 360)	2 (0.20)	10 (0.36)
Attributable risk	10	31
Education		
Did not graduate (N = 146)	9	43
High school graduate (N = 425)	5 (0.08)	15 (0.30)
Attributable risk	4	28
Alcohol use		
Problem use (N = 158)	14	44
No problem use (N = 419)	3 (0.22)	13 (0.35)
Attributable risk	11	31
Parental arrest		
Parent arrested (N = 56)	15	71
No parent arrested (N = 515)	5 (0.12)	18 (0.39)
Attributable risk	10	53

[a] Phi coefficient shown in parentheses.

FIGURE 4

Relationship of Preservice Drug Use to Post-
Vietnam Depression in Nonwounded and
Wounded Veterans.

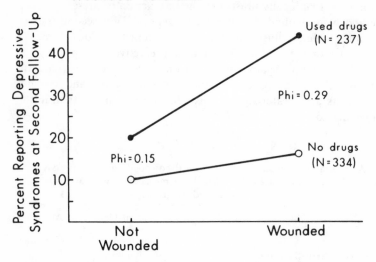

Discussion

This investigation provides a unique opportunity to examine the
relative influence of predisposition and stress in the later development of psychiatric symptomatology. The veterans sample we
studied is large and was randomly selected from men who served in
Vietnam at the height of the military campaign. Selection for United
States military duty at this time in history was relatively impartial
because of the draft lottery. Although men who had serious physical
or emotional illness, those with prison records, and those few who
were able to obtain educational or religious deferments did not fall
into our sample, deferments were more difficult to obtain in the late
1960s, and the draft lottery was probably reasonably equitable for
the vast majority of draft-eligible American youth. The follow-up
examination of the selected veterans was by personal interview
which was given by trained examiners using a structured instrument. The extreme events about which we inquired were memorable
ones and in contrast to many extreme events, were experienced by

TABLE 4

Attributable Influence of Preservice Predisposition on Depressive
Syndromes at Second Follow-Up Among Wounded and
Nonwounded Veterans.

	Percent Depressed Among	
Preservice Predisposition	Nonwounded (N = 494)	Wounded (N = 77)
Drug use		
Used drugs (N = 237)	20%	47%
No drug use (N = 334)	10 (0.15)[a]	16 (0.29)
Attributable risk	10	31
Childhood deviance		
High (N = 211)	18	44
Low (N = 360)	12 (0.09)	14 (0.33)
Attributable risk	6	30
Education		
Did not graduate (N = 146)	22	45
High school graduate (N = 425)	12 (0.13)	21 (0.26)
Attributable risk	10	24
Parental psychiatric problems		
Parental problem (N = 137)	22	32
No parental problem (N = 434)	12 (0.18)	27 (0.14)
Attributable risk	10	5

[a]Phi coefficient shown in parentheses.

large segments of the population under study. The outcome was
operationally defined, and the frequency of serious depressive
symptoms such as weight loss and suicidal thoughts suggest that the
outcome we focused on was more than just a transient dysphoric
mood state.

Perhaps the greatest advantage of the present study is the fact that
it gives us the opportunity to study the outcome of extreme events at
all. By definition, extreme situations occur rarely. They are obviously not events that one can cause to occur experimentally. It is
necessary to wait for a "natural experiment," and this the Vietnam
War provided.

The present study allows a reasonably straightforward consideration of the impact of events and the role of predisposition because it
minimizes many of the criticisms of life events-research reviewed
above. First, since we interviewed all of the veterans in the identified
sample and did not rely upon health records for medical informa-

tion or upon care-seeking to identify respondents, we ascertained prevalences of illness and not the tendency to seek consultation.

Second, although the study was retrospective, there was a clear change in setting between predisposition and extreme stress marked by military induction and transport to Vietnam, and an equally dramatic change in setting between stress events and the period of follow-up marked by return to the United States. Thus, temporal antecedents can be easily differentiated from outcomes. Finally, the stresses about which we inquired, combat and being wounded, are events that were outside the individual's control, were not symptoms of psychiatric disorder, and were unlikely to be consequences of psychiatric illness.

As we discussed above, predisposition can influence the occurrence of even extreme events. In the present study, it is not difficult to conceptualize how the predispositions we examined might have predicted exposure to combat. For example, of all the antecedents we studied, civilian antisocial behavior prior to entering the military was the strongest predictor of seeing combat. Assignment by a platoon leader or a company commander to a combat mission is presumably not a random event, and it is not difficult to imagine that men who had behavior problems tended to get undesirable duty assignments more frequently. The fact that some of our antecedent variables did predict seeing combat complicates the analysis of the relative influence of predisposition and extreme events on outcome. For these antecedents, part of the relationship between predisposition and outcome may be explained by the association between predisposition and level of combat stress. However, as we have shown, some of the antecedents did not predict level of combat but still were more strongly associated with outcome at high levels of combat stress than at low levels. In addition, only one of the antecedent variables which we studied, parental psychiatric problems, predicted being wounded in Vietnam. The fact that predisposition is a more important predictor of depressive illness for both types of extreme stress suggests that predisposition is an independent predictor interacting with extreme events.

Using this same sample of veterans, Robins (1978) examined the relative strength of the influence of setting and predisposition in predicting which veterans would initiate illicit-drug use. As in the present study, it initially seemed illogical to assume that the abundance of inexpensive illicit drugs in Vietnam would tend to attenuate the influence of predisposition on drug initiation. However, Robins (1978) found that preservice predispositions "were even more important in determining who would begin drug use in the high availability setting of Vietnam than in the lower availability conditions of the United States" (p. 193). Thus, in two different types of investigation we find that there is a synergistic effect rather than an attenuation of predisposition in extreme situations. Although it seems logical to assume that as stress becomes more severe, the influence of distant antecedents that also predict later illness will become of lesser relative importance, at least in the present sample this appears not to be the case.

This finding has theoretical implications for such questions as whether each individual has a "breaking point" in situations of extreme stress. We did find that the proportion reporting later depression rose with increased levels of Vietnam stress regardless of predisposition. However, as illustrated in Figs. 2, 3, and 4, the increase in depression under conditions of more extreme stress is much less for those without the predisposing factors, i.e., the slopes of the two curves in each figure are different. If these curves were to continue in the same fashion under conditions of even more extreme stress, "breaking points" would be reached considerably more quickly in those with predisposition than in those without. We examined predispositions individually, and men without a particular one may have had another. In future analyses, we plan to look for combinations of predispositions that are particularly likely to predict later breakdown among men who experienced extreme situations in Vietnam and also to examine men who had none of the predispositions we studied to see what the effects of increased stress are in them. From the present findings, it is not difficult to speculate that men who had none of the predispositions might show very few later effects of stress at all.

Our findings also have important practical implications for studies that attempt to quantify the effect of stress on later outcome. If a stressful event is strongly predictive of later depression, it may be misleading to conclude that the particular stress under consideration is especially deleterious without considering what role predisposing variables played in predicting who would be exposed to the stress event and further the interactive role of stress and predisposition in predicting the emotional aftermath. The fact that we have demonstrated that extreme events do not necessarily lessen the influence of distant antecedents does not preclude stress as a causative agent in later depression. But our results do render questionable any study that fails to consider the contribution of predisposition to later illness in those who have faced extreme stress on the assumption that because stress was so extreme, the relative influence of predisposition must be minimal.

Acknowledgments

This work was supported in part by United States Public Health Service Grants DA 01120, MH 14677, and DA 00013.

I wish to thank Eric Wish, Ph.D. for assistance in data analysis and Kathryn Strother Ratcliff, Ph.D. and Lee N. Robins, Ph.D. for reviewing the manuscript and offering many helpful suggestions.

References

Beebe, G. W. (1975), Follow-up studies of World War II and Korean War prisoners. II. Morbidity, disability, and maladjustments. *Amer. J. Epidemiol.*, 101:400–422.

Brill, N. Q. & Beebe, G. W. (1955), *A Follow-Up Study of War Neuroses.* Veterans Administration Medical Monograph, Washington, D.C., U. S. Government Printing Office.

Clayton, P. J., Halikas, J. A., & Maurice, W. L. (1972), The depression of widowhood. *Brit. J. Psychiat.*, 120:71–77.

DeFazio, V. J. (1978), Dynamic perspectives on the nature and effects of combat stress. In: *Stress Disorders Among Vietnam Veterans*, ed. C. R. Figley. New York, Brunner/Mazel, pp. 23–42.

Dohrenwend, B. P. (1974), Problems in defining and sampling the relevant population of stressful life events. In: *Stressful Life Events: Their Nature and Effects*, ed. B. S. Dohrenwend & B. P. Dohrenwend. New York. Wiley pp. 217–243.

Dohrenwend, B. P., & Dohrenwend, B. S. (1978), Psychiatric disorders and susceptibility to stress: Reactions to stress of varying magnitudes and varying origins. Read at the World Psychiatric Association Section Committee on Epidemiology and Community Psychiatry Triennial Meeting, St. Louis.

Figley, C. R., ed. (1978), *Stress Disorders Among Vietnam Veterans.* New York, Brunner/Mazel.

Helzer, J. E., Robins, L. N., & Davis, D. H. (1978), Depressive disorders in Vietnam returnees. *J. Nerv. Ment. Dis.*, 163:177–185.

Helzer, J. E., Robins, L. N., Wish, E., & Hesselbrock, M. (1979), Depression in Vietnam veterans and civilian controls. *Amer. J. Psychiat.*, 136:526–529.

Hocking, F. (1970), Psychiatric aspects of extreme environmental stress. *Dis. Nerv. Syst.*, 31:542–545.

Hudgens, R. W. (1974), Personal catastrophe and depression. In: *Stressful Life Events: Their Nature and Effects*, ed. B. S. Dohrenwend & B. P. Dohrenwend. New York, Wiley pp. 119–134.

Hunter, E. J. (1978), The Vietnam POW veteran: Immediate and long-term effects of captivity. In: *Stress Disorders Among Vietnam Veterans*, ed. C. R. Figley. New York, Brunner/Mazel, pp. 188–206.

Mechanic, D. (1974), Discussion of research programs on relations between stressful life events and episode of physical illness. In: *Stressful Life Events: Their Nature and Effects*, ed. B. S. Dohrenwend & B. P. Dohrenwend. New York, Wiley, pp. 87–97.

Rabkin, J. G. & Struening, E. L. (1976), Life events, stress, and illness. Science, 194:1013–1020.

Robins, L. N. (1978), Interaction of setting and predisposition in explaining novel behavior: Drug initiations before, in, and after Vietnam. In: *Longitudinal Research in Drug Use: Empirical Findings and Methodological Issues*, ed. D. Kandel, Washington, D.C., Hemisphere Publishing Co., pp. 179–196.

Wish, E. D., Robins, L. N., Hesselbrock, M., & Helzer, J. E. (1980), The course of alcohol problems in Vietnam veterans. In: *Currents in Alcoholism*, vol. V, ed. F. X. Seixas. New York, Grune & Stratton, in press.

Worthington, E. R. (1978), Demographic and preservice variables as predictors of postmilitary service adjustment. In: *Stress Disorders Among Vietnam Veterans*, ed. C. R. Figley. New York, Brunner/Mazel, pp. 173–187.

Yager, J. (1976), Postcombat violent behavior in psychiatrically maladjusting soldiers. *Arch. Gen. Psychiat.*, 33:1332–1335.

Personal Dispositions Related to the Life Stress Process

Each of the chapters in this section deals with a particular personal disposition and its relation to the life stress process. Richard S. Lazarus presents a careful analysis of the complex process of denial and discusses the circumstances in which it may be a beneficial mode of response versus circumstances in which it may be a harmful mode of response to life events.

Herbert M. Lefcourt presents results from his investigation of locus of control, conceived as a multidimensional construct, as an indicator of vulnerability to particular stressors. His results provide a model of the way in which personal dispositions and life events may interact to effect individuals' psychological states.

In their chapter on the relation of the Type A behavior pattern to cardiovascular disease, Karen A. Matthews and David C. Glass propose that this behavior pattern interacts with uncontrollable life events to affect cardiovascular health. They report research that supports this hypothesis.

The Costs and Benefits of Denial*

RICHARD S. LAZARUS

When I was just starting out as a psychologist about thirty years ago, it seemed important to be sophisticated in the fashion of the day, although one never thinks of the day's outlook as anything so trivial as a fashion. To be sophisticated meant accepting *accurate reality testing* as the hallmark of mental health (cf. Erikson, 1950, 1963; Jahoda, 1958; Maslow, 1954; Menninger, 1963). Self-deception was tantamount to mental disorder. If one wished to manage life successfully, it was necessary to know the truth, however painful; not only know it, but revel in it and even drown in it if necessary. One recent form this doctrine has taken is that we must always be "in touch with our feelings" and absolutely honest about them with others. This outlook about reality is still dominant today (cf. Haan, 1977; Vaillant, 1977), though I no longer believe it is sound. One can argue, in fact, that illusion is necessary to mental health.

Illusion and self-deception are closely related concepts. To have an illusion is to believe something that is not so and therefore, assuming that there is an adequate basis for assessing reality (an assumption often unwarranted), it is a self-deception. But if we equated having illusions with being crazy (as Freud did with the defense mechanism of denial), most or all of us would have to be condemned to the asylum. We have collective illusions, for example, that our society is free, moral, just; that successful people work harder, are smarter, more favored by God than others, and so on. We believe in a God (which we capitalize to express the reification) just as the Greeks believed in many gods. And we believe that our God is the true one while someone else's is not, or that there is no god. We also believe, to some degree, in personal immortality; Becker (1973) has argued that all our striving and products stem from a single, powerful psychological force: the denial of death. True, these notions may be only partly illusory, working assumptions, so to speak, but the line separating a working assumption from an illusion is difficult indeed to draw.

People not only have systems of belief they share with others in their culture and social group, but they also maintain their own

131

idiosyncratic set of beliefs about themselves and the world in which they live (Bem, 1970). Many of these beliefs are passed down from forebearers, and they may never be challenged or examined. They are what Rokeach (1968) calls primitive beliefs. Other beliefs and belief systems are forged out of the experiences of living. Some are implicit and barely accessible to awareness, others are formal and fully conscious, and form central personal themes affecting expectations and commitments. Some run counter to accepted wisdom, while others fit in comfortably with those shared by our peers.

In any case, one finds a genuinely unsettling discrepancy between the way most mental health professionals view reality-testing and self-deception and the outlook of many writers of fiction and poetry who maintain that life is intolerable without illusion. It is instructive to consider how these fiction writers have treated the issue.

Illusion and Reality in Fiction

The idea that illusion is essential to life is the core theme of Eugene O'Neill's *The Iceman Cometh*. In this play the protagonist, Hickey, who has unmasked himself and zealously wants to free the other blighted denizens of a saloon from their self-deceptions, destroys one man in the process and distresses all the others severely. An acceptable mode of living does not return until reality testing is abandoned in favor of illusion.

Ibsen's play *The Wild Duck* is built on the theme that one must protect and nurture illusions or, in Ibsen's terms, "the saving lie." Through the character of Gregers, Ibsen has created a neurotic moralist who presses his own destructive truths on a peer, shattering the latter's illusions about his past and present, inadvertently encouraging the suicide of his 14-year-old daughter, and shattering his family's happiness and morale.

In *Man of La Mancha*, author Wasserman tells us that instead of writing a cynical commentary on the remarkable human capacity for self-deception, his musical adaptation of Cervantes' *Don Quixote* is a plea for illusion as an important and powerful sustaining force in life. We are urged to "dream the impossible dream," "fight the unbeatable foe." "Facts," says Wasserman's Don Quixote, "are the enemy of truth."

Consider also the vignette below from Allen Wheelis's (1966) *The Illusionless Man*, which clearly implies that without illusions our lives are empty. Speaking of their wedding to his bride to be, Lorabelle, for whom illusion is all, Henry, the illusionless man, says:

God won't be there, honey; the women will be weeping for their own lost
youth and innocence, the men wanting to have you in bed; and the priest
standing slightly above us will be looking down your cleavage as his mouth
goes dry; and the whole thing will be a primitive and preposterous attempt
to invest copulation with dignity and permanence, to enforce responsibility
for children by the authority of a myth no longer credible even to a child.
[p. 17]

At the end of the story, when Henry and Lorabelle are near the end
of their lives, Wheelis clearly tells us that illusion is the only
workable way of life:

. . . he could see himself striving toward a condition of beauty or truth or
goodness or love that did not exist, but whereas earlier in his life he had
always said, "It's an illusion," and turned away, now he said, "There isn't
anything else," and stayed with it; and though it cannot be said that they
lived happily, exactly, and certainly not ever after, they did live. They
lived—for a while—with ups and downs, good days and bad, and when it
came time to die Lorabelle said, "Now we'll never be parted," and Henry
smiled and kissed her and said to himself "There isn't anything else," and
they died. [p. 44]

Dürrenmatt's powerful play *The Visit* is another illustration of
how writers have often treated illusion and reality. The setting is a
post-World War II town in Italy that has neither vitality nor
economic viability. The townsfolk see hope in the anticipated return
visit of an aging millionairess who had grown up there in poverty.
They hope she will give them financial aid. As part of her offer of a
huge sum, however, she stipulates a terrible condition, namely, the
execution of her lover whose treachery had eventuated in the death
of her child, jail, and ultimate banishment from the community. She
now wants retribution, or "justice," as she puts it. At first the town
leaders seem reluctant to accept the immoral bargain, but little by
little it becomes apparent that everyone has been living on the
anticipated windfall. The climax comes with the acceptance and
formal celebration of the evil bargain and the execution of the lover.
The town now thrives economically and socially. The mayor
emphasizes that the money is not being accepted for its own sake,
but for justice, and the townsfolk cheer. Dürrenmatt offers two
social messages here: first that prosperity and social vitality generally rest on evil; second, the evil is denied and disguised in the cloak
of justice. In effect, he is saying that our most cherished social values
depend on self-deception; they are illusions, little better than sugar-
coated distortions of social reality which is, at root, evil.

Perhaps the most celebrated modern literary figure to deal with illusion and reality and to make it his trademark was Pirandello, whose plays offer multiple and complex variations on social and self-deception. For example, *Henry IV* deals with a man who lives out the fantasy of being a long-dead monarch with hired retainers, advisors, and the like but who confuses all participants and on-lookers about whether he is really insane or merely play-acting. *It Is So! (If You Think So)* concerns the efforts of a townspeople to decipher the relationships of three people, a husband, a wife, and her mother, each of whom has a very different conception of each other and their relationships. Not only does the husband and his mother-in-law view reality in diametrically opposing ways, but the wife, knowing that her spouse and mother cannot manage without their own self-deceptions, adapts herself to both simultaneously and thus, through a social deception, engages in a humanitarian act toward those whom she loves. One of the townsfolk, who has insight into what is going on and probably speaks for the author, argues that each set of illusion is as real as any other. It is, therefore, impossible to know external reality without viewing it through the eyes of the individual person.

Summarizing Pirandello's outlook on illusion and reality in the play *Liolà*, Bentley (1952, p. xiii) states:

The play is about appearance and reality and shows, in what readers have always regarded as Pirandello's characteristically tricky fashion, that reality is not more real than appearance. Further, there are real appearances and merely apparent appearances. And just as appearance may be more real than reality, so merely apparent appearance may be more real than real appearance.
. . . for Uncle Simone, to appear to be a father is enough: appearance will establish his paternity more surely than actually having done the deed. However, strictly speaking, he does *not* appear to be a father; for the whole town knows the truth. He only appears to appear to be the father. That he appears to be the father is a kind of social pact or legal fiction.

Pirandello himself (1939, as cited in Bentley, 1952, p. xiv) puts it as follows:

The harder the struggle for life and the more one's weakness is felt, the greater becomes the need for mutual deception. The simulation of force, honesty, sympathy, prudence, in short, of every virtue, and of that greatest virtue veracity, is a form of adjustment, an effective instrument of struggle. The "humorist" at once picks out such various simulations; amuses himself by unmasking them; is not indignant about them—he simply is that way!

And while the sociologist describes social life as it presents itself to external observation, the humorist, being a man of exceptional intuition, shows—nay, reveals—that appearances are one thing and the consciousness of the people concerned, in its inner essence, another. And yet people "lie psychologically" even as they "lie socially." And this lying to ourselves—living as we do, on the surface and not in the depths of our being—is a result of the social lying. The mind that gives back its own reflection is a solitary mind, but our internal solitude is never so great that suggestions from the communal life do not break in upon it with all the fictions and transferences which characterize them.

And in a vigorous assault on the concept of reality entitled, *How Real Is Real*, communications psychologist Paul Watzlawick (1977) cites Dostoevski and Kafka as particularly good literary exemplars of the "dissolution of reality." He observes that Hermann Hesse suggested that Prince Myshkin in Dostoevski's *The Idiot* "does not break the Tables of the Law, he simply turns them round and shows that the contrary to them is written on the other side." Moreover, Watzlawick considers the metaphysical argument between Alyosha and Ivan in *The Brothers Karamazov* as the supreme literary example of this dissolution of reality. Ivan speaks of the imaginary confrontation between the Grand Inquisitor and Jesus, whom he has arrested after his descent once again to earth. In the Inquisitor's view of reality, Jesus has betrayed humankind by wanting people to be free to choose, by rejecting miracles, and by refusing to rule the world as one unanimous and harmonious "ant heap." These three ideological positions have made the lot of humans miserable. On the other hand, the organized Church, says the Grand Inquisitor, keeps people happy by providing miracles, mystery, and authority. Thus do we see two diametrically opposite views of reality, that of Jesus and that of the Grand Inquisitor, in which the same virtue, humanitarianism, leads to quite logically opposite conclusions.

Illusion and Reality in Psychological Thought

The dominant view of psychiatry and clinical psychology has long been that accurate perception of reality is a hallmark of mental health. However, there have been numerous voices also expressing the constructivist view that people create their own realities. The New Look movement of the 1950s also emphasized individual differences in the ways events are perceived and cognized (cf. Folkman et al., 1980; Lazarus, 1978).

Some psychologists, such as Frankl (1955), have built entire psychological and therapuetic systems on the need for background meaning in our lives, and have emphasized the devastating effects of the loss of such meaning. In a recent treatment of stress and coping in the concentration camp and in survivors, my colleagues and I (Benner et al., 1980) also suggested that such meaning served as a coping resource during the Holocaust, and its loss helps account for the troubled pattern of adjustment among survivors. This also seems to be a time in the industrialized Western world that is characterized by a widespread loss of meanings that once served as anchors in people's lives, though the concept of alienation, which includes meaninglessness as a core concept (Kanungo, 1979), was important in sociological thought before the turn of the century.

The important point, however, is that the kinds of beliefs on which people depend have an uncertain reality basis regardless of the fixity with which they may be held. One person's beliefs can be another's delusions. Coming from a communications theory perspective, Watzlawick (1977), cited earlier, writes:

The reader will have noticed that I have been unable to avoid the use of terms like "really," "actually," "actual fact," and thus have apparently contradicted the main thesis of the book: that there is no absolute reality but only subjective and often contradictory conceptions of reality.

Very frequently, especially in psychiatry where the degree of an individual's "reality adaptation" plays a special role as the indicator of his normalcy, there is a confusion between two very different aspects of what we call reality. The first has to do with the purely physical, objectively discernible properties of things and is intimately linked with correct sensory perception, with questions of so-called common sense or with objective, repeatable, scientific verification. The second aspect is the attribution of meaning and value to these things and is based on communication.

This domain of reality, however, says nothing about the meaning and value of its contents. A small child may perceive a red traffic light just as clearly as an adult, but may not know that it means "do not cross the street now." The first-order reality of gold—that is, its physical properties—is known and can be verified at any time. But the role that gold has played since the dawn of human history, especially the fact that its value is determined twice daily by five men in a small office in the City of London and that this ascription of value profoundly influences many other aspects of our everyday reality, has very little, if anything, to do with the physical properties of gold. But it is this second reality of gold which may turn us into millionaires or lead us into bankruptcy.

. . . It is a delusion to believe that there is a "real" second-order reality and that "sane" people are more aware of it than "madmen." [Pp. 140–142]

Yet, in spite of the ambiguities in judging reality, strip us of beliefs in which we are heavily invested and we are deeply threatened, alienated, and perhaps even seriously disrupted in our life course and capacity for involvement and satisfaction. In effect, we pilot our lives by virtue of illusions that give meaning and substance to living. Life cannot easily be lived and enjoyed without both a set of shared deceptions and a set of self-deceptions, that is, without beliefs that have no necessary relationship with reality.

Alfred Adler's (see H. L. Ansbacher and R. R. Ansbacher, 1956) concept of "fictional finalism," which suggests that human actions are pulled by future considerations rather than pushed from the past, and which draws on Hans Vaihinger's *The Psychology of "As If"* (1925; original, 1911), is relevant here. Vaihinger argued that we live by fictional ideas that have no necessary connection with reality, for example, that "all men are created equal," "honesty is the best policy," and "the end justifies the means" (see also Hall and Lindsey, 1957, on Alfred Adler).

That living "as if" could be a workable strategy in the real world is not surprising when we realize that from early childhood on we are treated to two alternative and simultaneous modes of thought: fairy tales and magic on the one hand and the "real world" on the other. Yet both modes seem capable of residing comfortably together, and sometimes even of being fused. In his theory of cognitive dissonance, not only did Festinger (1957) fail to help us understand and predict which of many dissonance-resolving strategies people use, but I think he was wrong in presuming that it is always urgent for people to resolve dissonances. Quite the contrary, though some of us are more sensitive to them than others, we tolerate them very easily, and much of the time do not even notice when we or others engage in self-contradictions. Moreover, as Freud emphasized, humans have a great capacity for rationalizing or dispelling apparent contradictions.

Rather than equating the use of illusion with pathology, a more appropriate and interesting conclusion would be that mental health *requires* some self-deception. Otto Rank (1936) has also adopted this position, the problem of the neurotic person being that he or she senses the truth but cannot deal with it. Rank wrote:

With the truth, one cannot live. To be able to live one needs illusions, not only outer illusions such as art, religion, philosophy, science and love afford, but inner illusions which first condition the outer [i.e., a secure sense of one's active powers and of being able to count on the powers of others]. The more a man can take reality as truth, appearance as essence, the sounder, the better adjusted, the happier will he be . . . this constantly effective process of self-deceiving, pretending and blundering, is no psychopathological mechanism. [Pp. 251–252]

We must somehow face the apparent paradox that illusion or self-deception can be both adaptationally sound *and* capable of eliciting a heavy price. The paradox is: How is it possible for self-deception to be at once healthy and pathogenic? The paradox can be resolved by shifting to the more sophisticated question: What kinds and degrees of self-deceptions are damaging or constructive, and under what conditions? Or as Becker (1973) has put it, "On what level of illusion does one live?" (p. 189). Alternatively, maybe some illusions work better than others.

The Denial Process as a Form of Self-Deception

Denial is the negation of something in word or act, or more properly, both, since thoughts and actions are apt to be conjoined in any defense process. Logically speaking, the negation can be either of an impulse, feeling, or thought, or of an external demand or reality, although, as we shall see, Sigmund and Anna Freud both distinguished denial from repression as being focused on external rather than internal conditions. Examples of denial in the larger sense include: I am not angry; I do not love you; I am not distressed; I am not seriously ill, dying, or facing extinction; I am not in danger; he doesn't mean any harm; she is not a competitor, etc. Some of these denials refer to environmental realities, others to intrapsychic forces.

In speaking of the denial process, one is immediately faced with multiple ambiguities. One of the most common sources of confusion is the equation of denial with *avoidance*. Behaviorally speaking, for example, one may exhibit denial by not paying attention to or speaking of the threatening connotation of events. Thus, if we wish to deny that we are mortally ill, we will also avoid this idea in thought, deed, or word. This is what Anna Freud (1946) seems to have meant by denial "in word and act." So it is not an illogical presumption that a cancer patient who does not mention the terminal nature of the illness, particularly when there is provocation, is denying the imminence of death. Although the presumption is not unreasonable, it is incomplete. A terminal patient may know full well that he or she is dying, but prefer not to think or talk about it. This is not denial but avoidance, and there is a world of difference between the two.

Another source of ambiguity is that one cannot deny what is not *known*. Therefore, if physicians have evaded communicating the diagnosis and prognosis, or been excessively subtle with a person who is not particularly perceptive, then the impression that this person is denying may be incorrect, since what is being revealed is ignorance rather than denial. There is a considerable difference between shading things a bit and a full-fledged process of denying what clearly should be known and acknowledged. Only very careful, in-depth exploration is capable of providing the empirical basis for this distinction.

In saying this I have accepted the idea, at least provisionally, that there are "realities" to be denied, although we must be extremely careful about how we deal with this idea. Put differently, if we could not, at least provisionally, take this position, there would then be no basis for speaking about denial, or for doing research on it. We cannot become completely hamstrung by the metaphysical problems. Thus, subject to the usual diagnostic reservations, a rapidly developing carcinoma or a clogged coronary artery offer reasonable (realistic) bases for an appraisal that one's life is threatened. Similarly, the death of a loved one involves a reality that needs to be taken into account in living and for which a grief process would be appropriate. Whether the absence of grief is inappropriate is somewhat more difficult to assess.

Still another important source of confusion has to do with the extent to which the process of denial is tentative or well-entrenched, or as clinicians used to say, well-consolidated. A well-consolidated denial is presumably unshakable. Many, perhaps most, denials are tentative constructions, responsive to this or that bit of information, mood, or whatever. Many patients who seem not to "know" they are dying really do know at some level of awareness, perhaps only dimly, an idea expressed in the concept of "middle knowledge" (Weisman, 1972). Somehow, their declining physical fortunes, leakage from what has been said to them, contradictions in word and fact, all conspire to give the patient a sense, even if dim, of what is happening. As Oken (1961) has put it, "A patient who is sick enough to die knows it without being told," although he or she must often play along with the reassuring, denial-focused statements of physicians, friends and relatives (Hackett & Weisman, 1964). What is called denial in such cases may be, at best, only a *partial* denial process that depends on the social circumstances to sustain it. A partial denial involves the capacity to bring the "reality" being denied into awareness, or to act on the denied knowledge when it is necessary. It is not a full-fledged self-deception, but only a tentative "suspension of belief."

In his treatment of denial in terminal cancer patients, Weisman

(1972) also addresses the question, "What is being denied?" He describes first-order denial as a denial of facts, for example, that a loved one has died, that one has cancer, or that manifest symptoms imply an important life-threatening illness. Such denial is usually tentative, since in a life-threatening or progressive disease the facts ultimately make the first-order denial process untenable. In second-order denial, the potentially damaging or threatening primary facts are accepted, but the worst implications are denied. The distinction here is very much like that made by Watzlawick (1977) of first- and second-order realities, noted earlier. It is, after all, the ultimate meaning of the facts for one's well-being that constitutes the threat. Third-order denial refers to the refusal to accept the further implications of one's extinction or personal death.

We have had the unfortunate habit in the past of treating the processes of coping as static states of mind, as fixed cognitive achievements (or traits), expressing the idea that the person has arrived at a stable interpretation (or defense). A better way of thinking is that, except for relatively rare instances of consolidated defenses, people are constatnly seeking a way to comprehend what is happening to them; this ongoing process of construing reality is a constantly changing one, depending on many things going on within the person and on the outside. Thus, when we consider denial, or any other kind of self-deception or illusion, we are dealing with flux, and we must always be aware of the changing nature of the event we are trying to understand (Lazarus, 1978).

Consider the following excerpt from an interview from my own research on coping with stressful encounters, in this case the threat of being electrocuted:

There I was alone vacuuming up this water near all the exposed wiring. . . . I hoped I wouldn't get electrocuted. But then I thought: "Well, this thing is made to take water and I have on rubber soles," and so I felt I wouldn't get electrocuted and kept on doing it but made sure I didn't touch anything. As soon as Bernie came back I said, "You're sure this is safe, I'm not going to get electrocuted doing this." And he said, "I hope not, I don't think so." I know he was kidding. At least I hope he was. And he had been doing it before I arrived. He has a lot of common sense about these things so I shook off most of the fear and just ran the vacuum.

Then we drank our wine and laughed at each other and just let it go . . . knowing we had to face it again tomorrow. We changed the situation by working on it together. I got over my anxiety about the wires by being very careful and knowing that Bernie wouldn't have me do something dangerous. The glass of wine really made me feel better. What else can you do? I don't like to get all upset. That was the first time we'd had a glass of wine at work. After all, life is just a game. It wasn't severe anxiety and I moved to a safer spot and everything was okay. I just let go of the fear. I did it by concentrating on what I was doing. I am just glad I was wearing crepe soles.

Many things seem to be happening here, including recognition of the danger, and efforts to bring the fear under control by bravado and avoidance. Still, the coping process seems also to contain denial-like elements, including the effort to accept Bernie's reassurance ("He has a lot of common sense" and "Bernie wouldn't have me do something dangerous"). To anyone (an observer) aware of the danger of standing in water near exposed wiring, to be convinced so easily and reassured by the crepe soles seems to involve a tremendous degree of denial. Yet how can we assess the actual sense of danger the person speaking could have experienced on the basis of what she saw and knew?

Another lesson of importance is that denial is not a single act but a highly diverse set of processes that respond to different external and internal conditions, and that are inferred with varying degrees of confidence on the part of the observer. There can be no satisfactory answer to the question of the adaptational outcomes of denial without there also being a sound basis for identifying, describing, and measuring the defensive process itself. Hasty and superficial measurement is hardly the way to undertake research on the problem (see Horowitz et al., 1975, for an example of an in-depth process measurement approach).

A thorough exposition of the concept of denial in theoretical terms is impossible to undertake here. It would go back to Freud, follow his shifting conceptions of defense in general, and proceed to subsequent psychoanalytic writers. Such an account is currently available in a book by Sjöbäck (1973), who gives considerable space to the history of thought about denial. As was noted earlier, Freud actually saw denial as a "disavowal" (to use his term) of external reality. It was also assumed to occur only in psychosis. He and others, including Anna Freud (1946) and Otto Fenichel (1945), continued this conception in later writing. On the other hand, Anna Freud may have changed her view of the matter much later, and at least by implication appeared to regard denial as capable of having positive clinical significance. In a book by Bergmann (1958), on which Anna Freud is listed as collaborator, a case is reported of a child with polio whose father's very strong denial was said to have potentiated remarkable feats of physical function in the sick child. About this, Bergmann wrote:

It is interesting to realize that the physical and medical evaluation could not explain how this child managed to walk so well with or without the cane because tests of muscle strength revealed quite insufficient power for such an accomplishment. With Carl it was evidently a case of "mind over matter." What had also to be taken into account was the father's denial of the facts, his unfaltering belief that everything was going to be all right again. Actually, it must have been the influence of the father's unrealistic attitude (and not my sensible advice) which contributed to Carl's amazingly successful recovery, the degree of which could not be explained in physical terms. [P. 111]

Still others (e.g., Jacobson, 1957) extended the concept of denial to mean a defense against intrapsychic forces (i.e., instinctual fantasies, wishes and impulses). Such an enlargement of the concept, however, has produced confusion. For example, if denial is a defense against intrapsychic processes as well as external reality, how is it to be distinguished from repression? The problem has never been resolved satisfactorily, and is part of the continuing uncertainty and confusion about definition and measurement (see also Fine et al., 1969; Lipowski, 1970). Whether it is more useful to distinguish among many types of denial, as I do here, as well as among related processes such as avoidance, or to speak of a generalized process, a family of denial, as it were, that includes a large range of specific patterns, remains at issue.

What then is the resolution of the seeming paradox, stated earlier, that the use of denial is both harmful and beneficial, that although we venerate reality testing as a hallmark of mental health, life is intolerable without illusion? The resolution takes two forms. First, we must recognize that denial consists of many diverse forms, some of which are disavowals of clear realities and others merely implications, or avoidance. The latter merges with affirmations or positive thinking in the face of ambiguous circumstances; in short, it is what we mean by illusion. By carefully making such distinctions, both definitionally and in assessment, we can ultimately justify the seemingly contradictory assertion that sometimes denial-related processes have positive outcomes and sometimes negative. Second, we can recognize that the costs and benefits of denial and denial-like coping processes depend on the context in which the process occurs. That is, the adaptational outcome must be considered in relation to the situational demands and constraints on action, and the resources available to the person, in short, the coping alternatives. In the section that follows some of these contextual variables play important roles in producing positive or negative outcomes.

Research on Denial-like Processes and Their Consequences

The definitional and conceptual confusion that surrounds denial, as it does most other defensive processes, makes the problem of evaluating its outcomes even more difficult. For example, although there are a substantial number of research studies of denial-like processes, it is difficult to compare them because of variations in the way the coping process is understood and measured. To measure denial in coronary care patients Hackett and Cassem (1974) used a rating scale that was based on Anna Freud's concept that denial is a general psychological goal that can be achieved in many diverse ways. Hackett and Cassem's scale includes some items that express denial explicitly in words, and others in which the denial is implicit, as in the item, "The patient avoids talking about the disability." We have already seen that combining alternative tactics such as avoidance and denial in word under the same general rubric risks confusion about which process is actually being used by the person. It may be a much better research strategy carefully to differentiate diverse denial-like processes so that their respective impact on adaptational outcome can also be distinguished.

Nevertheless, it is worth trying to wade into some of this research in an effort to extract whatever hypothetical principles we can, recognizing that they must be tentative, at best. To undertake this I have chosen the device of examining two types of studies, those in which denial seems to have damaging adaptational outcomes and those having constructive ones. No attempt has been made to provide a thorough review of all research. The citations were chosen to be illustrative. A fuller list of studies has been offered, with a different purpose than here, by Wortman and Dunkel-Schetter (1979). In making this categorization I have also had to overlook some of the definitional and measurement problems. This is why I have used the term "denial-like processes" in all headings in place of denial per se. The studies cited below vary greatly in their methods of assessing the coping process, although the word denial is used in all. Strictly speaking, one cannot treat them as studies of denial without evading the very definitional issues I raised earlier.

Studies in Which the Denial-like Processes Had Damaging Outcomes—An important line of thought about denial has come from the work of Lindemann (1944) and Bowlby (1961) on grieving. Lindemann found denial of pain and distress a common feature of the grief process among the bereaved. Other observers have suggested a similar pattern among those sustaining an incapacitating loss such as spinal cord injury (Dembo et al., 1956; McDaniel and Sexton, 1970; Wright, 1960). Implicit in Lindemann's concept of "grief work" was that if the bereaved person was prevented from grieving fully by processes such as denial and avoidance, he would fail to negotiate the bereavement crisis, which requires emancipation from the emotional bondage to the deceased and the formation of new relationships.

A parallel theme was also stated later by Janis (1958, 1974) in the concept of the "work of worrying." Janis's finding, that low fear prior to surgery was associated with high distress and behavioral difficulties during the later recovery period, was consistant with the view that denial of threat prevented the patient from anticipating realistically and working through the postsurgical discomforts. Although there was no direct measure of denial, and the findings on which this concept was based have not been replicated in a number of like studies, the concept has had good staying power because of its ring of truth and the existence of supporting findings from other types of investigation. (A recent review of research on coping with surgery and other illnesses, and of intervention research to aid surgical stress management, is available in a chapter by Cohen and Lazarus (1979).)

In their more recent writings about decision making Janis and Mann (1977) view vigilance as desirable because it potentiates a search for information and the weighing of alternative coping strategies in the face of threat. Research by Horowitz (1975) makes use of an idea similar to the work of worrying, namely, the tendency for unresolved threats (in the form of thoughts and images) to enter into awareness as unwanted intrusions (see also Freud's concept of repetition compulsion). In Horowitz's view, this process alternates with its opposite, denial. And Breger's (1967) treatment of dreams as efforts by the person to cope cognitively with unresolved conflicts clearly falls within the same conceptual tradition.

Another direct descendant of this line of thought is the series of studies generated and reviewed by Goldstein (1973) using a sentence completion test measure of vigilance (or sensitization) and avoidance (repression) as the opposite extremes of a coping continuum. Vigilants are those who accept and elaborate fully on the threatening meaning conveyed by incomplete sentence stems (e.g., to the stem *I hate*, they write, "my parents," "nosey people," "anyone who is smarter than me," etc.); avoiders seem to evade or deny what the researcher presumes is the threatening content (e.g., to the stem *I hate*, they write, "to be caught in the rain without an umbrella," or "no one"). Nonspecific defenders fall into neither extreme category, and are said to adapt their form of coping flexibly to the circumstances. To oversimplify this research (cf. Andrew, 1970; Delong, 1970) a bit, avoiders do not do well in anticipatory threat situations, or when they are exposed to repeated threats (e.g., when they are shown the same stressful movie more than once). The assumption is that their characteristic mode of coping prevents their coming to terms with the threat. Avoiders and vigilants seem also to be differentially benefited by diverse interventions in anticipatory stress situations, avoiders doing better when left alone and vigilants responding best to detailed preparation. Although, as is usually the case, the data are more complicated and less clear than one would wish, they seem consistent with the concepts of grief work and the work of worrying, and point to avoidance or denial as processes that can interfere with successful mastery by preventing appropriate cognitive coping prior to a stressful confrontation.

A recent study of asthmatic patients (Staudenmayer et al., 1979) further supports the above ideas, but adds an important behavioral dimension. Asthmatics were divided into those who respond to symptoms with vigilance and those who disregard them. When the slightest sign of a developing attack is noticed, the former grow fearful and vigilant; the latter evade or deny the seriousness of the symptom and wait out the situation, expecting or hoping that the attack will not materialize and the symptoms will disappear. Staudenmayer et al. found that the high-fear, vigilant patients were far less likely to be rehospitalized over a six-month period than the low-fear, denial-oriented patients. The former tended to take action quickly when breathing difficulties ensued, while the latter tended to disregard these difficulties, and hence allowed the attack to progress too far to treat without hospitalization. Here too we see the value of vigilance and the high cost of avoidance and/or denial in a medical situation; in this case the denial-like coping process leads to the failure to act in one's own best interest.

An oft-cited and even clearer demonstration of this theme that denial may interfere with actions necessary to survival may be found in the research of Katz and his colleagues (1970) concerning women who discovered a breast lump. Denial, mixed with rationalization, was reported to have been the most common form of coping employed (11 of 30 subjects). Katz et al. found that there was often considerable delay in getting medical attention, which in the event the lump was malignant would have added greatly to the danger of metastasis and reduced the chances for surgical care. Delays in seeking medical help for a heart attack have also been reported (Von Kugelgen, 1975), and Hackett and Cassem (1975) cite cases of men who, while undergoing such an attack, did vigorous pushups or climbed flights of stairs to convince themselves that what they were experiencing was not a heart attack.

Studies in Which Denial-like Processes Had Constructive Outcomes—Clinical thought has, in recent years, shifted considerably from an emphasis on intrapsychic conflict to environmental conditions such as catastrophic illness as factors in adaptational crises in ordinary people (Lipowski, 1970). In all likelihood, this shift reflects, partly, the positive mental health movement and a retreat from a preoccupation solely with inner dynamics and pathology. A series of studies influenced by the research and theorizing of Roy Grinker, Sr. (e.g., Offer and Freedman, 1972) has been particularly influential in the growing acceptance of the idea that denial-like processes can have positive as well as negative adaptational consequences. Defensive processes are not treated as the exclusive property of "sick" minds but as an integral feature of healthy coping as well.

Included in this research are studies of the victims of severe and incapacitating burns (Hamburg et al., 1953), of paralytic polio (Visotsky et al., 1961), and other life crises, summarized analytically by Hamburg and Adams (1967). A major thesis has been that self-deception, for example by denying the seriousness of a problem, was often a valuable initial form of coping, occurring at a time when the person was confused and weakened and therefore unable to act constructively and realistically. In a severe and sudden crisis, "time for 'preparation' is likely to be bought by temporary self-deception, in such a way as to make recognition of threatening elements gradual and manageable" (Hamburg and Adams, 1967, p. 283). Davis (1963), too, has observed that denial of the gravity of the illness (polio) and its damaging implications permits the parents to have a longer time perspective about their child's recovery, and to be able to accept as milestones comparatively small steps toward recovery. In writing about the atomic holocaust at Hiroshima, Lifton (1964) has suggested that early denial might facilitate ultimate adjustment by allowing the survivors to engage in a "psychic closing off" from "the threat [of psychosis] posed by the overwhelming evidence of actual physical death" (p. 208). These examples offer a stage-related concept of denial in which the "disavowal" of reality is temporary and helps the person get through the devastating early period of loss and threat, setting the stage for later acknowledgement (Kubler-Ross, 1969) of the situation and the mobilization of more realistic coping efforts.

A number of research studies have suggested that there is a high incidence of denial-like coping processes in severe, incapacitating illness, and that these coping activities can have positive adaptational consequences. Denial of the danger and its imminence has been reported as common in cancer illness by Cobb, Clark, McGuire, and Howe (1954), with denial inferred from retrospective depth interviews and identified in some degree in 90% of a sample of 840 patients. In patients with spinal cord injuries, Dinardo (1971) used the Byrne questionnaire scale of repression-sensitization, a dimension akin theoretically to Goldstein's (1973) sentence-completion measure, and found that repressors displayed greater self-esteem than sensitizers, although the latter type of injured persons were significantly less happy. Dinardo also obtained ratings of adjustment from physical therapists, occupational therapists and nurses, and found that repressors seemed to do better, although the difference was not statistically significant. In considering this type of evidence we must, of course, be wary of the measure itself (see also Lefcourt, 1966). First, the Byrne scale is a trait measure rather than process measure. Second, it can be as readily regarded as a measure of anxiety as of a coping process, though these concepts are quite interdependent. Third, there appears to be no correlation among the three diverse trait measures of presumably the same process (Lazarus et al., 1974).

Stern, Pascale, and McLoone (1976), on the other hand, assessed the coping process through interview techniques following acute myocardial infarction. What are called deniers by the authors (representing 25% of the sample) were more generally optimistic and did very well in returning to work and sexual functioning, and they suffered less from postcoronary depression and anxiety. This finding is consistent with Hackett, Cassem, and Wishnie's (1968) claim that denial of the danger of death may be associated with decreased mortality and better postcoronary adjustment in the coronary care unit.

Cohen and Lazarus (1973) have reported a study of vigilance and avoidance of relevant information by patients the night before surgery. Patients who avoided such information showed a more rapid recovery postsurgically, fewer minor complications, and less distress than vigilant patients, a finding opposite to that of Janis.

The process measure did not correlate at all with a trait measure of repression-sensitization (similar to Byrne's), which in turn failed to correlate with outcome. The authors offer both an institutional and psychological interpretation. With respect to the former, it is possible that physicians were guided in their decision to send patients home by virtue of their manifest attitude; pollyanna avoider-deniers would seem better candidates for early dismissal than worried, complaining vigilants. As to the psychological interpretation, a hospital environment encourages passivity and conformity, which would make vigilance a useless coping strategy since little or nothing one does will affect one's actual fate.

More equivocal concerning the outcome of denial is the research of Wolff, Friedman, Hofer, and Mason (1964) with the parents of children dying of leukemia. This well-known study found that parents who were "well-defined" (largely through denial-like forms of cognitive coping) showed lower levels of corticosteroid secretion during the child's illness than those who were poorly defended. Thus, to the extent that lowered stress levels can be considered a positive consequence, denial-like coping had positive adaptational value. On the other hand, a follow-up study with the same parents (Hoffer et al., 1972) obtained data suggestive of a later reversal: Those who had high secretion levels prior to the child's death showed lower levels many months after; alternatively, those who had low prior levels had higher ones later.

If this finding turns out to be solid and does not merely represent regression to the mean, it also points up the idea that one must be time-oriented in evaluating adaptational outcomes of coping. One might say, for example, that the well-defended parents were benefited *during* the illness but were more vulnerable *after* the child's death because they failed to do "grief work"; in contrast, those who continued consciously to struggle with the impending tragedy were better off later because of the anticipatory coping. To complicate matters further, Townes, Wold, and Holmes (1974) suggest that fathers did the work of grieving prior to the child's death while mothers did not, so that subsequent mourning was sustained and more intense for the latter. Although such data as these are suggestive (the difference did not reach statistical significance in the study of Townes et al.), none of the studies cited in this research arena is capable of clearly settling the issue of denial and the passage of time. Nevertheless, they are consistent with the concepts of anticipatory coping and with the antithetical role denial might play in it. We are still left with the possibility that denial may be helpful only in a limited time frame, and might exact a price later on.

Recent observations by Levine and Zigler (1975) on denial in stroke victims may also be considered here. Measuring denial idiosyncratically by examining their real- versus ideal-self disparity, stroke victims were found to have the greatest use of denial (i.e., they showed a larger discrepancy between presumed loss of function and how it was appraised) compared with two other handicapped groups, namely, victims of lung cancer and heart disease. Denial, assessed in this way, appeared to produce a comparative state of emotional equanimity in the stroke patients despite the fact that they actually suffered the greatest damage to functioning among the three disorders. One could argue, moreover, that a more realistic self-assessment by the stroke victims would have had little value, adaptationally speaking, since little or nothing more could have been done about their deficits even with a more realistic appraisal. Perhaps it could be said in such an instance that ignorance is more functional than the bitter truth.

Before leaving studies in which denial has proved constructive, it is worth noting a recent neurohumoral discovery that, with a small leap of the imagination, seems to have a bearing. Biochemists (Guillemin et al., 1977) have discovered that, simultaneous with the secretion under stress of ACTH by the pituitary gland, another hormone is also secreted called endorphin-B. ACTH stimulates secretion of corticosteroids by the adrenals; endorphin-B seems to affect morphine-sensitive brain tissue, presumably acting like an analgesic and psychedelic. A severely wounded animal, or a badly frightened or enraged one, might well be expected to produce not only corticosteroids (as in Selye's GAS stage of resistance), but also this morphine-like substance. This may help explain why Beecher (1956-1957) and others have observed a remarkable absence of pain in wounded soldiers, or why in battle men sometimes throw themselves into combat seemingly oblivious of the consequences. It may not be altogether fanciful to suggest that chemicals such as endorphin-B could be the neurohumoral analogue of denial and other comforting cognitions (Mechanic, 1978) or, as I have elsewhere referred to them, palliative forms of coping. The analogy could be reassuring to those who believe that palliative forms of coping, denial among them, might play a valuable part in the overall human armamentarium of coping.

Principles Concerning Costs and Benefits of
Denial-like Coping Processes

A useful summary containing four principles, can be offered of the adaptational consequences of denial-like processes.

1. The first is a version of an old truth, namely, that circumstances alter cases. Specifically, if direct action to change the damaging or threatening person-environment transaction is adaptationally essential or useful, denial (when it undermines such action by avoiding or disavowing the threat or danger) will be destructive. On the other hand, when direct action is irrelevant to the adaptational outcome, then denial-like processes have no necessarily damaging consequences and could even be of value by reducing distress and allowing the person to get on with other matters.

This principle also allows us to extrapolate to other damaging circumstances, for example, illnesses such as kidney failure and diabetes. Control of these illnesses depends on vigilant attention to diet and exercise, and to behavioral and bodily signals of the need for dialysis or insulin. To the extent that successful denial of fact or damaging implications pushes the person to overlook such signals and therefore to evade suitable actions, it is counterproductive and could even be fatal. However, depression and disengagement are also enemies of efforts to stay alive and functioning well, and to mobilize the necessary vigilance over a long time requires relatively good morale and the feeling of hope. It could be argued, therefore, that some positive thinking in the face of a severe hardship might also prove of value and even be necessary.

The distinction implied in principle is between what my colleagues and I have been calling *problem-focused coping* and *emotion-focused coping*, and which I had earlier spoken of as direct action and palliation (Lazarus and Launier, 1978). They represent two of the most important functions of coping, namely, that of changing a damaging or threatening relationship between person and environment (problem-focused) and regulating the emotional distress produced by that relationship (emotion-focused). In current research in my laboratory, Folkman (1979) has found that in every complex stressful encounter people use a mixture of both kinds of coping. Moreover, when an encounter is appraised as permitting little or nothing to be done, there is a pull toward emotion-focused coping; and when it is appraised as permitting constructive actions, the shift is to problem-focused modes. Folkman also found that work pulls for more problem-focused modes and illness pulls for emotion-focused ones. Denial clearly falls within the emotion-focused function and, as noted below in principle four, when denial is partial, tentative, or minimal in scope, it does not necessarily undermine the simultaneous use of problem-focused forms of coping when these might have relevance to the person's plight.

2. The second principle is that, when a given type of stress must be encountered again and again, denial (which could keep up morale and keep down distress) will prevent ultimate mastery. In effect, there are time-related implications in the use of denial.

3. The third principle is also time-related. Denial can have positive value at an early stage of coping when the person's resources are insufficient to cope in a more problem-focused way. Severely injured patients gain from denial when their life hangs in the balance, when they are too weak or shocked to act constructively and so need to be supported by others. Thus, the patient with spinal-cord injury is helped for a while by believing that bodily functions that have been lost will return, or that the incapacitation is not as severe as it seems. Only later will the person be strong enough to come to terms with the reality of the condition and ultimately struggle to cope in a practical, problem-focused sense. There is no contradiction between principles two and three. Both agree that denial is valuable, but only in an early stage. Principle two concerns the price of denial for later similar encounters, while principle three treats denial as a temporary preservative before more problem-focused forms of coping can be brought to bear.

4. Some kinds of denial are more or less fruitless and dangerous while others may have considerable value. For example, of two objects of denial, emotional distress and the harm or threat inherent in some encounter, the former has less utility because it provides little reason for the person actually to feel better—while denying, the person still feels upset. On the other hand, if we can believe that we are not seriously ill, or not in some danger, there is no reason to be upset. The threat has been shortcircuited (Lazarus and Alfert, 1964; Lazarus et al., 1965). Furthermore, logically it would seem to be far more dangerous to deny what is clear and unambiguous than to deny what cannot be known for certain. The most obvious example is the difference between denial of fact and denial of implication. The fact that one is sick is harder to deny successfully than the implication that one is going to die soon, and still harder to deny than the notion that one will in some sense live on after death. There is an insightful joke that wherever one goes after death can't be such a bad place since no one has ever returned to complain about it. If one denies what is ambiguous, the fiction is more easily sustained and is apt to be less pernicious adaptationally.

This last pricniple also concerns instances in which denial is partial, tentative, or minimal in scope [as in Lipowski's (1970) term "minimization"]. Then it should be far less pernicious, and often quite useful. Some of the self-deceptions or illusions people live by are important for mental health. It is useful to remember that these self-deceptions are not usually challenged by evidence, nor do we even try to test them by the methods of science. This kind of denial is closer to the sense of "as if," to illusion in the more literary sense, or to working fictions or assumptions.

Moreover, throughout human history such working fictions have been regarded as useful not only in maintaining morale but in also aiding effective adaptation. An example from stress and coping theory is the distinction between two ways in which the same demanding or troubling event can be appraised. One person is threatened by it, the other challenged (Lazarus, 1978; Lazarus et al., 1979; Lazarus and Launier, 1978). Some people appear to have the happy faculty of viewing harsh experiences in a positive, challenging light while others seem constantly to view them dourly as threats. There is reason to think that the former persons feel better and perform more effectively in the face of adversity than the latter. It is an important and practical research issue.

The discussion of threat and challenge above might remind us of a popular inspirational book of several decades past by Norman Vincent Peale called *The Power of Positive Thinking* which exhorted the reader to think positively even about life's travails and setbacks as the most serviceable way of life. To propose that it is better to appraise a stressful encounter as a challenge rather than as a threat is not very different from arguing that we would all lead happier, more productive lives if we could learn to think positively. The problem with Peale's inspirational message is not that he was altogether wrong about this but, as in the case of all advice and inspirational messages, those who need them most are least able to use them effectively.

Acknowledgments

*This paper was published previously in S. Breznitz (Ed.), *Denial and Stress*. New York: International Universities Press, 1980.

Constructive criticisms of an earlier draft by Professor Gerald A. Mendelsohn and by members of my research group are appreciatively acknowledged.

Writing of this paper was supported in part by a research grant from the National Institute on Aging (AG 00799).

References

Andrew, J. M. (1970), Recovery from surgery with and without preparatory instruction for three coping styles. *J. Pers. Soc. Psychol.*, 151:223–226.

Ansbacher, H. L. & Ansbacher, R. R., eds. (1956), *The Individual Psychology of Alfred Adler*. New York: Basic Books.

Becker, E. (1973), *The Denial of Death*. New York: Free Press.

Beecher, H. K. (1956–1957), The measurement of pain, prototype for the quantitative study of subjective responses. *Pharmac. Rev.*, 8–9:60–209.

Bem, D. (1970), *Beliefs, Attitudes and Human Affairs*. Belmont, Calif.: Brooks/Cole.

Benner, P., Roskies, E., & Lazarus, R. S. (1980), Stress and coping under extreme conditions. In: *The Holocaust: A multidisciplinary study*, ed. J. E. Dimsdale. Washington, D.C.: Hemisphere, in press.

Bentley, E. (Ed.). *Naked masks: Five plays by Luigi Pirandello*. New York: Dutton, 1952.

Bergmann, T. (in collaboration with A. Freud) *Children in the hospital*. New York: International Universities Press, 1958.

Bowlby, J. (1961), Process of mourning. *Int. J. Psychoanal.*, 42:317–340.

Breger, L. (1967), Functions of dreams. *J. Abnorm. Psychol. Monogr.*, 72 (No. 5, Whole No. 641).

Cobb, B., Clark, R. L., McGuire, C., & Howe, C. D. (1954), Patient-responsible delay of treatment in cancer. *Cancer*, 7:920–926.

Cohen, F. & Lazarus, R. S. (1973), Active coping processes, coping dispositions, and recovery from surgery. *Psychosom. Med.*, 35:357–389.

Cohen, F. & Lazarus, R. S. (1979), Coping with the stress of illness. In: *Health Psychology*, ed. G. C. Stone, F. Cohen, & N. E. Adler. San Francisco: Jossey-Bass, pp. 217–254.

Davis, F. (1963), *Passage Through Crisis: Polio Victims and Their Families*. Indianapolis: Bobbs-Merrill.

Delong, D. R. (1970), Individual differences in patterns of anxiety arousal, stress-relevant information and recovery from surgery. Unpublished doctoral dissertation, University of California, Los Angeles.

Dembo, T., Leviton, G. L., & Wright, B. A. (1956), Adjustment to misfortune—a problem of social psychological rehabilitation. *Artif. Limbs*, 3:4–62.

Dinardo, Q. E. (1971), Psychological adjustment to spinal cord injury. Unpublished doctoral dissertation, University of Houston, Texas.

Erikson, E. H. (1963), *Childhood and Society*. New York: W. W. Norton.

Fenichel, O. (1945), *The Psychoanalytic Theory of Neurosis*. London: Routledge & Kegan Paul.

Festinger, L. (1957), *A Theory of Cognitive Dissonance*. New York: Harper & Row.

Fine, B. D., Joseph, E. D., & Waldhorn, H. F., eds. (1969) The Mechanism of Denial. *Monograph III, Monograph Series of the Kris Study Group of the New York Psychoanalytic Institute*. New York: International Universities Press.

Folkman, S. K. (1979), An analysis of coping in normal adults: A naturalistic investigation. Unpublished doctoral dissertation, University of California, Berkeley.

Folkman, S. D., Schaefer, C., & Lazarus, R. S. (1980), Cognitive processes as mediators in stress and coping. In: *Human Stress and Cognition: An Information-Processing Approach*, ed. V. Hamilton & D. M. Warburton. London: Wiley, in press.

Frankl, V. E. (1955), *The Doctor and The Soul.* New York: Knopf.

Freud, A. (1946), *The Ego and the Mechanisms of Defence.* New York: International Universities Press.

Freud, S. (1966), *The Standard Edition of the Complete Psychological Works.* London: Hogarth.

Goldstein, M. J. (1973), Individual differences in response to stress. *Amer. J. Commun. Psychol.* 1:113–137.

Guillemin, R., Vargo, T., Rossier, J., Minick, S., Ling, N., Rivier, C., Vale, W., & Bloom, F. (1977), B-endorphin and adrenocorticotropin are secreted concomitantly by the pituitary gland. *Science*, 197:1367–1369.

Haan, N. (1977), *Coping and Defending.* New York: Academic Press.

Hackett, T. P. & Cassem, N. (1974), Development of a quantitative rating scale to assess denial. *J. Psychosom. Res.*, 18:93–100.

Hackett, T. P., & Cassem, N. (1975), Psychological management of the myocardial infarction patient. *J. Hum. Stress*, 1:25–38.

Hackett, T. P., Cassem, N., & Wishnie, H. A. (1968), The coronary-care unit: An appraisal of its psychologic hazards. *New Eng. J. Med.*, 279:1365–1370.

Hackett, T. P. & Weisman, A. D. (1964), Reactions to the imminence of death. In: *The Threat of Impending Disaster*, ed. G. H. Grosser, H. Wechsler, & M. Greenblatt. Cambridge, Mass.: The MIT Press, pp. 300–311.

Hall, C. S., & Lindsey, G. (1957), *Theories of Personality.* New York: Wiley.

Hamburg, D. A. & Adams, J. E. (1967), A perspective on coping behavior: Seeking and utilizing information in major transitions. *Arch. Gen. Psychiat.*, 17:277–284.

Hamburg, D. A., Hamburg, B., & deGoza, S. (1953), Adaptive problems and mechanisms in severely burned patients. *Psychiatry*, 16:1–20.

Hofer, M. A., Wolff, E. T., Friedman, S. B., & Mason, J. W. (1972), A psychoendocrine study of bereavement, Parts I and II. *Psychosom. Med.*, 34:481–504.

Horowitz, L. M., Sampson, H., Siegelman, E. Y., Wolfson, A., & Weiss, J. (1975), On the identification of warded-off mental contents: An empirical and methodological contribution. *J. Abnorm. Psychol.* 84:545–558.

Horowitz, M. (1975), Intrusive and repetitive thoughts after experimental stress. *Arch. Gen. Psychiat.* 32:1457–1463.

Jacobson, E. (1957), Denial and repression. *J. Amer. Psychoanal. Assn.*, 5:61–92.

Jahoda, M. (1958), *Current Conceptions of Postive Mental Health.* New York: Basic Books.

Janis, I. L. (1958), *Psychological Stress.* New York: Wiley.

Janis, I. L. Vigilance and decision-making in personal crises. In: *Coping and Adaptation*, ed. G. V. Coelho, D. A. Hamburg, & J. E. Adams. New York: Basic Books, pp. 139–175.

Janis, I. L., & Mann, L. (1977), *Decision making.* New York: Free Press.

Kanungo, R. N. (1979), The concepts of alienation and involvement revisited. *Psychol. Bull.*, 86:119–138.

Katz, J. L., Weiner, H., Gallagher, T. G., & Hellman, L. (1970), Stress, distress, and ego defenses. *Arch. Gen. Psychiat.*, 23:131–142.

Kubler-Ross, E. (1969), *On Death and Dying.* New York: Macmillan.

Lazarus, R. S. (1978), The stress and coping paradigm. Read at conference entitled, "The Critical Evaluation of Behavioral Paradigms for Psychiatric Science," Gleneden Beach, Oregon.

Lazarus, R. S., & Alfert, E. (1964), The short-circuiting of threat. *J. Abnorm. Soc. Psychol.*, 69:195–205.

Lazarus, R. S., Averill, J. R., & Opton, E. M., Jr. (1974), The psychology of coping: Issues of research and assessment. In: *Coping and adaptation*, ed. G. V. Coelho, D. A. Hamburg, & J. E. Adams. New York: Basic Books, pp. 249–315.

Lazarus, R. S., Cohen, J. B., Folkman, S. K., Kanner, A., & Schaefer, C. (1979), Psychological stress and adaptation: Some unresolved issues. In: *Guide to Stress Research*, ed. H. Selye. New York: Van Nostrand Reinhold, pp. 90–117.

Lazarus, R. S., & Launier, R. (1978), Stress-related transactions between person and environment. In: *Perspectives in interactional psychology*, ed. L. A. Peruin & M. Lewis. New York: Plenum, pp. 287–327.

Lazarus, R. S., Opton, E. M., Jr., Nomikos, M. S., & Rankin, N. O. (1965), The principle of short-circuiting of threat: Further evidence. *J. Pers.*, 33:622–635.

Lefcourt, H. M. (1966), Repression-sensitization: A measure of the evaluation of emotional expression. *J. Consult. Clin. Psychol.*, 30:444–449.

Levine, J. & Zigler, E. (1975), Denial and self-image in stroke, lung cancer, and heart disease patients. *J. Consult. Clin. Psychol.*, 43:751–757.

Lifton, R. J. (1964), On death and death symbolism: The Hiroshima disaster. *Psychiatry*, 27:191–210.

Lindemann, E. (1944), Symptomatology and management of acute grief. *Amer. J. Psychiat.*, 101:141–148.

Lipowski, Z. J. (1970), Physical illness, the individual and the coping process. *Int. J. Psychiat. Med.*, 1:91–102.

Maslow, A. H. (1954), *Motivation and Personality*. New York: Harper & Row.

McDaniel, J. W., & Sexton, A. W. (1970), Psychoendocrine studies of patients with spinal cord lesion. *J. Abnorm. Psychol.*, 76:117–122.

Mechanic, D. (1978), *Students Under Stress*. Madison, Wisc: University of Wisconsin Press.

Menninger, K. (1963), *The Vital Balance*. New York: Viking.

Offer, D. & Freedman, D. X. (1972), *Modern Psychiatry and Clinical Research: Essays in Honor of Roy R. Grinker, Sr.* New York: Basic Books.

Oken, D. (1961), What to tell cancer patients: Study of medical attitudes. *J. Amer. Med. Assn.*, 175:1120–1128.

Pirandello, L. (1939), *Saggi*. Milano, Italy: Mondadori.

Rank, O. (1936), *Will Therapy and Truth and Reality*. New York: Knopf.

Rokeach, M. (1968), *Beliefs, Attitudes, and Values*. San Francisco: Jossey-Bass.

Sjöbäck, H. (1973), *The Psychoanalytic Theory of Defensive Processes*. New York: Wiley.

Staudenmayer, H., Kinsman, R. A., Dirks, J. F., Spector, S. L., & Wangaard, C. (1979), Medical outcome in asthmatic patients: Effects of airways hyperactivity and symptom-focussed anxiety. *Psychosom. Med.*, 41:109–118.

Stern, M. J., Pascale, L., & McLoone, J. B. (1976), Psychosocial adaptation following an acute myocardial infarction. *J. Chron. Dis.*, 29:513–526.

Townes, B. D., Wold, D. A., & Holmes, T. H. (1974), Parental adjustment to childhood leukemia. *J. Psychosom. Res.*, 18:9–14.

Vaihinger, H. (1925), *The Philosophy of "As If."* New York: Harcourt.

Vaillant, G. (1977), *Adaptation to Life*. Boston: Little, Brown.

Visotsky, H. M., Hamburg, D. A., Goss, M. E., & Lebovits, B. Z. (1961), Coping behavior under extreme stress. *Arch. Gen. Psychiat.*, 5:423–448.

Von Kugelgen, E. (1975), Psychological determinants of the delay in decision to seek aid in cases of myocardial infarction. Unpublished doctoral dissertation, University of California, Berkeley.

Watzlawick, P. (1977), *How Real is Real?* New York: Vintage Books.

Weisman, A. D. (1972), *On Dying and Denying.* New York: Behavioral Publications.
Wheelis, A. (1966), *The Illusionless Man: Fantasies and Meditations.* New York: Norton.
Wolff, C. T., Friedman, S. B., Hofer, M. A., & Mason, J. W. (1964), Relationship between psychological defenses and mean urinary 17-hydroxycorticosteroid excretion rates, Parts I and II. *Psychosom. Med.,* 26:576–609.
Wortman, C. B. & Dunkel-Schetter, C. (1979), The importance of social support: Parallels between victims and the aged. Read at workshop entitled, "The Elderly of the Future," Committee on Aging, National Research Council, Annapolis, Maryland.
Wright, B. A. (1960), *Physical Disability: A Psychological Approach.* New York: Harper.

Locus of Control and
Stressful Life Events

HERBERT M. LEFCOURT

Though research focusing upon the response to life stressors has been prominent in both psychological and psychiatric literature for a considerable length of time, the publication by Holmes and Rahe (1967), in which they presented a scale to quantify the impact of life changes, has served to accelerate research in this area dramatically. Their creation of the Schedule of Recent Experiences (SRE), containing an assortment of potentially stressful events such as death, divorce, marriage, and financial changes, has led to the creation of a considerable literature, linking the frequency and severity of life changes with physical illness and emotional difficulties. Much of this research has been summarized and critically reviewed in the volume edited by the Dohrenwends (B. S. Dohrenwend & B. P. Dohrenwend, 1974).

At the same time that investigators have reported upon the effects that common life experiences can have upon an individual's state of well-being, it has always been apparent that there are some persons who do not exhibit the predicted effects. Novels as well as biographies often focus upon the heroics that given persons have demonstrated in the face of seemingly insurmountable life problems. Most recently the autobiography of Alexander Dolgun (1975) has illustrated how an individual can summon up a host of strategies and techniques to aid his survival in confrontation with nearly unbelievable cruelty in the Soviet gulag. Most pertinent for this paper was Dolgun's concern for the maintenance of control. As long as he believed that he could in some way effect the conditions of his incarceration, even if it meant having the option of suicide, Dolgun felt that he would be able to withstand the torment that was his daily lot.

Similarly, in a chapter written by me (Lefcourt, 1980), a case study was presented that described how a particular individual had struggled to survive following a near-fatal plane crash. The series of life-threatening events, surgeries, and so on, were such that many persons would have died from despair whereas the protagonist in

157

question planned and actively worked toward his recovery. Again, this person stressed the importance of retaining some degree of control over the traumatic events that he encountered.

The interest in examining individual differences that account for variations in the way that individuals cope with stressors has a time-honored history. Investigators such as Coehlo, Hamburg, and Adams (1974), Lazarus (1966), Murphy and Moriarty (1976), and many others have written at length about personality characteristics that differentiate among persons who vary in their coping skills.

Most recently Johnson and Sarason (1978) have summarized an extensive literature in which they discuss a number of potentially powerful moderator variables that can affect the relationship between life-stress events and their emotional and health concomitants. Among those variables discussed was the locus-of-control construct. In brief, locus of control refers to the beliefs that individuals hold regarding the ways in which given outcomes occur. If a person believes, for instance, that people reject him because of the ways in which he acts, he can be said to have an internal locus of control for social rejection. On the other hand, if he regards such rejection as deriving from other persons' prejudices then he may be said to have an external locus of control for social rejection. If other concerns such as achievement, love, and affection were likewise to be assessed for the individual's beliefs regarding causes of outcomes it would become possible to describe the degree to which such persons hold internal or external locus-of-control beliefs in general.

One reason for suspecting that this construct should be of importance as a moderator of life stresses is that empirical research has indicated that aversive events in laboratory situations do not have the same impact upon persons who differ in their beliefs about the controllability of laboratory procedures. Aversive stimuli such as electric shocks do not have the same degree of debilitating effects upon performances when subjects believe they can effect the onset or offset of those shocks as they do when subjects have no ostensible means of altering their occurrence. For more extensive discussions of this literature there are several available sources (Lefcourt, 1976a, 1976b; Phares, 1976). The reason offered for these effects has most often been that if one holds some belief that he can affect the events at hand, then those events will not simply continue on indefinitely. In essence, one can tolerate considerable abuse and suffering if one believes that such pain will not be infinite or that the current unpleasantness is in the service of some future ends that are of positive value.

Most recently the locus-of-control construct has been used in two investigations as a possible moderator of life stresses. Johnson and Sarason (1978) found that the relationships between negative life changes assessed by their Life Experience Survey and measures of anxiety and depression were more prominent among subjects classified as external on Rotter's Locus of Control scale (Rotter, 1966). Similarly, Kobasa (1979) found that executives who exhibited a high stress-high illness association were rated as more external on Rotter's scale than those who were in a high stress-low illness group.

In recent years I have been involved in a number of investigations in which the locus-of-control construct has been used as an indicator of vulnerability to particular stressors. Our focus thus far has been aimed at predicting affiliative and achievement relevant behaviors with locus-of-control scales designed to assess causal beliefs about those goal areas. These scales, The Multidimensional-Multiattributional Causality Scales (MMCS), and information pertaining to them are available elsewhere (Lefcourt et al., 1979).

Most recently we have been attempting to predict more enduring moods among individuals from life-event measures and various measures of locus of control including the MMCS. Epstein (1977) has demonstrated empirically that if one obtains repeated measures of self-reports, seemingly elusive data such as self-described moods become progressively more reliably assessed. Thus, with enough measurements over time, persons may be accurately described as depressed, angry, etc. The study described below made use of repeated testing sessions in the study of moods. It was our expectation that locus of control would be found to be an even more robust moderator of life events than previous investigators have reported when the mood criteria were more reliably assessed and the data were subjected to multiple regression analyses.

Subjects

Fifty-nine subjects from two third-year psychology courses volunteered in response to the instructors' solicitations. All subjects were aware that they would be asked to record their moods for four consecutive weeks.

Method

All subjects completed Coddington's life-events measure (Coddington, 1972) which provides life-event scores for each of four eras of life—preschool, elementary, junior high, and senior high school. Though not assessing the immediately preceding years for our third-year university students, Coddington's measure was chosen for the exploratory possibilities offered by its focus upon the various eras. This scale requires the checking of weighted life events much as the SRE with the addition of affective ratings—the subject can describe whether each checked off event was positive, negative, or neutral in the affect that was aroused by it. For the present purposes, the high-school life-events scores were of primary interest given their nearer proximity in time to our subjects' current lives.

Secondly, subjects completed Rotter's I-E scale as well as our own MMCS providing scores of general locus of control achievement and affiliation. Finally, subjects completed the Profile of Mood States (POMS; Lorr et al., 1971) for each week during four consecutive weeks.

Results

Though some writers have found relationships between life-event measures and locus of control (Sarason et al., 1978), in the present sample the measures proved to be relatively independent. Scores on the MMCS, like Rotter's I-E scale, are scored in the external direction, high scores indicating an external locus of control for the respective goal area (see table 1).

The POMS is comprised of six mood scores, one each for tension, depression, anger, vigor, fatigue, and confusion. In addition, a total mood-disturbance score is derived from adding all moods with the exception of vigor, which is subtracted from the total of the other five scores. In this study each subject's mood scores were a composite from the four weeks of testing. Means and standard deviations for the moods are presented in table 2.

The major analyses consisted of a series of hierarchically arranged

TABLE 1

Correlations between Negative and Positve Life Events during High School form the Coddington Scale, the MMCS and I-E Scales.[a]

Life Events	MMCS Affiliation	MMCS Achievement	I-E
Positive	−0.08	0.18	0.10
Negative	0.01	−0.16	−0.07

[a]N = 59.

TABLE 2

Means and Standard Deviations of POMS Scores

	Tension	Depression	Anger	Vigor	Fatigue	Confusion	Total Mood Disturbance
Mean	9.42	8.48	5.72	17.30	7.06	7.52	20.61
Standard deviation	5.02	7.66	3.93	5.47	4.11	3.46	22.01

Averaged from four administrations of POMS.

multiple regression analyses with negative life events during the high school era serving as the first variable, one of the three locus of control measures as the second, and the product of the two (indicating the interaction between the two main effect variables) as the third variable. The use of the product term as the equivalent or approximation of the interaction in an analysis of variance is a relatively recent statistical advance described by Kerlinger and Pedhazur (1973) and Cohen (1978). Because the presentation of all six moods for each of three regression analyses would be too cumbersome, only the overall "Total Mood Distrubance" analyses are presented in detail. As noted in table 3 both main effects and the interaction terms, the products of the negative life events and Rotter's I-E, and the MMCS affiliation scale attain some level of statistical significance, the Rotter scale producing the higher magnitude results. On the other hand, the MMCS achievement scale fails to produce either main effects or interactions. To illustrate the meanings of these interactions, the means of the total mood disturbance scores are plotted for each of the predictor variables divided at their respective medians (see fig. 1).

This figure shows that persons classified as external on either Rotter's I-E scale or the MMCS affiliation scale reveal the strongest association between negative life events and mood-distrubance scores. Also in table 3 are the multiple correlations which indicate that Rotters I-E scale and the MMCS affiliation scale add substantially to the predictive power of the life event scales.

With regard to specific mood scales, Rotter's I-E scale was found to interact with negative life events in the prediction of depression ($F = 6.21$ $p < 0.025$), fatigue ($F = 3.67$, $p < 0.10$) and confusion ($F = 4.90$, $p < 0.05$). The MMCS affiliation measure produced interactions with Tension ($F = 4.08$, $p < 0.05$) and depression ($F = 3.49$, $p < 0.10$) while the MMCS achievement scale failed to produce any significant interactions with negative life events in the prediction of moods. In each case where significant interactions

TABLE 3

Hierarchically Arranged Multiple Regression Analyses Between Negative Life Events, Locus of Control, and Mood Disturbance.

Variables	Simple Correlation	Cumulative r^2	Increase in r^2	F test on Increment	p Value
Negative life events	0.37	0.13	0.13	9.95	0.005
Rotter's I-E	0.20	0.19	0.06	4.44	0.05
Negative life events x I-E	0.27	0.26	0.07	4.90	0.05
Multiple $R = 0.51, p < 0.001$					
Negative life events	0.37	0.13	0.13	9.41	0.005
MMCS affiliation	0.21	0.18	0.04	2.96	0.10
Negative life events x MMCS affiliation	0.13	0.22	0.04	2.94	0.10
Multiple $R = 0.47, p < 0.005$					
Negative life events	0.37	0.13	0.13	8.58	0.005
MMCS achievement	-0.07	0.13	0.00	0.00	—
Negative life events x MMCS achievement	0.06	0.14	0.01	0.49	—
Multiple $R = 0.38, p < 0.05$					

were obtained the distribution of means were much like those presented in fig. 1.

Though the data were not presented it should be noted that no main effects were obtained with those life events that had been evaluated as positive. The highest correlation obtained between positive life events and moods was approximately 0.20 though each

FIGURE 1

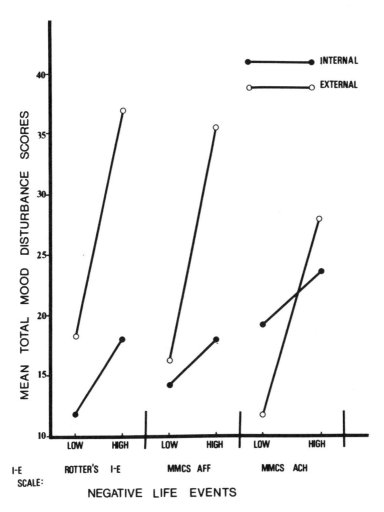

Mean Total Mood Disturbance Scores as a Function of
Negative Life Events and Various Locus of Control Scales

correlation was in the expected direction, negative with all moods excepting vigor with which it related positively.

Discussion

As was anticipated, locus-of-control variables, as assessed by Rotter's I-E scale and the MMCS affiliation measure, afforded rather sizable multiple correlations and even more notably produced significant interactions that conform to theoretical expectations. In brief, locus-of-control scales operated effectively as moderator variables between negative life events and the composite index of mood disturbance obtained over a four-week period. Those subjects who were more external with regard to generalized expectancies of control (Rotter's I-E) or with regard to affiliation outcomes were more likely to exhibit distress as indicated by the total mood-disturbance scores.

These findings are particularly impressive when considering the fact that the life events in question were not immediate, but had occurred approximately three to five years prior to the current assessment of moods. These life events, therefore, were not those characterized as having "triggering effects" but, given their time separation from the criteria, were more similar to those that are referred to as having "formative effects" (Brown and Harris, 1978). The latter more often have lesser effects upon moods and health than the former.

Questions may be raised regarding the independence of the life-events scale and the locus-of-control measures as well as the mood scales since they are cross-sectional data collected at one time period. It can be argued that the life-events measure, which requests that a subject recall past events as well as his affective responses to them, may be biased by the same moods that are assessed by the mood scales; and, in turn, locus-of-control scores may likewise reflect current moods. As was noted in the results section, however, correlations between the locus-of-control variables and both positive and negative life-events scales were found to be negligible. In addition, Sarason, Johnson, and Siegel (1978) have found that life-event scores do not vary with mood states per se. Though it is possible to contend that the evaluation of life events may change with present circumstances, it seems unlikely that subjects will falsify the actual noting of events that have a demographiclike character; and since most such events have modal affective responses (death of a close relative most often should be rated as a negative event) the evaluations of those events should also be less subject to momentary influences. The present study also adds considerably to the literature because of the multiple assessments of moods. The likelihood that singular measurements of mood are unreliable is high, and it is unfortunate that most studies using mood scales do rely on single assessments. As Epstein (1977) has noted, the larger the sampling of assessments the more reliable they are likely to become.

Finally, it should be noted that the current findings bear similarity to those obtained in several other investigations in which very different methodologies and criteria have been used. Langer and Rodin (1976) and Reid and Ziegler (1977) have found that a belief in control operates as a moderator of the stresses encountered in living in senior citizens' residences. In those studies ill health and death were predictable from conditions suggesting an absence of control and beliefs held regarding the uncontrollability of desired outcomes. Brown and Harris (1978) similarly have contended that the four factors that they have found to be powerful moderators of the effects of life stressors, the absence of a confidant, having 3 young children at home, not working outside the home, and having lost one's mother during one's formative years, can be subsumed by a construct akin to that of locus of control. These writers suggest that hopelessness, which results from the four factors, is the likely precursor of emotional difficulties; and that hopelessness is most apt to develop if a person does not have a sense of "mastery." The latter is defined as evident when "loss and disappointment is mediated by a sense of one's ability to control the world and thus to repair damage" (p. 235).

If one perceives that life events can be modified by one's own behavior, "that damage can be repaired," then the likelihood that negative events will continue unabated, that pain will continue indefinitely, becomes lessened. If man perceives that the tides may turn in his favor, even if in the far-off future, he should be better able to survive his daily travails with composure.

Acknowledgments

This research was supported by a research grant from the Social Sciences and Humanities Research Council of Canada #410-78-0297. Appreciation is expressed to Ed Ware, Debbie Sherk, and Rickey Miller for their help at various stages of this research.

References

Brown, G. W. & Harris, T. (1978), *Social Origins of Depression.* London: Tavistock.

Coddington, R. D. (1972), The significance of life events as etiologic factors in the diseases of children. *J. Psychosom. Res.* 16:7–18.

Coehlo, G., Hamburg, D. A., & Adams, J. E., eds. (1974), *Coping and Adaptation.* New York: Basic Books.

Cohen, J. (1978), Partialed products *are* interactions; Partialed powers *are* curve components. *Psychol. Bull.* 85:858–866.

Dohrenwend, B. S. & Dohrenwend, B. P., eds. (1974), *Stressful Life Events: Their Nature and Effects.* New York: Wiley.

Dolgun, A. (1975), *Alexander Dolgun's Story: An American in the Gulag.* New York: Knopf.

Epstein, S. (1977), Traits are alive and well. In: *Personality at the Crossroads: Current Issues in Interactional Psychology,* ed. D. Magnusson & N. S. Endler. Hillsdale, N.J.: Lawrence Erlbaum Associates.

Holmes, T. H. & Rahe, R. H. (1967), The social readjustment scale. *J. Psychosom. Res.* 11:213–218.

Johnson, J. H. & Sarason, I. G. (1978), Life stress, depression and anxiety: Internal-external control as a moderator variable. *J. Psychosom. Res.* 22:205–208.

Kerlinger, F. N. & Pedhazur, E. J. (1973), *Multiple Regression in Behavioral Research.* New York: Holt, Rinehart & Winston.

Kobasa, S. C. (1979), Stressful life events, personality, and health: an inquiry into hardiness. *J. Pers. Soc. Psychol.* 37:1–11.

Langer, E. J. & Rodin, J. (1976), The effects of choice and enhanced personal responsibility for the aged. *J. Pers. Soc. Psychol.,* 34:191–198.

Lazarus, R. S. (1966), *Psychological Stress and The Coping Process.* New York: McGraw-Hill.

Lefcourt, H. M. (1976a), *Locus of Control: Current Trends in Theory and Research.* Hillsdale, N.J.: Lawrence Erlbaum Associates.

Lefcourt, H.M. (1976b), Locus of control and the response to aversive events. *Canad. Psychol. Rev.,* 17:202–209.

Lefcourt, H. M. (1980), Locus of control and coping with life's events. In: *Personality,* ed. E. Staub. Englewood Cliffs, N.J.: Prentice-Hall.

Lefcourt, H. M., von Baeyer, C. L., Ware, E. E., & Cox, D. J. (1979), The multidimensional-multiattributional causality scale: The development of a goal specific locus of control scale. *Canad. J. Behav. Sci.,* 11:286–304.

Lorr, M., McNair, D. M., & Droppleman, L. F. (1971), *The Profile of Mood States.* San Diego: EDITS.

Murphy, L. B. & Moriarty, A. E. (1976), *Vulnerability, Coping, and Growth From Infancy to Adolescence.* New Haven & London: Yale University Press.

Phares, E. J. (1976), *Locus of Control in Personality.* Morristown, N.J.: General Learning Press.

Reid, D. & Ziegler, M. (1977), The contribution of personal control to psychological adjustment of the elderly. Read at Canadian Psychological Assn. Convention, Vancouver.

Rotter, J. B. (1966), Generalized expectancies of internal versus external control of reinforcement. *Psychol. Monogr.,* (Whole No. 609).

Sarason, I. G., Johnson, J. H., & Siegel, J. M. (1978), Assessing the impact of life changes. Development of the Life Experiences Survey. *J. Consult. Clin. Psychol.* 46:932–946.

Type A Behavior, Stressful Life Events, and Coronary Heart Disease

KAREN A. MATTHEWS

DAVID C. GLASS

The nature of the relationship between stressful life events and the subsequent onset of coronary heart disease (CHD) is still under debate (Andrews and Tennant, 1978; B. S. Dohrenwend and B. P. Dohrenwend, 1978; Rahe and Arthur, 1978). Although some studies suggest a positive association (Rahe and Romo, 1974), others have not replicated this result (Hinkle, 1974; Theorell et al., 1975). Differences between the various studies in design, sample, and disease endpoint do not permit precise identification of the sources of the discrepancy in results. However, the discrepancy does suggest that it is naive to expect life events to have the same impact on all individuals in all circumstances (B. S. Dohrenwend and B. P. Dohrenwend, 1978). Thus, a more profitable approach to understanding the life event-CHD relationship may be to specify mediating factors that determine the conditions under which life events do and do not have a negative impact on cardiovascular health.

In this chapter, one set of mediating variables is suggested, namely, the interaction of the Type A coronary-prone behavior pattern with uncontrollable stressful events. Uncontrollable stress involves the anticipation of psychic and/or physical harm which the individual believes he is relatively powerless to alter. The behavior pattern is a set of overt behaviors elicited in susceptible individuals by appropriate environmental conditions. It includes competitive achievement-striving, time-urgency and impatience, hostility and aggressiveness. Both uncontrollable stress and Type A behavior pattern have been implicated in the etiology of CHD (Friedman, 1969; Greene et al., 1972; Schneiderman, 1978).

This chapter is divided into several major sections as follows. First, Type A is defined and the evidence supporting its association with coronary disease endpoints is reviewed. Second, consideration is given to current approaches to identifying the underlying mechanisms associating Type A behavior pattern and coronary disease. One of these approaches emphasizes the importance of Type A responses to uncontrollable stress. The final substantive section of the chapter presents evidence for a joint effect of Type A behavior pattern and uncontrollable life events upon cardiovascular disease.

Definition of Type A

The concept of coronary-prone behavior has a long history, but a short scientific past. It is present in the writings of the Menningers, Flanders Dunbar (see Friedman and Rosenman [1969] for a review), and even a nineteenth-century cardiologist, Sir William Osler, who noted that, "It is not the delicate, neurotic person who is prone to angina but the robust, the vigorous in mind and body, the keen and ambitious man, the indicator of whose engine is always at 'full speed ahead'" (Osler, 1910, p. 839). Other cardiologists have noted the intense aggressiveness, drive to dominate and achieve goals, and hostility that characterize their patients (see Friedman, 1969).

A more systematic description of the coronary-prone behavior pattern has emerged from the laboratories of Friedman and Rosenman (Friedman, 1969; Rosenman and Friedman, 1974). The pattern, called Type A, is described by these investigators as" . . . a characteristic action-emotion complex which is exhibited by those individuals who are engaged in a relatively chronic struggle to obtain an unlimited number of poorly defined things from their environment in the shortest period of time, and, if necessary, against the opposing efforts of other things or persons in this same environment" (Friedman, 1969, p. 84).

This struggle is thought to be encouraged by contemporary Western society because it appears to offer special rewards and opportunities to those who can think, perform, and even play more rapidly and aggressively than their peers. Type A is not a set of personality characteristics leading to behavioral and physiological responses by some invariant process. Type A behavior is seen as the outcome of a set of predispositions interacting with specific types of eliciting situations, including those that might be defined as stressful.

Although individuals who exhibit pattern A behavior are called Type A's, whereas those who do not are called Type B's, in actuality, Type A is defined as a continuum ranging from extreme A to extreme B responses. A full description of the Type A side of the continuum has been developed, whereas the only available description of Type B is the relative absence of Type A. It seems obvious, however, that Type B is not merely the absence of a certain style of interacting with life's challenges and dilemmas. It probably represents a distinctly different set of coping responses. Such a view is consistent with the responses of Type A's and B's to uncontrollable stressful events (Glass, 1977). While A's are struggling to maintain control over their environment, B's are not simply struggling less, they appear to be coping in a different manner.

Operational Definitions—Two principal techniques are used currently to assess Type A behavior. One is called the structured interview. In this approximately 25-question interview, individuals are asked about their characteristic way of responding to a variety of situations, such as having to wait in long lines or to work with a slow partner. More importantly, the interviewee is deliberately provoked by the interviewer in order to elicit speech stylistics considered indicative of behavior pattern A. For example, a question may be asked in a hesitant and slow manner. The appropriate answer to the question is clear after the first few words are spoken by interviewer. A Type A person typically interrupts and answers the intended question. Another illustration is where the interviewer questions the accuracy of an answer, thereby arousing annoyance in a susceptible individual. Behavior pattern classification is thus based on self-reports of Type A behavior, as well as on behaviors observed during the interview itself. Although recent evidence suggests that the latter may be more critical in reaching a final assessment (Scherwitz et al., 1977; Schucker and Jacobs, 1977), both the style and content of a respondent's answers contribute to his behavior-pattern classification.

Individuals are classified into one of four categories; A1, or fully developed Type A; A2, or incompletely developed Type A; X, or an equal representation of Type A and Type B characteristics; Type B, or the absence of a preponderance of Type A characteristics. In a sample of approximately 3,500 men enrolled in the prospective Western Collaborative Group Study (WCGS) to be described below, approximately 50% were classified as Type A (Rosenman et al., 1964). In more recent studies, the percentage has been larger—e.g., 60% of the managers from 12 different Canadian firms were classified as Type A (Howard et al., 1976). If this preponderance of Type A classification continues to occur in future studies, large numbers of persons who will not develop CHD will be categorized as being at high risk for the disease. Consequently, the specificity of the interview for the prediction of coronary disease will be weakened.

The structured interview was developed with middle-class male populations. It is still an open question whether the technique can be used in different cultures and subcultures, and with women. Recent evidence suggests that the interview can be adapted for use with female subjects (Chesney, 1979; Waldron, 1978), but the influence of cultural factors has received little systematic attention (Cohen, 1978). Subcultural differences may also exert an important effect upon an A-B classification which emphasizes speech and voice stylistics. For example, it is by no means clear that A's and B's can be distinguished by such stylistics in populations like lower middle-class New York City residents. Loud and explosive speech, rapid and accelerated vocalizations are very much part of the New York manner of speaking, perhaps irrespective of whether the individual is Type A or Type B. This observation suggests the need for developing other assessment techniques that may be less susceptible to the influence of special subcultural speech stylistics.

A second technique for Pattern A assessment is the Jenkins Activity Survey for Health Prediction, commonly called the JAS (Jenkins et al., 1971). This questionnaire is a self-report measure that contains 54 questions similar to those used in the structured interview. Scoring of the items is based on optimal weights generated by a series of discriminant function analyses predicting the structured interview classification of large groups of subjects (Jenkins et al., 1971). The JAS scores were normally distributed in the validation sample. Consequently, a linear transformation applied to all scores was incorporated into the computer program that scores the test so that the mean of the A-B scores is 0.0 with a standard deviation of 10.0. Positive scores indicate the Type A direction; negative scores indicate the Type B direction.

Both the JAS and the structured interview show good reliability. For example, 80% of the subjects in the WCGS showed similar interview-based classifications over periods ranging from 12 to 20 months. Assessments of recorded interviews by two independent raters revealed agreement rates of the order of 75–90% (see Rosenman, 1978). Test-retest correlations of JAS A-B scores ranged between 0.60 and 0.70 across 1- to 4-year time intervals (Jenkins, 1978).

On the other hand, the association between the interview and the

JAS is less than impressive. The JAS agrees about 73% of the time with A-B assessments made from the structured interview of men who maintained the same A-B classification for two years (Jenkins et al., 1971). The agreement rate is reduced to 63% if men who were unstable in type classification are included in the calculation (Brand et al., 1978). Extreme JAS scores (1 standard deviation above and below the mean) agree with interview judgments 88–91% of the time.

A number of factors account for the discrepancy between structured interview and JAS assessments. First, the interview relies on the style as well as the content of a respondent's answers. The JAS by necessity relies exclusively on content. Second, the middle third of the JAS distribution agrees very poorly with the structured interview assessment (43–53%), probably because scores in this middle third, as well as interview Type X's, tend to be the most unreliable assessments (Jenkins, 1978). Third, and perhaps most important, the JAS, being a paper-and-pencil questionnaire, cannot create the appropriate setting needed to elicit Type A behavior. It must rely on recognition and recall of these behaviors on the part of the subject.

A note of caution needs to be introduced here. We do not mean to suggest the superiority of one assessment technique over the other. A variety of factors must enter into a decision of how to assess Type A. Among the more important is whether the assessment procedure leads to a classification that is systematically related to clinical CHD. Still another is whether the classification is linked to physiological and behavioral processes that might be routes to cardiovascular disease. Succeeding sections show that both JAS and interview assessments are related to these endpoints.

Type A and Coronary Disease

A large amount of research has indicated that the structured interview and the JAS are valid predictors of coronary disease. Consideration will be given, however, only to several representative studies. Readers interested in more extensive reviews of the literature are referred to Glass (1977), Dembroski et al. (1978b), and Jenkins (1971; 1976).

Coronary Heart Disease.—The major epidemiological study of relevance is the WCGS mentioned earlier. Beginning in 1960, approximately 3,500 healthy men between the ages of 35 and 59 were recruited into the project. All were employed by one of 11 California companies. This study used a double-blind procedure; that is, the researchers rating the behavior pattern via the interview had no knowledge of other risk factors and did not participate in the subsequent diagnosis of clinical CHD. After 8½ years, the results showed that subjects assessed as Type A in 1960 were twice as likely to develop CHD as their Type B counterparts (Rosenman, et al., 1975). Furthermore, the association of Pattern A with CHD was maintained when simultaneous adjustments were made for combinations of the traditional risk factors (e.g., serum cholesterol, hypertension, cigarette smoking). This latter finding suggests that Type A may not exert its major pathogenic influence through these other factors.

Jenkins, Rosenman, and Zyzanski (1974) reported data on 2,750 participants in the WCGS using the JAS as the basis for Type A assessment. High scorers on the JAS (5.0 and above) showed twice the incidence of new CHD as low scorers (-5.0 and below) over a four-year period. The JAS Type A score was also the strongest single predictor of recurrent myocardial infarction from an array of biomedical variables including the traditional risk factors (Jenkins et al., 1976). These findings indicate that the JAS, like the interview, has predictive value for measuring coronary-proneness. Note, however, that recent comparative work shows the interview procedure to be somewhat superior to the JAS in predicting clinical CHD (Brand et al., 1978).

Coronary Artery Disease.—Both interview and JAS assessments of Type A are related to the degree of atherosclerosis as measured by coronary arteriography (Blumenthal et al., 1978; Frank et al., 1978; Zyzanski et al., 1976), although at least one failure to replicate has been reported during the past year (Dimsdale et al., 1978). The JAS has also been related to progression of atherosclerosis over a mean 17-month interval in a sample of 66 male cardiac outpatients (Krantz et al., 1979). It would appear, then, that Type A behavior is linked both to the underlying disease process (atherosclerosis) and its clinical manifestations (CHD).

Mechanisms Underlying the Association Between
Pattern A and Coronary Disease

As noted earlier, Type A may not exert its pathogenic influence through the traditional risk factors. Therefore, several groups of investigators are attempting to identify other links between Type A behavior and coronary disease. There are at least three major approaches to this problem. The first notes that a classification as Type A does not require the individual to exhibit all forms of Type A behavior. Only a simple preponderance is necessary. A Type A diagnosis, in consequence, gives little information about an individual's actual behavior. It is possible that one person may be classified as Type A because he is competitive, and another because he suffers from a strong sense of time urgency. It is also possible that only certain Type A attributes are related to atherosclerosis and CHD. Knowledge of a global behavior-pattern classification might, therefore, result in a less-than-accurate prediction of disease.

Support for this view comes from a factor analysis of the structured interview responses of 186 men enrolled in the WCGS (Matthews et al., 1977). Although five primary factors were revealed, only two—competitive drive and impatience—were associated with the later onset of clinical CHD. Subsequent analyses indicated that of the more than 40 interview ratings, only seven items discriminated CHD cases from age-matched healthy controls. Of the seven, four items were directly related to hostility, one was concerned with competitiveness, and the remaining two dealt with vigorousness of voice stylistics.

Dembroski et al. (1978a) have developed a component scoring system for the structured interview based on the Matthews et al. (1978) findings. The same dimensions that predicted CHD were found to predict experimentally-induced elevations in systolic blood pressure and heart rate. These cardiovascular effects have also been obtained with the global measure of Type A. Relative to base-level values, Type A's show greater systolic blood pressure and heart-rate elevations than their Type B counterparts, when both types of subjects are exposed to environmental stresses and challenges. (Dembroski et al., 1978a; Glass et al., 1979; Manuck and Garland, 1979). These results take on added significance when viewed in the light of discussions about the role of episodic elevations in blood pressure in potentiating atherosclerosis and CHD (Herd, 1978).

A somewhat different approach to the association between Type A behavior and CHD comes from the work of Scherwitz, Berton, and Leventhal (1978). They identified and measured certain speech characteristics that occurred continuously in the structured interview. These characteristics were then correlated with simultaneously occurring changes in heart rate, finger-pulse amplitude, and blood pressure. Type A individuals who used many self-references (I, me, my, mine) in answering the interview questions showed the highest levels of systolic blood pressure. By contrast, the Type B group had very few significant correlates of self-references. These results have led to the suggestion that self-involvement might account for both the speech characteristics and autonomic reactions of Type A subjects. Indeed, there is evidence that individuals who are acutely aware of themselves behave like Type A's do. For example, individuals whose attention is focused on themselves are likely to be aggressive when provoked (Scheier, 1976). While performing a task, self-aware individuals compare their performance to their internal standards of excellence (Carver and Scheier, 1979; Carver et al., 1980). To the extent that these standards are high, salient discrepancies between performance and goals may lead to excessive striving, frustration, and helplessness. Thus, Scherwitz et al., 1978) suggest that the construct of self-involvement is useful not only because it may explain why Type A behaviors arise, but also because its correlations with cardiovascular and behavioral variables underscore its potential importance as a key construct in explaining the linkage between Type A behavior and CHD.

A third approach to the issue of mechanism comes from the work of Glass and his associates (Glass, 1977). These investigators have reported experimental evidence showing that Type A's work hard to succeed, suppress subjective states (such as fatigue) that might interfere with task performance, conduct their activities at a rapid pace, and express hostility after being frustrated or harassed in their efforts at task completion. It might be argued that these behaviors reflect an attempt by the Type A person to assert and maintain control over stressful aspects of his/her environment. Type A's engage in a continual struggle for control and, in consequence, appear hard-driving and aggressive, easily annoyed, and competitive. Furthermore, this struggle by Type A's may lead them, when confronted by a threat to that control, to increase their efforts to assett control. However, if these efforts meet with repeated failure, Type A's might be expected to give up responding and act helpless. Stated somewhat differently, brief exposure to threatened loss of control accelerates control efforts on the part of A's, whereas prolonged exposure leads to a decrement in these behaviors. This pattern of responding has been described elsewhere as hyperresponsiveness followed by hyporesponsiveness (Glass, 1977). It should be emphasized that the shift from hyper- to hyporesponsiveness is assumed to be a cyclical reaction to discrete events that occur repeatedly during the course of a Type A individual's life. We do not mean to suggest a permanent change in the Type A style of responding after one or even several experiences with prolonged stress. Evidence in support of the hyper- and hyporesponsiveness of Type A's is presented later in this chapter.

Central to the uncontrollability approach to Type A behavior are data concerning the physiological processes that accompany efforts to exert control and giving up. Recent data indicate that active coping with a stressor increases sympathetic activity and the discharge of catecholamines such as norepinephrine (Weiss et al., 1970). High levels of circulating catecholamines may elevate blood pressure, accelerate the rate of arterial damage, induce myocardial lesions, and facilitate the occurrence of fatal cardiac arrhythmias (Eliot, 1979; Haft, 1974; Raab et al., 1969). Catecholamines also potentiate the aggregation of blood platelets, which is considered to be an important factor in atherogenesis as well as in the genesis of thrombosis (Ardlie et al., 1966; Duguid, 1946). Other data show that severe depletion of norepinephrine, with a possible shift to parasympathetic dominance, is often associated with helplessness and giving up (Weiss et al., 1976). It has been suggested that abrupt shifts between sympathetic and parasympathetic activity may be implicated in the major cardiovascular disorders, including sudden death (Engel, 1970; Glass, 1977; Richter, 1957).

If a chronic struggle to exert environmental control accounts, even in part, for Type A behavior, the foregoing physiological processes might explain why Type A's are at greater risk for cardiovascular disease. Research does, indeed, suggest that Type A's exhibit elevated catecholamines in response to both experimental and day-to-day stresses and demands. For example, while working on an insoluble puzzle in order to win a prize, Type A middle-aged men showed greater elevations in plasma norepinephrine than did Type B's (Friedman et al., 1975). Extreme Type A's excrete considerably more norepinephrine in their urine during active working hours than do B's (Friedman et al., 1960). In a more recent study, Type A subjects who were harassed by a hostile competitor had significantly greater elevations in plasma epinephrine (and systolic blood pressure and heart rate) than did their Type B counterparts (Glass et al., 1979). If future research shows greater rises and falls in catecholamines among Type A individuals confronted by uncontrollable stressful events, the enhanced likelihood of coronary disease in these individuals might be explained, in part, by the pathophysiological effects of the catecholaminic changes.

Type A Behavior and Uncontrollable Events

Recall that an uncontrollable event was defined as one that an individual cannot influence or alter. Stated another way, lack of control occurs when a noncontingency is perceived to exist between one's behavior and outcomes. A controllable event, by contrast, implies a perceived contingency between behavior and outcomes. According to this definition, failure to terminate an aversive noise and failure to find the correct solution to cognitive problems are both instances of lack of control; that is, a noncontingency exists between efforts and outcome (Seligman, 1975). These events may also be considered stressful to the extent that they have the potential for causing physical and/or psychic harm to the individual.

Glass and his associates (Glass, 1977) have conducted a series of behavioral experiments in which Type A's and Type B's (based on the JAS) were exposed to uncontrollable stressful events. The paradigm typically involves a *brief* experience with either a controllable or uncontrollable task. Following this "pretreatment phase," efforts to control another task are measured in what is called the "test phase." It is assumed that enhanced responses following an uncontrollable event reflect an effort by the subject to reassert control over the environment.

In a prototypic study, Type A and Type B male college students were exposed to 12 bursts of loud noise. Half of the cases in each group were able to terminate the noise by an appropriate series of lever-pressing responses (Control), whereas the other half were unable to do so (No Control). Following pretreatment, subjects worked on a choice reaction time (RT) task with lengthy intertrial intervals and foreperiods. Previous research had demonstrated that Type A's respond more slowly than Type B's on this type of task, perhaps because their characteristic impatience distracts them from being appropriately attentive to the signal lights on the RT apparatus. In any event, it was expected that A's would perform more poorly than B's following pretreatment with controllable noise. By contrast, uncontrollable noise was expected to enhance the subsequent RT performance of Type A's. The study supported these predictions. Type A's had faster reactions times following exposure to uncontrollable compared to controllable noise, whereas Type B's had slower times after uncontrollable noise.

The same pattern of findings, enhanced performance by A's and deteriorated performance by B's following brief exposure to uncontrollable stress, has been obtained in a number of other studies using somewhat different experimental procedures, including earning points or money on a partial reinforcement schedule that was perceived as uncontrollable (Glass, 1977; Matthews, 1979).

Enhanced efforts on the part of A's to exert direct control over an uncontrollable event must meet with failure in the long run. According to theory, Type A's should, under these circumstances, give up responding and become passive. What is curious about this phenomenon is that the passivity may transfer to other tasks that Type A's can, in fact, master but do not. Thus, enhanced efforts to control may eventuate in ineffective coping strategies. This pattern of responding, termed hyporesponsiveness, has been discussed in other contexts as learned helplessness (Seligman, 1975).

Several studies have tested the notion that Type A's give up active responding after prolonged exposure to uncontrollable stress and do poorly on later tasks. One representative study (Glass, 1977) manipulated control by exposing subjects to 35 loud noise bursts that were either controllable or uncontrollable. (Selection of 35 and 12 noise bursts as constituting prolonged and brief stress exposure was based on procedures used in previous learned helplessness research [Seligman, 1975; Wortman and Brehm, 1975].) In the subsequent test phase of the experiment, all subjects were asked to terminate another series of noise bursts that were in fact controllable. The results showed that Type A's were slower in terminating noise following uncontrollable compared to controllable pretreatment. Type B's performed similarly after both forms of pretreatment.

These data can be interpreted as follows. Type A's learned that a lack of relationship existed between their lever-pressing responses and noise termination which generalized, albeit inappropriately, to the controllable test-phase task. It can, of course, be argued that depressed responding by A's in the test phase of the study occurred for reasons other than the belief that their behavior was having little impact on the environment. An obvious alternative is that they became bored and experienced a decrement in motivation to exert control in the experimental situation. Before accepting such an explanation, consider how Type A's appraise uncontrollable stress. An experiment by Brunson and Matthews (1979) is relevant here. Type A and B subjects were asked to solve a series of insoluble problems (a form of uncontrollability) while simultaneously verbalizing all thoughts, including those that were task irrelevant. At first, all subjects exerted about equivalent efforts to solve the problems. However, the Type A's showed an eventual deterioration in the sophistication of their problem-solving strategies and, moreover, reported that they were personally responsible for their failure. Type A's also became increasingly disappointed in themselves and pessimistic about reaching the correct solution on subsequent trials. By contrast, Type B's did not report such self-perceptions and negative feelings.

These results provide some support for the uncontrollability explanation of Type A hyporesponsiveness. Type A subjects appear to have learned the noncontingency between their behavior and outcomes through initial efforts to master the insoluble problem-solving task. This perception of lack of task control, which they attributed to their own lack of ability, led them to give up eventually and become pessimistic about succeeding on subsequent trials. It would seem, then, that the initial struggle of A's to control their environment may result, in the long run, in a tendency to relinquish control.

But what about the behavior of Type B subjects? Is Type B the mere absence of Type A, or does it represent an alternative way of coping with life's challenges and stresses? If Type B is the relative absence of efforts to exert environmental control, Type B's should respond similarly to uncontrollable and controllable events. On the other hand, they might be expected to respond differently to the two types of stressors if Type B represents a distinct style of response. Examination of Type B behavior in all of the studies cited in this section suggests the latter possibility. When B's are exposed to uncontrollable events, they respond initially by slowing down in their efforts to master the situation. (See the brief noise-exposure experiment). Recall, however, that they do not assume personal responsibility for their lack of control, and they do not believe that they are, in general, incapable of exerting environmental control. (see Brunson-Matthews, 1979). Instead, Type B's appear to respond veridically to the absence of an incentive implicit in an uncontrollable situation. Performance on subsequent tasks is, therefore, unaffected by their failure to master a previous task. It might be suggested, then, that the Type B style of coping with life events consists of being responsive to contingencies—to excel when possible and to relax when not. In this view, behavior pattern B would appear to be an alternative coping style rather than the absence of tendencies to exert environmental control.

Type A, Stressful Life Events, and Coronary Disease

Type A has been defined as a set of behaviors elicited by an appropriate set of environmental circumstances, yet precise specification of these circumstances has received little systematic attention. An exception to this observation is the work suggesting that uncontrollable stress, in which the potential for harm is salient, may be a specific variable eliciting Type A behavior. It is also possible that uncontrollable events in which the potential for reward is salient (i.e., challenge) can also elicit Type A behavior. The available evidence, albeit minimal, does support this possibility (Glass, 1977; Matthews, 1979). Other theoretically relevant factors might be inferred from studies designed to categorize life events and relate them to disease endpoints. For example, unpredictable life events may prove to be a useful category of situations that produce Type A behavior in susceptible individuals (B. S. Dohrenwend and B. P. Dohrenwend, 1978). Mundane and repetitive stressful life events, called daily hassles by Lazarus and Cohen (1977), also deserve special attention as possible releasers of Type A behavior. As other environmental factors are identified, models of specific person-situation interactions can be constructed that will allow for a more precise specification of the role of behavior pattern A in coronary disease.

Closely related to this point is the question of how knowledge of the interaction of Type A behavior pattern and uncontrollable events may assist in elucidating the processes by which stressful life events are related to coronary disease. Recall that the alternation of efforts to control followed by giving up may be accompanied by physiological processes that culminate in cardiovascular pathology. It seems reasonable to suggest that uncontrollable life events will trigger these pathophysiological processes in the Type A individual. What is more, Type A's may actually experience more uncontrollable life events than do their Type B peers. After all, they chronically push themselves to their limits where they are likely to fail and experience a loss of control. Consistent with this formulation are the findings of two studies, which indicate that Type A's report more stressful life events than do Type B's (Dimsdale et al., 1978; Suls et al., 1980). While data for specifically uncontrollable events were not available in either of these studies, we may at least hypothesize that the combination of Type A and frequent uncontrollable events are particularly deleterious to cardiovascular health.

A direct test of this hypothesis would require a prospective study. To our knowledge, research of this kind has not as yet been conducted. However, the results of a recent study in Sweden may be relevant here. Theorell (1975) selected, from a sample of over 9,000 participants, five groups of 40 subjects each who were healthy (no illness lasting longer than 30 days), employed, and in certain predetermined categories on a life-change index and a personal-discord index. Examples of these categories include the highest quartile on both the life-change and discord indices, the highest quartile on the discord index and the lowest on the life-change index, and so forth. Two years after the life-change and discord scales were administered, all participants but the two who had died were asked to return for medical testing. A total of 151 complied with this request. The group with both the highest discord and life-change scores had more cardiovascular symptoms than any other group. Examination of the items on the discord scale revealed two major clusters: hostility at slowness and job dissatisfaction. Thus, in this sample, those who reported some Type A behaviors *and* experienced the greatest number of life changes were at greatest risk.

Another study (Glass, 1977), although retrospective in design, deserves comment here because it is the most direct test of the joint effects of Type A and uncontrollable events. In this project, hospitalized coronary patients, noncoronary patients, and healthy controls were compared in terms of (1) JAS A-B scores, and (2) recall of life events for the year prior to disease onset. Before the study was begun, a 10-item loss index was developed from the life-events list used in the study. These items were agreed upon by three members of the research staff as reflecting stressful events over which minimal control could be exerted. Examples are "death of a close family member," and "being fired." A 7-item negative events index was constructed at the same time. These items were designed to reflect life events that would be experienced as stressful, but not necessarily as uncontrollable. Items in this index included "foreclosure on mortgage or loan" and "large increase in number of arguments with spouse."

Analysis of the loss-index responses showed that a reliable higher percentage of each patient group (coronaries and hospitalized noncoronaries) than healthy controls reported having experienced at least one major loss in the previous year. By contrast, percentages for the negative-events index did not differ between groups. It was also found that coronary patients had significantly higher Type A scores than either the hospitalized or nonhospitalized samples.

These data support the notion that uncontrollable life events— not just negative or stressful events—discriminate persons with illness from those without disease. Moreover, the relative presence of Type A characteristics seems to discriminate persons with coronary heart disease from those with other diseases. These findings are consistent with the reasoning presented earlier in this section, namely, an excess of life events involving a loss of environmental control, when experienced by Type A's, may be particularly damaging to their cardiovascular health. Prospective research is needed for a more unequivocal test of this line of thought.

Future studies should also address themselves to the relationship among Type A, uncontrollable life events, and those physiological processes implicated in cardiovascular disease. We refer here to hemodynamic changes and the catecholamines. It might be noted that one recent attempt to explore the role of Type A in the life event-physiological matrix has not produced encouraging results. While being in the expected direction, correlations between urinary catecholamines and life-changes for Type A subjects only approached statistical significance (Swan et al., 1979). However, the study did not fractionate life events into those that were stressful and those that were more benign. It also failed to distinguish between controllable and uncontrollable events. Moreover, there is other research (Theorell et al., 1972) that does report significant correlations between life change units and changes in epinephrine and norepinephrine in postinfarct patients (where presumably we might expect a higher than average number of Type A's). This line of research would seem, then, to be well worth pursuing with more systematic classification of life events into theoretically relevant categories.

Summary and Conclusions

The research reviewed in this chapter indicates that Type A's have a distinctive style of coping with uncontrollable stressors. When initially confronted by an uncontrollable event, they exert greater efforts than their Type B counterparts to assert control. As their efforts meet with repeated failure, Type A's blame themselves for not being able to succeed and eventually give up responding.

It was suggested that physiological processes associated with these reactions may be inimical to cardiovascular functioning. Although work in this area has only begun, preliminary data suggest that Type A's respond to challenge and stress with elevations in systolic blood pressure and plasma catecholamines. Both factors are believed to potentiate the major cardiovascular disorders.

We have also suggested that research on Type A may aid in understanding the processes by which stressful life events lead to coronary disease. To the extent that Type A's experience frequent uncontrollable life events, they may respond to them in ways that elevate CHD risk. The available data support the notion of a combined impact of Type A and uncontrollable events on cardio-vascular disease. Systematic prospective studies are now needed in this area. Such research may help, in addition, to identify relevant categories of life events that enhance the coronary risk of the Type A individual. A recommendation was also made that future studies examine the relationship among Type A, stressful life events, and those physiological variables that are believed to be implicated in the coronary-disease process.

References

Andrews, G. & Tennant, C. (1978), Being upset and becoming ill: An appraisal of the relation between life events and physical illness. *Med. J. Austral.*, 1:324–327.

Ardlie, N. G., Glew, G., & Schwartz, C. J. (1966), Influence of catecholamines on nucleotide-induced platelet aggregation. *Nature*, 212:415–417.

Blumenthal, J. A., Williams, R. B., Kong, Y., Schanberg, S. M., & Thompson, L. W. (1978), Type A behavior pattern and coronary atherosclerosis. *Circulation*, 58:634–639.

Brand, R. J., Rosenman, R. H., Jenkins, C. D., Sholtz, R. I., & Zyzanski, S. J. (1978), Comparison of coronary heart disease prediction in the Western Collaborative Group Study using the structured interview and the Jenkins Activity Survey assessment of the coronary-prone Type A behavior pattern. Read at the annual conference on cardiovascular disease epidemiology, American Heart Association, Orlando, Florida.

Brunson, B. I. & Matthews, K. A. (1979), The Type A coronary-prone behavior pattern and reactions to uncontrollable stress: An analysis of performance strategies, affect, and attributions during failure. Manuscript submitted for publication, University of Pittsburgh, 1979.

Carver, C. S., Blaney, P. H., & Scheier, M. F. (1979), Focus of attention, chronic expectancy, and responses to a feared stimulus. *J. Pers. Soc. Psychol.*, 37:1186–1195.

Carver, C. S. & Scheier, M. F. (1980), *Attention and self-regulation: A control theory approach to human behavior.* New York: Springer-Verlag, in press.

Chesney, M. (1979), Cultural and sex differences in the Type A pattern. Read at the annual meeting of the American Psychological Association, New York City.

Cohen, J. B., Matthews, K. A., & Waldron, I. (1978), The influence of culture on coronary-prone behavior. In: *Coronary-prone Behavior*, ed. T. M. Dembroski, S. M. Weiss, J. L. Shields, S. G. Haynes, & M. Feinleib. New York: Springer-Verlag, pp. 183–190.

Dembroski, T. M., MacDougall, J. M., & Shields, J. L., (1977), Physiologic reactions to social challenge in persons evidencing the Type A coronary-prone behavior pattern. *J. Hum. Stress*, 3:2–9.

Dembroski, T. M., MacDougall, J. M., Shields, J. L., PetiHo, J., & Lushene, R. (1978a), Components of the Type A coronary-prone behavior pattern and cardiovascular responses to psychomotor challenge. *J. Behav. Med.*, 1:159–176.

Dembroski, T. M., Weiss, S. M., Shields, J. L., Haynes, S. G., & Feinleib, M., ed. (1978), *Coronary-Prone Behavior*. New York, Springer-Verlag.

Dimsdale, J. E., Hackett, T. P., Block, P. C., & Hutter, A. M. (1978a), Emotional correlates of the Type A behavior pattern. *Psychosom. Med.*, 40:580–585.

Dimsdale, J. E., Hackett, T. P., Hutter, A. M., Block, P. C., & Catanzano, D. (1978b), Type A personality and extent of coronary atherosclerosis. *Amer. J. Cardiol.*, 43:583–586.

Dohrenwend, B. S. & Dohrenwend, B. P. (1978), Some issues in research on stressful life events. *J. Nerv. Ment. Dis.* 166:7–15.

Duguid, J. B. (1946), Thrombosis as a factor in the pathogenesis of coronary atherosclerosis. *J. Path. Bact.*, 58:207–212.

Eliot, R. S. (1979), *Stress and the Major Cardiovascular Disorders*. Mount Kisko, New York, Futura.

Engel, G. L. (1970), Sudden death and the "medical model" in psychiatry. *Canad. Psychiat. Assn. J.*, 15:527–538.

Frank, K. A., Heller, S. S., Kornfeld, D. S., Sporn, A., & Weiss, M. (1978), Behavior pattern and coronary angiographic findings. *J. Amer. Med. Assn.*, 240:761–763.

Friedman, M. (1969), *Pathogenesis of Coronary Artery Disease*. New York, McGraw-Hill.

Friedman, M., Byers, S. O., Diamant, J., & Rosenman, R. H. (1975), Plasma catecholamine response of coronary-prone subjects (Type A) to a specific challenge. *Metabolism*, 24:205–210.

Friedman, M., St. George, S., Byers, S. O., & Rosenman, R. H. (1960), Excretion of catecholamines, 17-ketosteroids, 17-hydroxy-corticoids and 5-hydroxyindole in men exhibiting a particular behavior pattern (A) associated with high incidence of clinical coronary artery disease. *J. Clin. Invest.*, 39:758–764.

Glass, D. C. (1977), *Behavior Patterns, Stress, and Coronary Disease*. Hillsdale, N.J.: Lawrence Erlbaum Associates.

Glass, D. C., Krankoff, L. R., Contrada, R., Hilton, W. F., Kehoe, K., Mannucci, E. G., Collins, C., Snow, B., & Elting, E. (1980), Effect of harassment and competition upon cardiovascular and catecholaminic responses in Type A and Type B individuals. *Psychophysiology*, in press.

Greene, W. A., Goldstein, S., Moss, A. J. (1972), Psychosocial aspects of sudden death: A preliminary report. *Arch. Intern. Med.*, 129:725–731.

Haft, J. I. (1974) Cardiovascular injury induced by sympathetic catecholamines. *Prog. Cardiovasc. Dis.*, 17:73–86.

Herd, J. A. (1978), Physiological correlates of coronary-prone behavior. In: *Coronary-Prone Behavior*, ed. T. M. Dembroski, S. M. Weiss, J. L. Shields, S. G. Haynes, & Feinleib, M. (1978), New York, Springer-Verlag, pp. 129–136.

Hinkle, L. E. (1974), The effect of exposure to culture change, social change, and changes in interpersonal relationships on health. In: *Stressful Life Events: Their Nature and Effects*, ed. B. S. Dohrenwend & B. P. Dohrenwend. New York: Wiley, pp. 9–44.

Howard, J. A., Cunningham, D. A., & Rechnitzer, P. A. (1976), Health patterns associated with Type A behavior: A managerial population. *J. Hum. Stress*, 2:24–32.

Jenkins, C. D. (1971), Psychologic and social precursors of coronary disease. *New Eng. J. Med.*, 284:244–255, 307–317.

Jenkins, C. D. (1976), Recent evidence supporting psychologic and social risk factors for coronary disease. *New Eng. J. Med.*, 294:987–994, 1033–1038.

Jenkins, C. D. (1978), A comparative review of the interview and questionnaire methods in the assessment of the coronary-prone behavior pattern. In: *Coronary-Prone Behavior*, ed. T. M. Dembroski, S. M. Weiss, J. L. Shields, S. G. Haynes, & M. Feinleib (1978), New York, Springer-Verlag, pp. 71-88.

Jenkins, C. D., Rosenman, R. H., & Zyzanski, S. J. (1974), Prediction of clinical coronary heart disease by a test for the coronary-prone behavior pattern. *New Eng. J. Med.*, 290:1271-1275.

Jenkins, C. D., Zyzanski, S. J., & Rosenman, R. H. (1971), Progress toward validation of a computer-scored test for the Type A coronary-prone behavior pattern. *Psychosom. Med.*, 33:193-201.

Jenkins, C. D., Zyzanski, S. J., Rosenman, R. H.: (1976), Risk of new myocardial infarction in middle-aged men with manifest coronary heart disease. *Circulation*, 53:342-347.

Krantz, D. S., Sanmarco, M. E., Selvester, R. H., & Matthews, K. A. (1979), Psychological correlates of progression of atherosclerosis in men. *Psychosom. Med.*, 41:467-475.

Lazarus, R. S. & Cohen, J. B. (1977), Environmental stress. In: *Human Behavior and Environment*, vol. 2, ed. I. Altman & J. F. Wohlwill. New York: Plenum, pp. 89-127.

Manuck, S. B. & Garland, F. N. (1979), Coronary-prone behavior pattern, task incentive, and cardiovascular response. *Psychophysiology*, 16:136-142.

Matthews, K. A. (1979), Efforts to control by children and adults with the Type A coronary-prone behavior pattern. *Child Devlpm.*, 50:842-847.

Matthews, K. A., Glass, D. C., Rosenman, R. H., & Bortner, R. W. (1977), Competitive drive, pattern A, and coronary heart disease: A further analysis of some data from the Western Collaborative Group Study. *J. Chron. Dis.*, 30:489-498.

Osler, W. (1910), The lumleian lectures on angina pectoris. *Lancet*, 1:839-844.

Raab, W., Chaplin, J. P., & Bajusz, E. (1969), Myocardial necroses produced in domesticated rats and in wild rats by sensory and emotional stresses. *Proc. Soc. Exper. Biol. Med.*, 116:665-669.

Rahe, R. H. & Arthur, R. J. (1978), Life change and illness studies: Past history and future directions. *J. Hum. Stress*, 4:3-15.

Rahe, R. H., & Romo, M. (1974), Recent life changes and the onset of myocardial infarction and coronary death in Helsinki. In: *Life Stress and Illness*, ed. E. K. E. Gunderson & R. H. Rahe. Springfield, Ill.: Charles C. Thomas, pp. 105-120.

Richter, C. P. (1957), On the phenomenon of sudden death in animals and man. *Psychosom. Med.*, 19:191-198.

Rosenman, R. H. (1978), The interview method of assessment of the coronary-prone behavior pattern. In: *Coronary-Prone Behavior*, ed. T. M. Dembroski, S. M. Weiss, J. L. Shields, S. G. Haynes, & M. Feinleib. New York: Springer-Verlag, pp. 55-69.

Rosenman, R. H., Brand, R. J., Jenkins, C. D. et al. (1975), Coronary heart disease in the Western Collaborative Group Study: Final followup experience of 8½ years. *J. Amer. Med. Assn.*, 233:872-877.

Rosenman, R. H., & Friedman, M. (1974), Neurogenic factors in pathogenesis of coronary heart disease. *Med. Clin. N. Amer.* 58:269-279.

Rosenman, R. H., Straus, R., Wurm, M., Kositcheck, R., Hahn, W., & Werthessen, N. T. (1964), A predictive study of coronary heart disease. *J. Amer. Med. Assn.*, 189:103-110.

Scheier, M. F. (1976), Self-awareness, self-consciousness, and angry aggression. *J. Pers.*, 44:627–644.

Scherwitz, L., Berton, K., & Leventhal, H. (1977), Type A assessment and interaction in the behavior pattern interview. *Psychosom. Med.*, 39:229–240.

Scherwitz, L., Berton, K., Leventhal, H. (1978), Type A behavior, self-involvement, and cardiovascular response. *Psychosom. Med.*, 40:593–609.

Schneiderman, N. (1978), Animal models relating behavioral stress and cardiovascular pathology. In: *Coronary-Prone Behavior*. ed. T. M. Dembroski, S. M. Weiss, J. L. Shields, S. G. Haynes, & M. Feinleib. New York: Springer-Verlag.

Schucker, B. & Jacobs, D. R. (1977), Assessment of behavior pattern A by voice characteristics. *Psychosom. Med.*, 39:219–228.

Seligman, M. E. P. (1975), *Helplessness: On Depression, Development, and Death*. San Francisco: W. H. Freeman.

Suls, J., Gastorf, J. W., & Witenberg, S. H. (1979), Life events, psychological distress and the Type A coronary-prone behavior pattern. *J. Psychosom. Res.*, 23:315–319.

Swan, G. E., Black, G. W., Chesney, M. A., Ward, M., & Rosenman, R. H. (1979), Life event-physiological relationships: Mediated by coronary-prone behavior? Read at the annual meeting of American Psychological Association, New York.

Theorell, T. (1975), Selected illnesses and somatic factors in relation to two psychosocial stress indices—a prospective study on middle-aged construction building workers. *J. Psychosom. Res.*, 20:7–20.

Theorell, T., Lind, E., & Floderus, G. (1975), The relationship of disturbing life-changes and emotions to the early development of myocardial infarction and other serious illnesses. *Int. J. Epidemiol.*, 4:281.

Theorell, T., Lind, E., Froberg, J., Karlsson, C. G., & Levi, L. (1972), A longitudinal study of 21 subjects with coronary heart disease: Life changes, catecholamine excretion, and related biochemical reactions. *Psychosom. Med.*, 34:505–576.

Waldron, I. (1978), Sex differences in the coronary-prone behavior pattern. In: *Coronary-Prone Behavior*. ed. T. M. Dembroski, S. M. Weiss, J. L. Shields, S. G. Haynes, & M. Feinleib. New York: Springer-Verlag, pp. 199–205.

Weiss, J. M., Glazer, H. I., & Pohroecky, L. A. (1976), Coping behavior and neurochemical changes in rats: An alternative explanation for the original "learned helplessness" experiments. In: *Animal Models in Human Psychobiology*, ed. G. Serban & A. Klihg. New York: Plenum, pp. 141–173.

Weiss, J. M., Stone, E. A., Harrell, N.: Coping behavior and brain norepinephrine in rats. *J. Comp. Physiol. Psychol.* 72:153–160, 1970.

Wortman, C. B. & Brehm, J. W. (1975), Responses to uncontrollable outcomes: An integration of reactance theory and the learned helplessness model. In: *Advances in Experimental Social Psychology*, vol. 8, ed. L. Berkowitz. New York, Academic Press, pp. 278–332.

Zyzanski, S. J., Jenkins, C. D., Ryan, T. J., Flessa, A., & Everist, M. (1976), Psychological correlates of coronary angiographic findings. *Arch. Intern. Med.*, 136:1234–1237.

Social Conditions Related to the
Life Stress Process

The social conditions in which a life event is experienced have received increasing attention in recent investigations of the life stress process. In this section several ways of conceptualizing and operationalizing these conditions are discussed.

George W. Brown presents the rationale for measuring the objectively conceived contextual threat of a life event experienced by a particular individual in order to understand its impact. He describes the program of research in which he has used this procedure and the way in which the concept and its measurement have evolved from its beginning in his studies of life stress and schizophrenia through his more recent work on life stress and depression.

In the next chapter Susan Gore provides a general overview of conceptual and methodological problems in the study of social support as a component of the life stress process. She presents and discusses a model of the various ways in which social support may enter into the life-stress process.

Susan L. Phillips and Claude S. Fischer then present results of their extensive empirical work on the measurement of social support networks in general populations. They provide a detailed description of measurement procedures as well as results indicating the utility of these procedures in the study of life stress.

In the final chapter in this section Ramsay Liem and Joan H. Liem broaden the conceptualization of social conditions that are related to life stress by considering the relation of the social system, particularly as conceptualized in terms of social class, to this process. They suggest a number of ways in which the relation between social class and life stress may be mediated.

Contextual Measures of Life Events

GEORGE W. BROWN

Most life-event research has been based on a dictionary approach to meaning. A birth is considered a birth and no more. But within such an approach there are two possibilities. The birth may be treated no differently from other events; it is treated as equivalent to, say, being dismissed from a job or a divorce. Alternatively such classes of "events" may be differentiated from each other. Thus in the well-known approach of Holmes and Rahe (1967) the birth of a child is given a score of 39 in terms of the readjustment required by the event, being dismissed from work a somewhat higher score of 47, and divorce a still higher one of 73. (The maximum score of 100 is given to death of a spouse). Both approaches however utilize a dictionary method in the sense that "birth" is seen in terms of a lexical decoding of the kind that it is "the production of offspring" with no further attempt at differentiation *within* the category of "birth." Indeed, Holmes and Rahe also include with the birth of a child, "adoption of a child" and "a relative coming to stay."

Encyclopedias and text-books would, of course, tell us more about births than a dictionary. Some births involve painful, and even life-threatening, complications, some mothers have twins and some a deformed child. However, even an encyclopedia approach to meaning would omit a great deal, inevitably leaving out many personal characteristics—say that the mother was a school-girl who was forced to give up her plans to go to university; a mother who already had a child and lived in only two rooms; another whose husband had not long before been admitted to prison; and one whose father had died just before the birth of what would have been his first grandchild. 'Social science' text-books dealing with this kind of variability do not exist, although all of us carry about with us a solid basis for such a publication.

In a previous publication I have criticized life-event instruments of the kind produced by Holmes and Rahe on methodological grounds and I will not go over this ground again in any detail (Brown, 1974). It is the conceptual shortcomings of most instruments that I now wish to emphasize. They basically deal with events as would a dictionary. Some years ago in research with schizophrenic patients a colleague and I also produced such an interview instrument. It had the advantage of avoiding most of the methodological pitfalls of questionnaire-type instruments. By using an interview approach it had the necessary flexibility to enable both a greater accuracy and rule out important potential sources of invalidity that had plagued such research and seriously threatened claims about the causal link between events and medical and psychiatric disorders. However, the instrument, while methodologically strong, was theoretically weak since it treated all types of events as equal (Brown and Birley, 1968).[1]

Some research workers using questionnaire-type instruments of the kind employed by Holmes and Rahe have recently attempted to deal with the problem of the variability of meaning of events such as a birth by asking individual respondents to rate the importance of particular events for *them* (e.g., Hurst, 1979; Uhlenhuth, 1979). This is a major departure from the earlier approach where the scores given to each type of event had been derived from a panel of judges rating the degree of readjustment involved when presented with short dictionary-type definitions of events. An arbitrary score of 500 was allocated to "marriage" and the rater had to ask himself how much more or less or perhaps equal the birth would be to marriage and then allocate a score to it. The *average* scores for each event for the whole series of a hundred or so judges was then taken to characterize the "event." The more recent approach avoids the catastrophic loss of sensitivity of this approach by asking the individual involved to score the event. It is clearly reasonable to expect that something of the true complexity of meaning of individual events will be reflected in such an approach—and, indeed, correlations of event scores with "outcome" measures have tended to be higher using such an approach.

Unfortunately the approach runs into formidable methodological difficulties. For instance, it is not clear just what the respondent will have in mind when rating the event. Will it be, for instance, at the time of the first occurrence of their child's illness when there seemed some risk of his dying or from the perspective a few days later when he clearly had not been suffering from a major illness? But there are more fundamental problems. I will deal only with those arising from

[1]Given the theory we held about schizophrenia—that such patients are vulnerable to any marked emotional arousal whether of a positive or negative kind—there was some justification for this crudity. However, the approach was clearly insufficient when we began to study depression.

retrospective research i.e. asking about events once the person is ill.[2] A problem with using questionnaires arises from the fact that reports about the "severity" of the event may be influenced by the fact that the illness had already happened when reporting the event. One way this can occur is by an "effort after meaning" (Bartlett, 1932). A man whose wife has developed a severe depressive illness may greatly exaggerate the importance to her of her pet dog who died two months before her illness as a means of coming to terms with what has happened. His wife might exaggerate for a similar reason or because of the fact of being depressed. We know that this kind of distortion can occur (see Brown, 1974). However, the critical point is not whether or not it has occurred but the inability of questionnaire-type instruments to rule out the possibility. They cannot do so because the approach is entirely based on the respondent's assessment of what has been upsetting.

My colleagues and I have developed various contextual measures as a way of dealing with this and other similar problems. Since a full account has been given in our recent book I will here only give enough detail to give an adequate grasp of what is involved (Brown and Harris, 1978).

The contextual ratings are intimately related to the issue of meaning and issues raised by the *Methodenstreit* controversy in German sociology. We have attempted to translate some of the ideas surrounding the notion of empathic understanding or *Verstehen* to a wide range of social situations met in everyday life. The fundamental need was to move from measurement based, as in questionnaires, on the respondent to that on the interviewer, as in the use of rating scales. This was made possible by using an empathic approach to measurement, and this in turn enabled us to make judgments about the meaning of events *while ignoring what the respondent said he or she felt*. It was only by ignoring such

[2]A prospective survey will not necessarily avoid these problems (Brown, 1974: 219-20); nor can some kind of retrospective design usually be avoided. If a person is interviewed at time A and 'events' established in the previous year and then the person seen again at time B six months later, events occurring before A will clearly form part of a *prospective* design. However, critical 'events' are likely to fall in the six month period A to B and this can only be established by retrospective questioning. Only when dealing with common conditions such as streptococcal infections of the throat (e.g., Meyer and Haggerty, 1962) or a wide range of disorders is it probably practical to interview sufficiently often to rule out the need for retrospective questioning. It is impractical because for rare conditions the sample requiring repeated interviews is far too large.

reports that we could avoid the possibility of the kind of circularity due to the reconstruction of meaning that I have outlined. It is perhaps worth adding that concern with the possibility of carrying out such measurement is not restricted to the measurement of life events but is a central and unresolved concern of sociology as a whole (Schutz, 1972).

The approach as a whole is firmly based on earlier work with schizophrenic patients in spite of my earlier comments on its limitations. At this point in our work we developed a method for obtaining units of change. Because we believed that a florid episode of schizophrenic symptoms could be brought about in a susceptible individual by marked emotion of any kind, we developed an instrument that conceived of life events in terms of the emotions they might arouse irrespective of whether the emotion was "positive" or "negative" or a mixture of both.

For this we made the critical decision to define life events in terms of their likelihood of producing strong emotion rather by the type or degree of emotion they actually produced. This is the first of two procedures we employ to move, using terms employed by Alfred Schutz, from subjective- to objective-meaning contexts. In order to establish such units we developed a comprehensive list of incidents which could be dated to a particular point in time and which we believed would for most people be likely to be followed by strong negative or positive emotion. It did not matter whether or not a particular incident was in fact followed by such emotion.[3] We largely restricted ourselves to events involving the respondent (henceforth called the subject) and "close ties" (i.e., spouse or cohabitee, parent, sibling, children, or fiance), but at times particularly dramatic incidents involving more distant relatives or even strangers were included as long as the subject had been present (e.g., witnessing a serious road accident). In the later depression study we also included confidants as close ties. A confidant was an especially close friend, defined as one to whom the subject felt able to confide problems or worries with complete trust.

The list contained 38 types of event falling into the following 8 groups:

1. Changes in a role for the subject such as changing a job and losing or gaining an opposite-sex friend for the unmarried.

---

[3]For the reader already worried by this apparent negligence, it seems worth anticipating our argument to state that this "contextual" approach will, if anything, underestimate the causal role of life events in etiology. Further, in spite of this constraint, that it has been shown to be capable of demonstrating powerful etiological effects. (Brown and Birley, 1968; Brown and Harris, 1978).

2. Changes in a role for close relatives or household members, such as a husband staying off work because of a strike.

3. Major changes in health, including admissions to hospital and development of an illness expected to be serious.

4. Changes similar to (3.) occurring in close relatives or household members.

5. Residence changes and any marked change in amount of contact with close relatives and household members.

6. Forecasts of change, such as being told about being rehoused.

7. Valued goal fulfillments or disappointments, such as being offered a house to rent at a reasonable price.

8. Other dramatic events involving (*a*) the subject, e.g., witnessing a serious accident or being stopped by the police when driving, or (*b*) a close relative or household member, e.g., learning that a brother had been arrested.

In every instance the events can be seen as involving change in an activity, role, person, or idea.

It was then necessary to define in some detail for each of the 38 types of event just what would be included, illustrating each definition with a range of examples. Therefore by no means all incidents reported by respondents were included as events. Indeed, they were quite often excluded and in practice our threshold for inclusion was sufficiently high for only quite rarely occurring events to be included. Women interviewed at random in Camberwell, an inner London population, experienced on the average only about 3 incidents in the year before we saw them—although this number ranged from 0 to over 20. An example of the approach is our definitions for "changes in health" where we included events occurring to those with whom the subject lived as well as close relatives. All admissions to hospital for the subject were included, but only those that were urgent or lasting one week for other persons. Illnesses not followed by admission were counted only if in our judgment they involved a possible threat to life or were alarming enough for serious implications to be suspected. Accidents were covered by similar criteria. There was one exception: we included a new contact with a psychiatric service by a close relative. We also included as an event the death of anyone living at home or of a close relative; all other deaths were excluded unless the subject had been present or involved in its immediate aftermath (such events were rare).

Such instructions guided the interviewer about what to include as an event. It was insufficient, for example, simply to ask about accidents. It was necessary to settle before the main study began whether to include, say, an accident to a woman's husband which required outpatient treatment but about which she knew nothing until he came home. But the definitions had a more fundamental purpose than accuracy of measurement. We were concerned that in the actual study if anything were left open in any way it might allow the decision of whether to include an incident as an event to be influenced by knowledge that it antedated a schizophrenic attack or any other type of disorder. The use of a comprehensive and detailed set of definitions allowed us to rule out this possibility. The interviewer was extremely tightly controlled in what could be counted as an event.[4] Of course a case could be made for both including or excluding the accident to the woman's husband. (We in fact included it.) The important point was to settle the matter *before* we began our main research and then apply a common set of standards to everyone whether in the patient or comparison group.

At this stage of the development of the instrument we were not only concerned to establish that an event in our terms had occurred but *when* it had occurred in the period before onset (or interview in the case of those without schizophrenia). We attempted to place an event within a week of its occurrence, although on occasions we were forced to record a range of weeks. Respondents often found it easier to describe onset when there was some anchor point to which they could relate; and when respondents did not give a suitable point we attempted to provide one such as a holiday or important public event. The respondent was in any case always encouraged to relate "events" to each other in a similar way and also to any onset of the "condition" with which we were concerned, but we did not question about the possibility of a cause and effect relationship.

When we came to extend the instrument to the study of depression it was essential to go beyond this kind of dictionary-level meaning since we had every reason to believe that depression would only relate to events with a *particular* kind of meaning. In the first stage of the instrument we had collected only scanty information about each event. We now needed some way of bringing meaning back into our research but at the same time avoiding the kind of

---

[4]This claim had empirical support in the schizophrenia study where the rate of events in the schizophrenic compared with the comparison group was much higher in the three weeks before onset, but exactly comparable in the three 3-week periods before this (Brown and Birley, 1968). If there was a tendency for bias, it is extremely unlikely that this would be restricted to events occurring just in the three weeks before onset.

circularity that can come from taking a respondent's account of his response to the event.

What we did was to first record events in the way I have already described. The interviewer then went on to cover in as informal a way as possible a lengthy list of questions about what led up to and what followed each event, and the full set of circumstances surrounding it. We were interested not only in describing in detail such circumstances but also in what each respondent told us about his reactions to the event. At this point it is important to note that we kept these aspects of event quite separate. The questioning was standardized only in the sense that there was a fairly lengthy list of topics to be discussed and a certain number of suggested probes. It was, however, the interviewer's job to question until he was confident that he had enough information to rate the various "qualities" of each event. For this there were 28 rating scales for each event. They dealt with (a) basic characteristics, (b) prior experience and preparation, (c) immediate reactions, and (d) consequences and implications. The scales took two years to establish, and several hundred depressed patients and close relatives were seen in the course of developmental work. Most emphasis was placed on obtaining a full account of the situation at the time of the event. While the material was obtained from the subject, it must be emphasized that it was the interviewer who carried out the job of measurement.

In the actual interview a good deal of the material that we required tended to come up spontaneously when discussing the events. Vague evidence was not enough and the interviewer had to be thoroughly conversant with a several hundred page manual to be able to decide at the time of the interview whether enough was known to complete the various scales.[5] The interviews were tape-recorded and the final ratings made after the completion of the interview.

However, by collecting this additional material we were open to the same kind of criticism as other instruments. How could we rule out potential sources of bias such as "effort after meaning"?

We therefore took the final step of measuring certain of the

---

[5]Appendix 5 of *Social Origins of Depression* (Brown and Harris, 1978) gives the full interview schedule and also some suggested probes for the 28 scales covering each event. But it will now be clear that this schedule cannot be used without the set of rating scales, and the accompanying manual giving definitions, instructions and examples and also participation in a training program.

28 scales in terms of an "objective-meaning context" or contextual ratings. We here followed, as we saw, the general spirit of discussions of *Verstehen* by ignoring anything concerning what the subject said he or she felt about the event—and indeed anything about the subject's clinical condition.

We believed that a critical element of meaning involved the person's plans for action. We cannot tell what something means for us until we can relate it to our plans. Since we knew a considerable amount about the person we felt we could make a reasonable estimate about how most people would react to the event given the particular set of current and biographical circumstances; further we could do this while knowing nothing of what the person said he had actually felt about the event.

We believe Alfred Schutz (1954), who has greatly influenced recent schools of interpretive sociology, takes a similar position when he writes of the use of common-sense experience of the world:

But the world of everyday life is from the onset a social cultural world in which I am interrelated in manifold ways with fellowmen known to me in varying degrees of intimacy and anonymity. To a certain extent, sufficient for any practical purposes, I understand their behaviour if I understand their motives, goals, choices and plans originating in their biographically determined circumstances. Yet only in particular situations, and then only fragmentarily, can I experience the other's motives, goals, etc.—briefly, the subjective meaning they bestow on their actions, in their uniqueness. I can, however, experience them in their typicality. In order to do so I construct typical patterns of actors' motives and ends, even of their attitudes and personalities, of which their actual conduct is just an instance or example. [P. 496]

In terms of the practical matter of carrying out effective research, the critical decision is to decide at which point we are willing as investigators to begin constructing such "typical patterns of motives and ends." Schutz leaves no doubt that we as investigators must at some point build on knowledge of typical patterns, established in our daily lives. As we have seen in our own work on contextual threat we only did so after collecting a good deal of information about each woman.

Two of the most important scales in which we followed this procedure were those concerning contextual threat, measuring the degree of threat and unpleasantness at two points in time. For example, the consequences of an event, such as one's child unexpectedly developing a high temperature and being admitted to the hospital in an emergency with suspected meningitis, may well be resolved by the following day when his temperature returns to normal. However, other events such as learning quite unexpectedly of one's husband's infidelity have longer-term implications. We defined short-term threat as that implied on the day the event occurred or soon after, and long-term threat as that implied by the event about one week after its occurrence. We rated each on a 4-point scale of severity: "marked," "moderate," "some," or "little or none." In practice the interviewer read to the rest of the research team an account of the event and its surrounding circumstances, leaving out any mention of reactions and whether or not the subject was psychiatrically disturbed. The threat ratings were then made independently by each member of the team without discussion. Ratings were then compared and if there was any disagreement a consensus rating was agreed upon. The raters were helped in three ways. First, there were a series of anchoring examples to illustrate the four points on each scale. Second, a rating was followed by a discussion about any discrepancy, and a final rating agreed upon. Third, fairly "standard" ratings were applied to events such as routine childbirths. These were not subtle and on the whole we kept strictly to them. We had a convention, for instance, that childbirth was only rated high on long-term contextual threat when it occurred in obviously difficult circumstances such as poor housing, acute financial shortage, or very poor health of the mother. These we considered to be integrally part of the context of the birth and therefore relevant to its degree of threat. In practice what was or was not taken into account as relevant for contextual threat rarely caused any difficulty and was rarely the topic of discussion.

However, to underline the point that certain things are excluded we will quote from an already published discussion:

The death of a parent antedating the birth would not be relevant to the context; for even though the new mother might herself repeatedly refer to the close juxtaposition of the death and the birth as having caused even more upset than she thought she would have felt with either singly, according to our rating the earlier event would not be part of the context of the second one. The rating was based on our view about women's usual plans and expectations at the time of birth; in our geographically mobile society the presence and support of a husband at the time of a birth is expected in a way in which that of a parent usually is not. We might, however, have made exceptions: a woman whose husband, although in no way estranged, was often away for weeks at a time on his job might plan, in the absence of a substantial income, to continue her job soon after the birth, leaving the new baby with her mother-in-law who would receive no payment for this. The mother-in-law's unexpected death six weeks before the birth now becomes part of the context of the birth in the sense that it crucially affects the young woman's plans and life-style; she may not be able to afford an au-pair or find a suitable baby-minder, and so now she may be unable to continue working, with all the attendant financial problems. (Brown and Harris, 1978 p. 92).

To summarize: the contextual measures of threat were made in three stages. First, the event was obtained by a method that ignored the respondent's judgment of its impact on her (as in the schizophrenic study). Second, the interviewer collected extensive background material about the event. Third, the rating was made by people not involved in the interview, taking into account only biographically relevant circumstances surrounding the event and how they thought most people would react given this configuration of factors. Since self-reports of threat were controlled both at the stage of enquiry about the event itself and also at the later stage of rating threat, we believe we greatly reduced the risk of the various kinds of invalidity that I discussed in detail in the earlier account (Brown, 1974).

Life events occurring at one point in time are, of course, not the only form of adversity relevant to stress research. A woman may live in a dismal, overcrowded, and damp flat without necessarily having an "event" in our terms during the year of enquiry. Life-event research has been muddled and unsystematic about this, often including a handful of ongoing difficulties with questions about events. We have collected such material systematically and extended the principal of contextual ratings to such difficulties (Brown and Harris, 1978, chap. 8). Since we date the time the difficulty has lasted and in particular its course during the year before interview, it is possible to use these measures to document the outcome of events occurring in the year.

The interrater reliability of the various ratings concerning events and difficulties is high, both in terms of whether or not an event or difficulty is present and for the ratings of their various "qualities" (Brown and Harris, 1978). This has been recently confirmed by others for the contextual threat scales (Tennant et al., 1979). The issue of validity is more complicated and ultimately, we believe, depends on the persuasiveness of theory stemming from research using the measures. However, two sets of results are encouraging. For 50 depressed patients we interviewed an additional respondent who knew the patient well. Agreement about the occurrence of particular events in the year before interview was 79%; and agreement about long-term markedly and moderately threatening events even higher at 92%. Moreover the reporting of more severely threatening events, which formed approximately a fifth of the total events, did not fall-off with length of recall (Brown and Harris, 1978). However, after the thirty-third week there was a fall-off in reporting for the less threatening events of about one-third. (It is of interest that it was only the more severe events that were capable of provoking a depressive disorder.) The "construct validity" of the instrument is equally encouraging but its discussion requires a broader compass than is possible here (Brown and Harris, 1978, 1979).

The measures have now been used in a series of studies which have demonstrated large associations between social stressors and the onset of psychiatric disorder. For instance, 53% of women developing depression in a random sample of women living in London had an event that had brought about an onset of depression in the year before we saw them and 83% had an event or difficulty that had done so. These events and difficulties involved for the most part important losses and disappointments.[6]

The size of these associations is, of course, large given that the contextual ratings of threat were based on estimates of what most women would have experienced in the circumstances. The results are perhaps less surprising when it is realized that there is a large association between the contextual ratings and the degree of threat the women reported they felt about the event (Brown and Harris, 1978). However, given these results it seems important to underline

[6]The proportions of 53% and 83% we have just quoted are based on an index we call 'x'. This takes into account the juxtaposition by chance of an event or difficulty with onset, i.e., the actual proportions with events or events and difficulties are greater than quoted (Brown and Harris, 1978). We have since found that similar measures have been independently developed by statisticians working in epidemiology (see Markush, 1977, on Levin's Attributable Risk Statistic). Ordinary correlation coefficients will provide much lower associations because they take into account the fact that most important losses and disappointments do not lead to depression. The use of such an index of association has led two reviewers to the conclusion that life events explain less than 10% of the variance in depression and that published results are "unlikely to have clinical or preventive importance" (Andrews and Tennant, 1978). If a correlation coefficient is used, a similar conclusion would be reached about lung cancer and smoking: it is highly misleading because it neglects the critical point that most instances of depression are brought about by events and difficulties and most instances of lung cancer by heavy smoking. It merely indicates that factors that "buffer" the impact of such factors must also be considered (see Brown and Harris, 1978, chap. 11).

our view that use of contextual-type ratings, if anything, has underestimated the size of the associations. The logic of our argument holds for the way we establish the presence of an event and for the ratings of contextual threat, but I will deal only with that for contextual threat. In discussing the death of a parent and a mother-in-law in the context of a birth we do not always include everything of possible relevance in rating contextual threat. We might take into account the death of a mother-in-law if her death meant that the new mother could not now go out to work since she now lacked child care for the infant. If the attendant financial problems were serious enough the birth might be rated as highly threatening whereas it would not have been so rated without the mother-in-law's death. This is an instance of "raising" a rating above what we would ordinarily rate by taking into account something of the woman's plans and life-style.

The converse, however, would not apply. For instance a separated woman giving birth to a child would be rated high on contextual threat because we have accepted that there is some conventional expectation that birth should occur in a two-parent context. Thus we would not lower the severity rating even if she had a doting mother nearby and an au-pair girl to help her. In this sense there was a slight imbalance in our estimates of threat: we might raise a standard rating in the light of other circumstances but we would not usually lower such a rating despite other circumstances that might mitigate its impact. If this introduced bias it would be in the direction of *underestimation* of the size of the causal link; for it would be among women whose plans were less threatened than average for whom we would not be lowering the threat rating, and, given there is a causal link, they would be expected to be, if anything, less depressed just because their plans were less threatened. They would therefore be expected to be in the comparison group and this would, if anything, raise the level of threatening events for this group and thereby reduce the association between threatfulness of events and depression. In fact we do not believe that this kind of effect occurred to any great extent: the point is that it is possible to argue that given we did not know who was depressed when we made the contextual threat ratings, our estimates of causal influence are, if anything, an underestimate.

The general conclusion is that when contextual threat ratings are used there is no reason to believe that bias could ever increase the size of an association between stressors and onset of a condition and that under certain circumstances it might decrease it. (Brown and Harris, 1978).

We have now trained a number of research workers in Europe and North America in our methods and an instrument based on our life-event approach is currently being used in research in India. We have also used the instrument in a rural setting in the Outer Hebrides in Scotland. In order to assist such training and enable us to retain satisfactory levels of agreement between research centres we have developed dictionaries of both life events and difficulties which describe the majority of those we have so far obtained and give the contextual-threat ratings under some 200 headings such as "news of impending death," "abortion," and "separations or decreases in interaction, not including marital separations or departures from household." The dictionaries are particularly helpful for someone working alone. Basic training in the instrument involves rating from tape-recorded interviews and can be given in a week, although it takes a few weeks in the field for a worker to feel fully conversant with the instrument.

Another important characteristic of the instrument is its flexibility. This allows it to be used in different cultural settings with only minor amendments; it also makes it possible easily to add to it. One function of social measures is to define the unit to be studied: what is to count as a social contact, a close relative, a separation from parents, and so on. This took about a year's developmental work in the original work with schizophrenic patients and established what was to count as an event. We have seen that once this stage is completed the task of describing qualities such as an event's unexpectedness or threat can be undertaken (Brown and Harris, 1978). A unit can vary in terms of many such qualities.

It is therefore possible to add dimensions once a unit has been defined, and this means that the present instrument can be extended and elaborated. What can be added is limited only by the ingenuity and patience of the investigator. Moreover, there is no reason why the present instrument (including ongoing difficulties), which takes on average about $1\frac{1}{2}$ hours to administer, cannot be reduced by dropping a number of the scales describing "qualities" of events and difficulties. (We have in fact done this in the research in Scotland). Equally there is no reason why new scales should not be added. (We have done this in recent work on the etiology of anxiety scales).

However, while we do not see the present instrument in any sense as a final one, we believe it important to keep a core of comparable measures, including the definition of the basic units, so that comparisons between studies can be made. These are already providing interesting material, for instance about the lower frequency of stressors in rural settings (Brown and Prudo, 1979). At the same time this need not inhibit new ideas as long as the constraints of the method are remembered. This we have seen requires moving firmly away from the blandishments of the standard questionnaire and using interviews that have some of the characteristics of ordinary conversation; it means harnessing the tremendous potentialities of the human mind as a measuring instrument and providing the necessary infrastructure and training for interviewers to do this; it is also essential to spend time developing additional rating scales and making a case for their reliability and validity.[7] These desiderata require time and this is probably the main reason why the standardized questionnaire has managed to retain its ennervating and unhappy grip for so long on systematic social research.

Acknowledgments

The development of the measures I have described was carried out with the support of the Medical Research Council. Work was begun in 1958 but mostly done between 1965 to 1966 and 1968 to 1969. J. L. T. Birley played an important part in the first and Frieda Sklair in the second stage. Tirril Harris, who is co-author of *Social Origins of Depression* in which the measures are described more fully, has had a great influence in developing ideas surrounding the contextual threat ratings and our methods of training and has also made valuable comments on this paper. The work in India on life events is being carried out by Dr. Richard Day and Dr. Julian Leff in collaboration with WHO.

References

Andrews, J. G. & Tennant, C. (1978), Life event stress and psychiatric illness. *Psychol. Med.*, 8:545–549.
Bartlett, F. (1932), *Remembering: A Study of Experimental and Social Psychology.* Cambridge: Cambridge University Press.
Brown, G. W. (1974), Meaning, measurement and stress of life events. In: *Stressful*

---

[7]A general discussion of the approach can be found in Brown and Rutter, 1966; Rutter and Brown, 1966; and Richardson, Dohrenwend, & Klein, 1965.

Life Events: Their Nature and Effects, ed. B. S. Dohrenwend & B. P. Dohrenwend. New York: Wiley, pp. 217–243.

Brown, G. W. & Birley, J. L. T. (1968), Crises and life changes and the onset of schizophrenia. *J. Hlth Soc. Behav.*, 9:203–214.

Brown, G. W. & Harris, T. (1978), *Social Origins of Depression: A Study of Psychiatric Disorder in Women*. London: Tavistock.

Brown, G. W. & Harris, T. (1979), A sin of subjectivism: a reply to Shapiro. *Behav. Res. Ther.*, 17:605–613.

Brown, G. W. & Prudo, R. (1979), Psychiatric disorders in rural and urban population. 1. Aetiology of depression. Unpublished manuscript.

Brown, G. W. & Rutter, M. (1966), The measurement of family activities and relationships: a methodological study. *Hum. Relat.*, 19:241–263.

Holmes, T. H. & Rahe, R. H. (1967), The social readjustment rating scale. *J. Psychosom. Res.*, 11:213–218.

Hurst, M. W. (1979), Life changes and psychiatric symptom development: issues of content, scoring, and clustering. In: *Stress and Mental Disorder*, ed. J. E. Barrett, R. M. Rose, & G. L. Klerman. New York: Raven Press, pp. 17–36.

Markush, R. E. (1977), Levin's attributable statistic for analytic studies and vital statistics. *Amer. J. of Epidem.*, 105:401–406.

Meyer, R. J. & Haggerty, R. J. (1962), Streptococcal infections in families. *Pediatrics*, 29:539–549.

Richardson, S. A., Dohrenwend, B. S., & Klein, D. (1965), *Interviewing: Its Forms and Functions*. New York: Basic Books.

Rutter, M. & Brown, G. W. (1966), The reliability of family life and relationships in families containing a psychiatric patient. *Soc. Psychiat.* 1:38–53.

Schutz, A. (1954), Concept and theory formation in the social sciences. *J. Philosophy*, 51:257–273, 1954.

Schutz, A. (1972), *The Phenomenology of The Social World*. London: Heinemann.

Tennant, C. & Bebbington, P. (1978), The social causation of depression: a critique of Brown and his colleagues. *Psychol. Med.*, 8:565–575.

Tennant, C., Smith, A., Bebbington, P., & Hurry, J. (1979), The contextual threat of life events: the concept and its reliability. *Psychol. Med.*, 9:525–528.

Uhlenhuth, E. H. (1979), Life stress and illness: the search for significance. In: *Stress and Mental Disorder*, ed. J. E. Barrett, R. M. Rose, & G. L. Klerman. New York: Raven Press, pp. 55–60.

Stress-Buffering Functions of Social Supports: An Appraisal and Clarification of Research Models

SUSAN GORE

There appears to be increasing frustration with prospects for investigating the stress-buffering functions of social supports, and yet the literature grows with such efforts. The paradox in this state of affairs is that the appearance of several reviews (Gore, 1973; Pinneau, 1975; Cobb, 1976; Dean and Lin, 1977; Lin et al., 1979b) and a sizable number of papers and journals devoted precisely to this issue indicate a field well out of infancy; but there is still no agreement on the existence, magnitude, and mechanism of a stress-moderating effect, and there has been no coherent statement of what more-promising research directions might be pursued.

The problem, it seems ot me, stems from our failure to systematically consider the most fundamental question, and that is: what constitutes evidence for a stress-reducing function of support?

In tackling this question, the existing research paradigms serve as the point of departure for considering the range of conceptual and operational choices and constraints which have defined stress research. Given these designs, study of the data in light of the central question noted above should indicate the limitations of existing models and of the types of formulations that are needed to explore the stress-related functions of support.

The Stress-Vulnerability Model

The model which articulates the etiological relations between life stress, social supports, and health is illustrated in fig. 1. It depicts the role of social relational variables in stress processes through three sets of arrows. The central hypothesis of most current work in the area of social supports has been the expectation that supportive interventions function to moderate or buffer the impact of life stress. This possibility is symbolized by arrows 1 (a) and 1 (b) which denote an effect of support on a relationship rather than on a particular

202

FIGURE 1

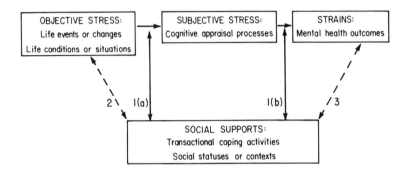

The Functions of Social Supports in Stress Processes

variable. Arrows 2 and 3 indicate other support-related functions. These are represented as tentative because the relationships have not been the focus of systematic research activity. Each, however, suggests possibilities for a broadened study of the stress-support-health nexus. Arrow 2 indicates a reciprocal relationship between social supports and stress experiences. On the one hand, the nature of ongoing support activity may determine vulnerability to the occurrence of those stress events that are not totally fortuitous happenings. This may be defined as a preventive support function. Conversely, stressful events and conditions impact on the support system and determine the nature and degree of its responsiveness. The concepts of support mobilization and support deterioration (Lin et al., 1979b) point to the consequences of stress for support process and structure.

Arrow 3 indicates a relationship between social support variables and mental health status, one which has been observed in the absence of a significant stress-support interaction (Gore, 1973,

Pinneau, 1975; Lin et. al., 1979b). Such an additive, as opposed to interactive, effect of social support, constitutes disconfirming evidence for a stress-buffering function of support. As will be indicated later, this distinction between statistical patterns may be somewhat artificial, and it is overly rigorous in light of the state of methodological sophistication in the field. The support functions represented by arrows 2 and 3 (leading from social support) suggest the significance of ongoing support activity for the prevention both of stress and mental disorder. Empirically, support activities that are ongoing and preventive may be intermingled with those that are responses to stress and are crisis-oriented. Notwithstanding this complexity, the prevailing research conception of supports operating solely in response to stress events has resulted in the study both of a limited range of questions and of empirical situations. In this regard, the second causal path represented by arrow 3 also indicates an overlooked concern of relevance to mental health practitioners, that being how mental health status affects the nature and function of support systems.

Objective Stress—The question of whether and how social support variables moderate the impact of life stress has been addressed to date exclusively through reliance on the "life crisis" or "events" paradigm. Stressful events are discrete happenings that can be located in time, and can, in theory, be measured in a relatively objective fashion, i.e. through self-reports that are independent of subjects' evaluations and perceptions of the events and their meaningfulness. Such evaluations would confound features of the person, including mental health status, with those of the environment, a violation of the requirements of a situation-based definition of stress (McGraph, 1970). In most studies in which support variables are explicitly examined, ratings of the independent variable, aggregate stressful life events, are made with the Holmes and Rahe (1967) Social Readjustment Rating Scale (SRRS). The alternative strategy has involved selection of an at-risk population which can be studied during the course of a single known stressful experience, for example, involuntary job loss (Gore, 1979; Cobb and Kasl, 1977). A fundamental assumption underlying the events paradigm is that it is through disruption of the usual activity of most people that events set in motion the adaptive processes that are the link between life changes and health status. The approach implicitly de-emphasizes the importance of both circumstances surrounding events and the substance of particular events, instead favoring estimates of overall magnitude of change.

An alternative research strategy has been proposed recently by Gersten et al. (1977), who present evidence that indicates a stronger relationship between ongoing stressful life conditions and mental health than that between life changes and health. The validity of these analyses has been the subject of some debate (Link, 1978; Gersten et al., 1978), but the focus of attention on a second dimension of stress, life circumstances or conditions, will broaden the scope of future research activity. The significance of this modification of the stress-illness paradigm for the present discussion is reflected in fig. 1 through the incorporation of life condition variables under the objective stress rubric.

From the viewpoint of assessing the role of social support in etiological processes, there are two major problems regarding the measurement of stress. Although these issues have been identified with the events paradigm they would also surface in research defined by the alternative concept of stress. The first problem is the tendency to confound stress and support measurements. A large number of life events are indicators of a loss of potential support resources through death, mobility or role change, or through a change in the content of relationships (e.g., increased fighting with a spouse). Since assessments of these dimensions of relationships are also typically made in support measurement (e.g., stability, number of roles and affiliations, quality of relationships), there is an apparent operational and conceptual confounding of stress and social supports, with the latter being a simple converse of the former. Although this issue will be considered in detail at a later point, here it is sufficient to note that the confounding is symptomatic of current approaches to the study of social supports. The origin of this problem is not in the events concept *per se*, nor in the population of stress events which have been studied. In fact, regarding the latter, there has been consistent epidemiologic evidence that among the most virulent stress experiences are those involving the loss, disruption, or deterioration of social ties. These data have led B. P. Dohrenwend and Egri (1979) to propose that loss of supports may be considered one component of a "pathogenic triad" of recent events, ". . . whose co-occurence in close proximity to one another over a relatively brief period of time may induce psychopathology in previously normal persons in much the same way that extreme situations involved in natural or manmade disasters are known to do" (p. 12).

A second methodological issue involves strategy in developing weights for assigning a magnitude of change or disruption to particular events or classes of events. B. S. Dohrenwend et al. (1978 p. 206) emphasize the need for a "clean measure of environmental input . . ." in the stress process, that is, in a priori, empirically derived, and generalized system of weightings which accurately reflects group differences. The alternative procedure would involve subjects' reports of both their life events and the extent of the adjustment they necessitate. Such subjective estimates of stressfulness, although not features of the objective environment, are in the domain of intervening variables in fig. 1 identified as Subjective Stress.

Subjective Stress—This domain of variables broadly denotes the cognitive threat appraisal processes that are triggered by the recognition of environmental events. According to this theory of psychological stress (Cofer and Appley, 1964, Lazarus, 1966, Lazarus et al., 1974), these cognitive processes, and specifically the threat of negative expectations, determine coping behaviors that in turn regulate secondary and subsequent appraisals of threat. The sequence of appraisal and coping activity constitutes the "etiological pathway of psychopathology and psychosomatic disorders . . ." (Pinneau, 1975, p. 45).

The distinction between the objective event and subjective, or individual, appraisals of it, is the source of some confusion in the stress literature. Determining what types of environmental stimuli provoke the stress response is not interchangeable with the question of their subjective, idiosyncratic meaning, as measures of the latter are not "clean measures of environmental input." It is not surprising, as B. S. Dohrenwend et al. (1978) also note, that these subjective, post hoc measures of stress are significantly correlated with self-reported outcome measures of psychological strain. The same cognitive and emotional processes that define the disorder are also relied upon in defining the conditions leading to the disorder. Thus, stress and outcome dimensions would be confounded in measurement in a parallel manner that certain life events are evidently not independent of the psychiatric symptoms in which they are expected to result (B. S. Dohrenwend and B. P. Dohrenwend, 1974).

The possible confounded rather than causal relation between intervening subjective variables and outcome variables has implications for the measurement of social support and the interpretation of evidence regarding its stress-moderating effect. First, the inclusion of support variables which are themselves subjective assessments of trust or reliance in others (a dimension of the concept frequently investigated), may measure the same variance as the subjective stress variable, and for that matter, as the outcome variable. In this case, adding support variables to the model would increase the problem of redundancy.

The second issue regards which causal relationship social support is expected to condition, whether it is that between objective and subjective stress, or that between subjective stress and outcome variables. In fig. 1, both mediating processes are depicted as possibilities. Researchers have assumed that support might function to curtail overreaction to the stress situation (arrow 1a), or (arrow 1b) it might attentuate the relationship between appraisals and health responses (Gore, 1973; Pinneau, 1975; Pearlin and Schooler, 1978; Lin et al., 1979b). In light of the operational similarities between broad subjective estimates of stress and reports of symptomatology, the most frequently used outcome variable, it might be most appropriate to observe whether the traditionally weak associations between objective and subjective environments might vary with differences in supports.

The Social Support Variables—In a recent formulation of a strategy for investigating variability in the psychological consequences of life stress, Kessler (1979) has proposed that social support be conceived as a determinant of vulnerability factor, with vulnerability expressed as an impact coefficient, and defined as "the force with which a stress impacts on the distress of an individual" (p. 101). Supports are not the only variable comprising this dimension. Vulnerabilities are determined by a potentially wide range of constitutional and environmental factors. Kessler's discussion of vulnerability and the strategies for measuring its components elucidates the major weakness in approaches to conceptual and operational definitions of social supports. Essentially, there are two symptoms of a single problem of validity, structural nonspecificity and behavioral overspecificity.

Structural nonspecificity manifests itself in the selection of mediating variables thought to indicate or stand for social support processes, and which are equivalent to virtually the entire vulnerability dimension (constitutional factors aside). Because such variables are surrogate measures, the specific factor (i.e., the vulnerability component) that accounts for the differential impact of stress is not measured. Thus, a mediating effect, if present, cannot be assumed to be a function of social support (Gore, 1978).

Behavioral overspecificity manifests itself in the multiplicity of ad hoc measures, that, taken singly or in indices, stand for features of situation-specific support potential, or actual transactions or perceptions. In this case, some one or more support-related variable is measured as the vulnerability component, but the validity of the indicator(s) is questionable.

In both cases, if there is evidence to suggest differential vulnerability of contrast groups under the same stress conditions, adequate interpretation of this effect is severely jeopardized. If the evidence does not seem to confirm the model, poor measurement of the appropriate dimension of social support may account for the inability to reject the null hypothesis.

Briefly, the first tendency is evident in the definition of support as those social statuses, roles, and contexts likely to determine or shape supportive interaction, or more generally, adaptive behavior. The second tendency results from a more microscopic focus on features of interpersonal interaction that are thought to constitute social support and that would be expected to affect the outcomes of specific adaptational challenges. In contrast to the former, this behavioral approach emphasizes the key transactions which are thought to occur within the wider contexts of vulnerability.

Structural Nonspecificity—The source of this tendency lies in the classic epidemiologic studies of Durkheim (1951), Faris and Dunham (1939), Hollingshead and Redlich (1958) Kohn and Clausen (1955), and others, all of which have empirically demonstrated both at the micro- and macrosocial levels an association between particular social statuses and situations, and indicators of morbidity and mortality. This tradition continues to serve as the foundation for epidemiologic study as it has generated a significant and intriguing research agenda, one which includes the support question in a new but not unfamiliar fashion. The major weakness evident in this body of research is the absence of attention to intervening variables, the features of these socially structured life situations which would bring about the health responses. For example, much attention has focused on the consistent findings since mid-nineteenth century that singles, including the divorced, widowed, and never married, have less favorable rates of mortality and morbidity than do their coupled counterparts. Recent explanations for these findings (within a theory of social causation) have incorporated notions of differential stress and support resources (Gove, 1973), but in the absence of actual measurement of these variables the causal link between marital status and disorder has not been firmly established.

Even in the most current research on stress mediation, the major thrust has been to measure structural conditions under which there would be a likelihood of social support mobilization. This is evident in the definition of social support provided by Lin et al. (1979b, p. 109): "Social support may be defined as support accessible to an individual through social ties to other individuals, groups, and the larger community." A similar view is evident in my work (1973, 1978), that of Lowenthal and Haven (1968), Nuckolls et al. (1972), Myers et al. (1975), Eaton, (1978), Dooley et al. (1979), and many others. These studies used one or more of the following types of support indicators: number of social roles; network size; marital, occupational, and residential status; affiliative frequency; and perceptions of life, job, and marital satisfaction. In each design, analysis focused on the separate and joint effects of stress and support variables on psychiatric symptomatology. The Myers et al. study has received considerable attention because the data are longitudinal and derived from a community sample (Paykel et al., 1969). In addition, their measure of social integration, which is the study's equivalent of a social support index, has come under scrutiny due to the inclusion of economic variables under the rubric of social resources.

Eaton's reanalysis (1978) of the Myers et al. data is particularly instructive as his pattern of findings best meets the expectations for confirming a conditioning effect of social support on the stress-strain relationship. Essentially, his data show that the effect of life events on symptoms differs in the predicted direction by level of social support when controlling for earlier symptoms and event levels, and background characteristics. All available support indicators, however, do not have the moderating influence. Only for marital status and residential aloneness is there a strong interaction, and the effect is stronger for those living alone, which would be expected by the conceptual overlap of the two support indicators.

Eaton's interpretation that the question of aloneness is one of a support dynamic is a reasonable one. But there is no assurance that this is the variance being measured, because the specific support dynamic is unobserved. His findings, nevertheless, constitute the most promising point of departure to date in support research, because he has isolated a *single* structural variable—living alone—that is both immediately relevant to the question of social support and is a link with a tradition of epidemiologic research on the health

210   STRESSFUL LIFE EVENTS

effects of social isolation (Jaco, 1954; Holmes, 1956; Myers and Roberts, 1959; Langner and Michael, 1963). In these studies, the concept of social isolation might be thought to stand alternatively for stress, social support, or some unknown ratio of the two. Eaton's work, like that of others using the events model as a research tool, marks progress toward establishing the operational independence of stress and social support variables.

Behavioral Over-Specificity—A number of support researchers have argued that measures of support should reflect attention to the expected stress-mediation functions of such resources. It has been assumed that life stress provokes two classes of problems for which supports are relevant, these being task-related (or concrete) and person-related (or psychological), both of which have their counterparts in types of helping behaviors. Thus, a distinction is usually made between *instrumental support*, consisting of help with the tasks that are generated by the stress events, and *expressive support*, consisting of help with feelings aroused by the event or its consequent tasks. Although there has been some tendency to characterize relationships as having one or the other quality (see Lin et. al., 1979a) most research has been directed toward establishing the role of these types of actions and interactions as stress-reducing mechanisms. The problem has been in their measurement.

Under the stress-buffering model, environmental stress is assumed to precede in time the use of supports, which are understood to constitute a class of coping resources (with support defined statically as a potential) or of coping activity (with support defined transactionally). Although there is currently no theory of coping or statement of the role of supports in the wider complex of coping activity, coping is generally understood as individual efforts to manage the demands, whether affective or instrumental, that ensue from the stress situation.

The problem of measurement overspecificity becomes manifest in the selection of support measures thought to reflect facets of coping activity and coping success. These indicators are in turn examined for their effect on the stress-strain relationship. Because each measure is only a partial examination of the multiplicity of actions involved in coping, focus on any single measure expected to produce a statistical support effect may be misleading.

Two measurement strategies are particularly problematic. The first, as noted earlier, involves measuring an affective component of social supports. This may be a dimension of satisfaction with people or with the help they give. These perceptions may be assumed to be a consequence of supportive activity that has occured, or they may reflect an expectation or sense that support, when needed, will be forthcoming, a generalized sense of interpersonal security. The latter dimension closely approximates features of Cobb's (1976) two-faceted definition of support. On the one hand, support is information. But it is information that results in persons believing that they are "cared for and loved," or "esteemed and valued," or that they belong to "a network of community and mutual obligation." If support is to be defined in terms of the cognitive security it brings, it is likely that this sense of support would buffer the negative expectations intrinsic to psychological stress.

However, if the socio-emotional quality of support is measured through subjective reports of this affective quality, the correlations between support, subjective stress, and outcome (mental health) variables are likely to be spuriously high, with each variable measuring a portion of the same variance, such as variance in well-being. This problem may be evidenced in studies in which the sense of being supported is a major support measure (Gore, 1973, 1978; Dooley et al., 1979; Lin et al., 1979b). The analyses tend to indicate a weak or moderately significant stress effect on health, a significant support effect, but no support-stress interaction. On the face of it, it would seem that support is explaining such a high proportion of the variance in mental health because the measures are redundant. This being the case, it is difficult to interpret the absence of the predicted stress-support interaction.

A second measurement strategy is to assess directly the coping behavior that is understood to short-circuit the stress. Pearlin and Schooler (1978) do this in their analysis of coping responses and resources in different domains of life problems. The one support-related coping variable is a measure of engaging in help-seeking versus self-reliant behavior. The findings viewed from a causal perspective seem to indicate that help seeking per se is a poor coping technique which results in higher levels of psychological distress. I have interpreted these data to mean that there is a reverse causal relationship, with level of distress preceding and determining help-seeking behavior (Gore, 1979). Alternatively, Pearlin and Schooler (1979) propose that having to ask for help may in itself indicate the unavailability of a supportive network. Truly supported individuals may be "so thoroughly embedded in a supportive network that they [do not] have to solicit help in order to receive it . . ." (p. 204). The plausibility of both interpretations underscores the problem of focusing on a single facet of coping, in this case help-seeking, and a single outcome variable (mental health) as a basis for drawing inferences about support process.

This point is similarly made by Carveth and Gottlieb (1979) who are faced with interpreting an unexpected direct relation between social support (measured as amount of contacts and problem-centered interactions, and importance of network members) and distress. They argue that relationships between variables in the coping process cannot be assumed to be equivalent to those bearing on etiological questions. For example, at some time in the coping process there will be a direct causal relation between distress and support, one that reflects support mobilization in response to distress. The direction of these correlations may differ when the sequence of support utilization and its mental-health impact can be studied through improved research designs.

The Support-Stress Interaction—The basis for arguing that an interactive effect of stress and support on health must be evidenced derives from the definition of stress as exceeding or taxing the adaptive resources of most individuals. Illness response is assumed to be a function of ability to meet these new demands, an ability that may be enhanced by social supports. The emphasis by some researchers on the extent of familial and affiliative networks or social roles rests on the assumption that to meet these new demands a flexible supply of resources must be available. A similar case can be made for the more subjective measures of network intensity, which indicate a readiness or immediacy of help. The effect of support, it follows, will manifest itself in reducing the levels of strain, but not at a constant rate. The support effect should be observed disproportionately under the high-stress condition where demands are excessive.

This focus on a stress-support interaction for confirmation of a buffering or conditioning effect of social support is problematic both from substantive and operational viewpoints. On a conceptual level, both stress and support concepts have been largely tied to the notion of crisis or change as the fundamental dimension of stress. But social networks analysts have for some time emphasized the contrast between "every day" support and "emergency" support (Wellman, 1972). That there is no basis for examining the functions of such everyday or maintenance support activity within the major paradigms of stress research suggests a significant omission in thinking about adaptation. Not only is continuing support relevant to chronic stress situations, but such support activity is also relevant to the crisis or events model. How relationships function and are maintained in everday situations probably shape methods of mobilization and the success of mobilization in crisis situations. That there is a complex background or history of support activity is the basis for Pearlin and Schooler's remark that measures of help-seeking per se are too far removed from the broader support context to be meaningful.

Thus, the requirement of a statistical interaction calls for a narrow expression of a stress-buffering process, one which eliminates from our purview significant research questions, namely the mental-health functions of on-gong social activity. (see fig. 1, arrows 2 and 3). Thus, if it can be inferred that significant interaction effects indicate coping (through support) under stress, it can also be interpreted that significant additive effects indicate generalized support activity and perceptions that are also health enhancing. That this takes place is evident from nonetiologically oriented research on what constitutes support. In one such study, Gottlieb (1978) used detailed reports about help in a wide range of problem situations as a basis for developing a classification scheme of informal support. From these data, he identified a pattern of "indirect influence" on the basis of frequent indications that supporters had not said or done anything, but would "be there" if needed. Such perceptions of "milieu reliability" in addition to the three categories of emotionally sustaining behavior (talking, listening, and showing understanding) would be expected to be ongoing and health promoting in noncrisis situations.

In addition, while the statistical interaction is a useful benchmark for evaluating findings, its value reflects the quality of stress and support measures. Specifically, failure to evidence the expected interaction may coincide with a weak or insignificant stress effect on the outcome measure. As evidence of coping behavior presupposes a meaningful stress differential, there would be a lower likelihood of observing the interaction if the stress-illness relation is poorly established. For example, one problem in stress measurement is the possible conceptual narrowness of taking change to be the significant facet of stress. If it is also appropriate to characterize continuing life conditions along a dimension of stress experience, as Gersten et al. (1977) have demonstrated, there could be unobserved variance in stress in the study population. Thus, comparison groups that are equivalent on magnitude of life change may differ in extent of more chronic stress which derives from ongoing life circumstances.

Finally, as noted earlier, the limitations of the analysis of variance model and the research it has generated lie in the approach to support measurement in which proxy measures are substituted for processes that are not directly observed. As noted in the discussion of Eaton's analysis, there is some risk in attributing the interaction to a support dynamic. It is also the case that failure to evidence an interaction may be due to the invalidity of the chosen support indicator.

Research Recommendations

The research problem is to understand the differential health impact of ostensibly similar stress experiences. It is evident, in my opinion, that social support plays a role in the processes set in motion by life stress. The question is what research strategies would facilitate a better understanding of the so-called support effect. The most general recommendation that can be made is that the field calls for more microscopic, descriptive, and processual study of stress mediation. The following are three operational definitions of this recommendation, which are justified by the research problems they address.

The Disaggregation of Stress and Support Indices—This is already taking place in events research, as attention is turning to the study of stimulus parameters in the stress situation. In the measurement of support, however, most of the recent large-scale investigations have relied upon indices that include a hodge-podge of objective and subjective social relational variables. The term disaggregation refers not only to the problems posed by these indices, but also to the use of more limited sets of social characteristics or features of social roles as social support indicators. It is difficult to reconcile the study of support process with such proxy measures. The overall goal of disaggregation is to link support and coping behaviors more closely to the stresses they are hypothesized to affect. This goal would be maximized through study of particular at-risk populations. For example, Eaton's analysis indicated that people who live alone may have special difficulty in mobilizing support systems. The study of persons in specific life situations is a more optimal starting point for focusing on intervening process than is reliance on assessments of aggregate stress in representative samples. The demands of particular situations or stresses can be linked more closely with the resources for dealing with them.

This strategy would begin to remedy two problems which are obstructing progress in the field:

1. Because many stress events might alternatively be seen as support events (e.g., all changes in relationships, including exits, entrances, and any change events which would impact on social relationships, as in job loss), the redundancy of concepts has been troubling. The problem, however, is pronounced only through use of methodologies in which both concepts are defined as an aggregate experience. The result is a double-counting, so to speak, of social support. First, aspects of relationships are assessed as a stress variable, and then as a support variable. It is the false equivalence of social-support process with a static and multidimensional assessment of qualities of the entire relational system that makes double-counting inevitable. Instead, the real question should concern the implications of life stress, however directly or indirectly these events are linked to social relationships, for the viability and mobilization of the (remaining) relational system.

2. While the use of single indicators of support such as help-seeking often lead to unexpected findings (e.g., a direct association between support and distress), global indices, by virtue of the multiplicity of indicators they include, cannot be understood to measure any definition of support. They are inevitably strongly correlated with self-report outcome measures, often through variable confounding, thus trivializing the research effort.

The Focus on Mediating Variables Through Processual Rather than Static Analyses—This recommendation is based on the view noted earlier that there is no single support variable that would account for any meaningful support effect. Also, the idea of a support effect is a dubious notion, for at any point subsequent to the occurrence of stress there are a variety of relevant outcomes to consider. Here, processual refers to the types of questions asked and not to the method of longitudinal or prospective study, although the latter does facilitate the former. For example, a central processual issue in support analysis is that of network mobilization. It is typically the case in support research that extent of potential support is measured (through reports of network size, etc.) *or* actual supporters or types of helping behaviors are identified; but the conditions under which the former is translated into the latter is undetermined. This would provide the contextual key to predicting coping effectiveness. This issue of mobilization underlies Pearlin and Schooler's (1978) query about the meaning of having to ask for help, versus receiving it in an unsolicated manner.

The case to be made here parallels that made by Lazarus and Launier (1978) who see the analysis of variance model as falsely representing the person-environment transactions we seek to study. The approach fosters measurement of assumed stable or fixed characteristics. Then, the stress-support interaction is examined statistically, but not empirically.

The following are some familiar problems that are exacerbated by inattention to mediating processes.

1. Processual study fosters a view of the support concept as standing for a variety of questions about the role of others in a complex of coping activity. Alternatively, a static, factorial approach leads to ad hoc operationalizations of support as a potential, characteristic, or a consequence, i.e., a sense of support. These unsystematic efforts to articulate the support vulnerability components fail to capture process, which is the black box of support research. Instead, data that indicate differential vulnerability under identical stress conditions are used to confirm what is assumed: that support activity accounts for this effect. Thus, the criticism that support tends to be defined in a circular fashion in terms of its effect (Hammer, 1979) is well taken. In addition, as noted earlier, specific subjective measures of feeling supported that also tap psychological well-being may also be regarded as circular; in this case, support is equivalent to the mental health it fosters. The problem lies not in general definitions of support that stipulate a positive function. For example, Tolsdorf (1976) defines support as "an act or behavior that functions to assist the focal person in meeting his personal goals or in dealing with the demands of the particular situation" (p. 410). To examine the function of support in ameliorating the impact of stress, support activity and impact must be operationally independent, and the relationship between the two must be clearly demonstrated.

   A secondary critique of the support concept is that it implies a characterization of social relationships as uniformly helpful. Consequently, the nonsupportiveness of affiliates is excluded from study. This conceptual narrowness also derives from the false equivalence of social-support process with assessments of static social-relational characteristics. The problem is then compounded through use of global or aggregate (across all interactions or relationships) measures of support. The values at the low end of these support scales may indicate a distinct second dimension of support. While the values at the low end of these support scales may indicate a distinct second dimension of interpersonal difficulty or stress, the measures are defined as support variables and analytically treated as unidimensional. Another facet of this problem is that of "categorical typing" (Liem and Liem, 1978b), the tendency in the measurement stage "to treat the functions and qualities of specific relationships as if they are stable over time and situations" (p. 6). Processual study takes for granted that social realtionships are nonstable, especially in the context of life stress. Thus, if the concept of support is understood to imply process, then network stress and deterioration, and alternatively, network mobilization are appropriate subjects of investigation.

2. Until intervening processes are clearly documented, etiological arguments will be questionable either due to lack of adequate explanation or to a failure to eliminate the possibility of reverse causation. The study of mediation calls for the specification of the mechanisms through which particular social statuses and situations have a negative impact on health. Once there is evidence of causality the emphasis shifts to study of the specifics of adaptation. The necessity of this reorientation is voiced by Kasl (1978) in reviewing the literature on the relation between job satisfaction and health. He refers to the "tiresome repetitiousness in many studies that have looked at the intercorrelations among job satisfaction, performance, turnover and absenteeism . . ." in lieu of the ". . . *process* of adapting to unfulfilling and unchallenging jobs . . ." (p. 30, my italics).

3. Although the study of social-support processes requires an implicit or explicit stress situation, the dependent variables need not be so consistently conceived as mental-health outcomes. There are causally prior evidences of distress, negative appraisals and illness behavior, which are relevant to the pragmatic goal of preventing the more profound subsequent effects. In other words, the study of mediation draws attention to the existence of outcomes or responses at each stage of coping.

This alteration in thinking also implies that different analytic goals would be maximized by longitudinal designs. Heretofore, prospective study has been used to obtain stress and mental-health measurements at two points in time, with the interval between observations allocated for the occurrance of illness episodes. Illness or illness behavior is then retrospectively assessed, or coded from medical records. The lag time between measurements should be given more serious attention in the research design. In fact, prospective study of stress mediation and support process means that the lag time should be the immediate research focus. Specifically, through observation using variable time frames it would be possible to track the coping process as it occurs. It is the study of pathways to illness, with the emphasis on pathway rather than illness, that allows stress researchers to benefit from the advances in social network analysis.

Study of the Stress-Support Relationship.—The modeling of stress and support as orthogonal and unrelated dimensions of social life is the source of considerable superficiality in the investigation of stress-amelioration processes. While it is the case that measures of stress and support must be independent, they are reciprocally interrelated on an empirical level. The consideration of the impact of support on stress and stress on support raises new research issues that are essential to the study of stress mediation.

1. First, as indicated in the discussion of fig. 1 (arrow 2), support functions not only to ameliorate stress but also to prevent its occurrence. Lin et al. (1979b) have most recently articulated this latter "structural" function of supports (see also Gore, 1973; Pinneau, 1975; Pearlin and Schooler, 1978). The structural support mechanism falls outside a stress-mediating model, since support is examined as an independent variable that determines the distribution of stress events. Moderate negative correlations between stress and support variables may indicate that supports causally precede and determine stressful happenings. Most research on supports has not addressed this hypothesis, but attention to this problem is inherent in the work of researchers who are calling for the study of stress contexts rather than discrete events (Liem and Liem, 1978a). It is evident that in this conception only a minority of life events can be regarded as fortuitous, and that the study of etiology would require a significant shift in both time frame and perspective.

2. Investigation of a stress-prevention function of social support is important in itself, but it is also necessitated for an exhaustive treatment of the mediating issue. Kessler (1979) noted that the evidence of a vulnerability effect assumes equivalent reporting of events by contrast groups, i.e., high versus low support, and equivalent exposure to events of different magnitude. The assumption of equivalent starting points in terms of the stress experience is problematic in the absence of analyses that demonstrate this to be the case.

3. The other side of the stress-support relationship involves consideration of support processes as a series of dependent variables. Since events are felt throughout the wider social context, the question is what are the patterns of social response. A first research issue has been explored in a preliminary fashion by Lin et al. (1979b) who hypothesize that stress results in support mobilization for high-status persons, but support deterioration for low-status persons. (In the former case, the impact of stress is moderated, but in the latter a vicious cycle of stress, network deterioration, and psychological distress is set in motion.) Their data do not evidence this social class-stress interaction, but further analyses of this kind are warranted to examine the tenuousness or conditional nature of support.

A second issue in mobilization is that of timing. In some cases the support intervention may be so coincident with the event that the subjective impact of stress is immediately buffered. The question of timing also underscores the thin line between stress-prevention and stress-amelioration functions of social support.

These recommendations are not intended to exhaust the possibilities for exploration of support processes, but instead to direct attention to some points of departure for the study of supports in stress mediation. The challenge is to redirect attention from evidencing a presumed support effect, to one of documenting the nature of support mechanisms. In summary, this entails closer study of the links between particular stresses and supports (through addressing processual in addition to structual questions) toward descriptive, in addition to explanatory, goals.

References

Carveth, W. B. & Gottlieb, B. H. (1979), The measurement of social support and its relation to stress. *Canad. J. Behav. Sci.*, 11:179–186.

Cobb, S. (1976), Social support as a moderator of life stress. *Psychosom. Med.*, 38:300–314.

Cobb, S. & Kasl, S. (1977), *Termination: The Consequences of Job Loss*. Cincinnati, Ohio, U.S. Dept. of Health, Education and Welfare, P.H.S. Center for Disease Control, National Institute of Occupational Safety and Health.

Cofer, C. N. & Appley, M. H. (1964), *Motivation: Theory and Research*. New York: Wiley.

Dean, A. & Lin, N. (1977), The stress-buffering role of social support: problems and prospects for systematic investigation. *J. Nerv. Ment. Dis.*, 165:7–15.

Dohrenwend, B. P. & Egri, G. (1979) *Recent stressful life events and schizophrenia*. Read at the Conference on Stress, Social Support and Schizophrenia. Burlington, Vermont, September 24–25.

Dohrenwend, B. S. & Dohrenwend, B. P. (1974), Overview and prospects for research on stressful life events. In: *Stressful Life Events: Their Nature and Effects*, ed. B. S. Dohrenwend & B. P. Dohrenwend. New York: Wiley, pp. 313–331.

Dohrenwend, B. S., Krasnoff, L., Askenasy, A. R., & Dohrenwend, B. P. (1978), Exemplification of a method for scaling life events: the PERI Life Events Scale. *J. Hlth Soc. Behav.*, 19:205–229.

Dooley, D., Catalano, R., & Barthrop, A. (1979), *The relation of economic conditions and individual life change to depression: towards a cross level analysis of behavioral disorder*. Read at the annual meetings of the American Psychological Association, New York.

Durkheim, E. (1951), *Suicide*. Tr. J. A. Spaulding & G. Simpson. Glencoe, Ill.: The Free Press.

Eaton, W. (1978), Life events, social supports and psychiatric symptoms: a reanalysis of the New Haven data. *J. Hlth Soc. Behav.*, 19:230–234.

Faris, R. & Dunham, H. W. (1939), *Mental Disorders in Urban Areas*. New York: Hafner.

Gersten, J. C., Langner, T. S., Eisenberg, J. G., & Simcha-Fagan, O. (1977), An evaluation of the etiologic role of stressful life-change in psychological disorders. *J. Hlth Soc. Behav.*, 18:228–243.

Gersten, J. C., & Simcha-Fagan, O. (1978), The power of time. *J. Hlth Soc. Behav.*, 19:345–346.

Gore, S. (1973), *The influence of social support and related variables in ameliorating the consequences of job loss*. Doctoral dissertation, The University of Pennsylvania. Dissertation Abstracts International, 34, 5330-A-5331A (University Microfilms No. 74-2416).

Gore, S. (1978), The effect of social support in moderating the health consequences of unemployment. *J. Hlth Soc. Behav.*, 19:157–165.

Gore, S. (1979), Does help-seeking increase psychological distress? *J. Hlth Soc. Behav.*, 20:201–202.

Gottlieb, B. H. (1978), The development and application of a classification scheme of informal helping behaviors. *J. Behav. Sci.*, 10:105–115.

Gove, W. R. (1973), Sex, marital status and mortality. *Amer. J. Sociol.*, 79:45–67.

Hammer, M. (1979), *Social supports, social networks and schizophrenia*. Read at the Conference on Stress, Social Support and Schizophrenia. Burlington, Vermont, September 24–25.

Hollingshead, A. & Redlich, F. (1958), *Social Class and Mental Illness*. New York: Wiley.

Holmes, T. (1956), Multidisciplinary studies of tuberculosis. In: *Personality, Stress and Tuberculosis*, ed. P. J. Sparer. New York: International Universities Press, pp. 65–152.

Holmes, T. H. & Rahe, R. H. (1967), The social readjustment rating scale. *J. Psychosom. Res.*, 11:213–218.

Jaco, E. G. (1954), The social isolation hypothesis and schizophrenia. *Amer. Sociol. Rev.*, 19:567–577.

Kasl, S. (1978), Epidemiological contributions to the study of work stress. In: *Stress at Work*, ed. C. L. Cooper & R. Payne. New York: Wiley, pp. 3–48.

Kessler, R. C. (1979), A strategy for studying differential vulnerability to the psychological consequences of stress. *J. Hlth Soc. Behav.*, 20:100–108.

Kohn, M. L. & Clausen, J. A. (1955), Social isolation and schizophrenia. *Amer. Sociol. Rev.*, 20:265–273.

Langner, T. S. & Michael, S. T. (1963), *Life Stress and Mental Health*. New York: The Free Press.

Lazarus, R. S. (1966), *Psychological Stress and the Coping Process*. New York: McGraw-Hill.

Lazarus, R. S., Averill, J. R., & Opton, E. M., Jr. (1974), The psychology of coping: issues of research and assessment. In: *Coping and Adaptation*, ed. G. V. Coelho, D. A. Hamburg, & J. F. Adams. New York: Basic Books, pp. 249–315.

Lazarus, R. S. & Launier, R. (1978), Stress-related transactions between person and environment. In: *Perspectives in Interactional Psychology*, ed. L. A. Pervin & M. Lewis. New York: Plenum Publishing Co., pp. 287–327.

Liem, G. R. & Liem, J. H. (1978a), Social class and mental illness reconsidered: the role of economic stress and social support. *J. Hlth Soc. Behav.*, 19:139–156.

Liem, G. R. & Liem, J. H. (1978b), *Social support and stress: some general issues and their application to the problem of unemployment*. Read at the National Institute of Mental Health Conference on Mental Health and the Economy. Hunt Valley, Maryland, June 1–3.

Lin, N., Dean, A., & Ensel, W. (1979a), *Constructing social support scales*. Read at the Third Biennial Conference on Health Survey Research Methods. Reston, Virginia, May.

Lin, N., Simeone, R. S., Ensel, W., & Kuo, W. (1979b), Social support, stressful life events and illness: a model and empirical test. *J. Hlth Soc. Behav.*, 20:108–119.

Link, B. (1978), On the etiologic role of stressful life-change events. *J. Hlth Soc. Behav.*, 19:343–345.

Lowenthal, M. & Haven, C. (1968), Interaction and adaptation: intimacy as a critical variable. *Amer. Sociol. Rev.*, 33:20–30.

McGraph, J. E. (1970), A conceptual formulation for research on stress. In: *Social and Psychological Factors in Stress*, ed. J. E. McGraph. New York: Holt, Rinehart, and Winston, pp. 10–21.

Myers, J., Lindenthal, J., & Pepper, M. (1975), Life events, social integration and psychiatric symptomology. *J. Hlth Soc. Behav.*, 16:421–427.

Myers, J., & Roberts, B. (1959), *Family and Class Dynamics in Mental Health*. New York: Wiley.

Nuckolls, K., Cassel, J., & Kaplan, B. (1972), Psychosocial assets, life crisis and the prognosis of pregnancy. *Amer. J. Epidemiol.*, 95:431–441.

Paykel, E., Myers, J., Dienelt, M. N., Klerman, J., Lindenthal, J., & Pepper, M. (1969), Life events and depression: a controlled study. *Arch. Gen. Psychiat.*, 21:753–760.

Pearlin, L. I. & Schooler, C. (1978), The structure of coping. *J. Hlth Soc. Behav.*, 19:2–21.

Pearlin, L. I. & Schooler, C. (1979), Some extensions of "The Structure of Coping." *J. Hlth Soc. Behav.*, 20:202–204.

Pinneau, S. R., Jr. (1975), *Effects of social support on psychological and physiological strains.* Doctoral dissertation, The University of Michigan, Ann Arbor.

Tolsdorf, C. (1976), Social networks, support and coping: an exploratory study. *Fam. Proc.*, 15:407–417.

Wellman, B. (1972), *Community Ties and Support Systems.* Toronto: University of Tornoto Centre for Urban-Community Studies. Research Paper #11.

Measuring Social Support Networks in General Populations

SUSAN L. PHILLIPS

CLAUDE S. FISCHER

Evidence suggesting that social networks offer support crucial to psychological well-being has been mounting (Cobb, 1976; Dean and Lin, 1977); many of the studies to date, however, have been quite global in nature. In order to understand the relationship between social networks and well-being in all of its intricacy, more research is necessary. We need to specify the types of networks most conducive to well-being; we do not yet, for example, know whether large networks or close-knit networks are more beneficial. To answer such questions, we must develop network measures that are comprehensive and accurate. Toward that end, we will describe a method of gathering network information that improves upon many techniques used to date; second, we will present a brief illustration of the range of network measures and the type of analysis this method affords.

Method

Our method of mapping personal networks was developed for use in a large-scale survey of small town–large city differences (Fischer, 1980). For those purposes 1050 people were asked, among other things, to describe their social networks.

Many earlier techniques of mapping networks suffered from a lack of precision and accuracy. For example, some methods involved asking rather vague questions such as, "Whom do you feel closest to?" This technique invited a wide degree of measurement error since respondents may interpret terms such as "closest to" in a variety of ways. Other techniques involved asking about only a few types of network members. For example, subjects might be asked "Who are your best friends?" or "How many neighbors do you know?" This method underestimated persons outside the role relations mentioned who might actually be significant to the respondent. We improve upon these methods by asking respondents to tell us about a wide spectrum of specific persons.

Eliciting Names of Significant Network Members—Since it is infeasible, if not impossible, to ask about all the persons in a given network, the first step in network measurement is to delimit the concept of network. Our goal was to gather information on the set of people who were significant in respondents' lives; an exchange theory of relations (Thibaut and Kelley, 1959; Homans, 1974) suggests that the significant network members are likely to be those who provide some type of support or exchange (the rationale for the use of exchange theory can be found in McCallister and Fischer, 1978; more detail is available in Jones and Fischer, 1978). We therefore, developed questions that elicited from respondents an accurate list—or at least a representative sample—of people who provided them with specific forms of material, social, and emotional support. We tried to select commonly exchanged types of support so that the networks would be comparable across different types of individuals. Of all the exchanges we could have asked about, and of the thirty or so we pretested, we chose to ask respondents to tell us:

1. Who would care for their homes if they went out of town;
2. (If the respondents worked) to whom they talked about decisions at work;
3. Who had helped with household tasks in the last three months;
4. With whom they had engaged in social activities (such as having someone over for dinner or going to a movie);
5. With whom they discussed mutual spare-time activities;
6. (If the respondents were not married) who were their fiances or "best friends";
7. With whom they discussed personal worries;
8. Whose advice they considered in making important decisions;
9. From whom they would or could borrow a large sum of money;
10. Who over fifteen years of age lived in the same household.

Persons named in answer to question number ten were assumed to be involved in tacit exchanges. Respondents were allowed to name as many people as they wished in response to each question. Interviewers, however, recorded only the first eight names for each (actually ten for question four and four for question nine). In the end, an average of 18.5 network members were reported, though networks ranged from a low of 2 to a high of 67.

Measuring Attributes of Network Members—In addition to gathering names of network members, we measured attributes of the network members. After the name-eliciting questions had been asked and the solicited names written down, the interviewer went back over the questions to select a special subsample of up to 5 names. This subsample was used to obtain the kind of detailed information that we could not obtain for all the relations. The subsample was picked from names, excluding household members, given first (or second, or third, if the prior names had been already picked) in answer to several "key" questions: those numbered 1, 4, 5, 7, 8, and 9 above. The interviewer used these up-to-five names to measure network density (the degree to which network members are interconnected) by asking the respondents whether each pair of people in the subsample "know each other well." Then, the interviewer put each subsample name of a separate self-administered questionnaire, which she handed, with a pencil, to the respondent. The form asked the respondent:

1. How they had met the person;
2. How many years they have known each other;
3. What city the person lives in;
4. How often they "get together";
5. The person's age;
6. The person's employment status;
7. The person's marital status; and
8. Whether the person has children and how old they are.

While the respondent filled out this questionnaire, the interviewer compiled all the names—typically over a dozen—onto a list form. This form included an automatic (noncarbon) copy, which was given to the respondent when he or she finished the self-administered questionnaire. Then the interviewer asked the respondent to look over the list and tell her if there was "anyone else important to you who doesn't show up on this list?" Any such people were added. In the end, most respondents had between ten and thirty names on their lists.

Using these lists, the interviewer asked the respondent:

1. The sex of each person;
2. All the role relations of ego with the named people (e.g., cousin, co-worker, fellow union member, "friend");
3. Which persons respondents "feel especially close" to;
4. Which persons live within a five-minute drive;
5. Which live more than an hour's drive away;
6. Which they see at a favorite "hang-out";

7. (For homemakers) which are also full-time homemakers;
8. (For workers) which are in the same line of work;
9. (For respondents with an ethnic identity) which are of the same ethnicity;
10. (For respondents with a religious affiliation) which share the same religion; and
11. (For respondents with a favorite pasttime) which share the favorite pasttime.

In addition, we knew from the name-eliciting questions which exchanges the respondents claimed to receive from each person named. The technique of asking respondents to select names from a list—that is, asking, "Which of the people on the list are _____?"— permitted us to obtain more descriptions than would be feasible by asking about each person directly—that is, by asking, "Is John _____?" We chose to accept the potential inaccuracies of this approach (names the respondents may have inadvertantly skipped) in return for its greater efficiency. This method of collecting detailed network information typically took between twenty and thirty minutes.

The primary advantage of our procedure is that it permits us to focus on people who are important sources of valued exchanges. Our evaluation of the method suggests that it identifies these people reliably (Jones and Fischer, 1978); the names we miss tend to be "specialists," sources of only one kind of exchange. As a result, we are confident that the networks we identify are comparable across respondents. In addition, this method allows the researcher to create a multitude of network variables. To demonstrate this, in the next section we examine several aspects of social networks in order to determine which has the greatest impact on well-being.

Illustration Analysis

Numerous studies indicate that the structure and composition of a network may affect its supportiveness. Several researchers have noted that people with large networks tend to score high on measures of well-being (Brim, 1974; Henderson et al., 1978; Fischer and Phillips, 1979); those with networks low in density or high in multistranded relations also tend to score higher on well-being (Hirsch, 1979, 1980). Women with more sources of instrumental support tend to be happier (Brim, 1974); number of casual friends, as opposed to intimates, has also been found to be related to the well-being of women (Miller and Ingham, 1976). The presence of a confidant appears to buffer the effects of age-linked social losses among the elderly (Lowenthal and Haven, 1968; Moriwaki, 1973; Miller and Ingham, 1976); and, among the elderly, those with a large proportion of kin in their networks tended to have low morale (Arling, 1976). In order to assess which of these several network variables has the most important contribution to well-being, however, their independent effects on a single measure of well-being must be examined. Our method allows us to create all the measures mentioned above—size, density, multistrandedness, number of kin and number of non-kin, social companions, number of confidants, and number of instrumental supporters—and to measure their effects on the well-being scores of respondents whose networks we mapped.

Sample—In Fall and Winter of 1977, we interviewed 1050 randomly chosen adults in fifty Northern Californian communities— urban census tracts or small towns ranging from central San Francisco to agricultural regions over a hundred miles away. For reasons discussed elsewhere (Fischer, 1980), the sample excluded towns under 2500 in population, neighborhoods that were forty percent or more black, and people who did not speak English. The sample overdrew respondents from smaller places, but, for the analysis reported here, we weighted the data to approximate the English-speaking population living in nonblack urban areas of Northern California in 1977. In addition, the analysis was performed on the 950 members of the total sample who had at least three names selected for the special subsample (see above). It was necessary to eliminate those with two or fewer subsample names in order to obtain an accurate measure of network density.

The Measures—Our data included several indices of well-being, indices measuring the tendency of respondents to report feelings of happiness, distress, or anger. For the purposes of our illustration, however, we will present only findings for the Happiness Index. The items comprising this index are as follows:
1. How often do you feel particularly excited or pleased? (a lot of the time; some of the time; only once in a while; or never).
2. How often do you feel that things are going the way you want them to?
3. How often do you feel pleased with what you're doing these days?
4. Thinking of your life as a whole, how happy would you say

you are these days—very happy, pretty happy, pretty unhappy, or very unhappy?

Our method of mapping social support networks allowed us to create a multitude of network characteristics. An examination of several measures of network structure (including its size, density and multistrandedness) and several measures of its composition (including the number of kin vs. non-kin in the network and the number of social companions, instrumental supporters, and confidants in the network) indicated the range of network possibilities. The measures of network structure to be examined here are defined below.

Size: A count of all individuals reported in response to the ten name-eliciting items and the "Is there anyone else . . . ?" question.

Multistrandedness: The average number of specific exchanges a respondent receives from each one of his or her network associates. The exchanges involved were those mentioned in the name-eliciting questions number 1 through 5 and 7 through 9. The higher the number of average exchanges per associate, the greater the degree of multistrandedness.

Density: The density measure is based on the subsample of up to five persons described in the self-administered questionnaires. For these three to five people, respondents reported, among other things, which of the named persons knew each other well. The density measure is the number of relationships among this subset of people divided by the number of possible relationships.

Because we asked respondents to describe their role relations (whether the person named is a co-worker or a relative, for example), we were able to distinguish kin from non-kin. For the analysis presented here, the number of kin measure included only kin living outside the household. (We excluded relatives living within the household in order to avoid redundancy with marital status, which will also be introduced into the analysis.)

Since we know the specific exchanges provided by each network member, we were able to construct measures of the range of material, social, and emotional support available in a network.

Number of Instrumental Supporters: This variable is the number of persons named in response to one or more of the name-eliciting questions number 1 through 3 and 9, that is, the questions concerning home care, work, household tasks, and borrowing money. In this analysis we were interested in only those instrumental supporters living outside the household.

Number of Social Companions: This measure is the number of persons living outside the household who were named in response to question number 4, that is, persons with whom the respondent engaged in social activities. (Again, those living within the household were excluded in order to avoid redundancy with a measure of marital status which will also be introduced into the analysis.)

Number of Confidants: Similarly, our measure of confidants is the number of persons living outside the household named in response to either name-eliciting question number 7 or number 8, that is, persons with whom personal worries are discussed or whose advise is considered.

The Findings

In order to choose the best predictors of our Happiness Index from among these several measures of network characteristics, we performed a stepwise regression analysis. Because we knew certain background characteristics and that a measure of stressful life events were also related to scores on the Happiness Index, we first controlled for these factors. As Table 1 shows, the background characteristics (age, income, race, marital status, number of children, and number of stressful life events) were introduced into the first equation simultaneously. When controlling for the background variables, number of non-kin in the network was the strongest predictor of happiness (partial $r = 0.22$, $p \leq 0.001$) while number of social companions (partial $r = 0.19$, $p \leq 0.001$) and total network size (partial $r = 0.18$, $p \leq 0.001$) run a close second and third in terms of predictive strength. Though the partial correlations of number of instrumental supporters (partial $r = 0.09$, $p \leq 0.01$) and number of confidants (partial $r = 0.07$, $p \leq 0.05$) with happiness are low, they are still significant. Since the network variables under consideration are colinear, however, it is necessary to control for the effects of the network measures themselves on one another in order to assess their independent effects on happiness; in order to do this, the network measures were entered into the second equation sequentially according to their predictive strength. This procedure shows number of non-kin (Beta = 0.17, $p \leq 0.001$) to be the strongest predictor of happiness when the relevant background factors are taken into consideration. Once both background factors and number of nonkin are held constant, number of social companions (Beta = 0.09, $p \leq 0.05$) is the only other network variable which remains significantly related to happiness; the associations of all other network variables drop to nonsignificance.

TABLE 1

Stepwise Multiple Regression of Happiness Index on Background
Variables, Number of Stressful Life Events,
and Network Variables (N = 950).

Variables	Zero-Order r's	eq $(1)^a$ Betas	eq (2) Betas
Age	−0.06	$−0.14^b$	$−0.09^c$
Income	0.30	0.21^b	0.15^b
White/nonwhite	0.14	0.11^b	0.09^c
Married/single	0.18	0.12^b	0.13^b
Number of children	−0.02	0.08^d	−0.06
Number of stressful life events	−0.20	$−0.16^b$	$−0.15^c$
		Partial r's	Betas ^{e}
Number non-kin	0.29	0.22^b	0.17^b
Number of companions	0.28	0.19^b	0.09^d
Multistrandedness	−0.06	−0.04	NS ^{f}
Number of instrumental supporters	0.16	0.09^c	NS
Number of kin	0.05	0.03	NS
Number of confidants	0.04	0.07^d	NS
Density	−0.04	0.02	NS
Network size	0.27	0.18^b	NS
R^2		0.14	0.19

^{a} Background variables and number of stressful life events were entered into the equations (1) and (2) simultaneously.
$^b p \leq 0.001.$
$^c p \leq 0.01.$
$^d p \leq 0.05.$
^{e} In equation (2), the network variables were entered consecutively in order of their predictive power.
^{f} NS = not significant.

Discussion

To summarize, when only the effects of the background variables
were held constant, network size, number of non-kin, and number
of social companions were the three strongest predictors of happiness. Number of kin, confidants, and network density were notably
insignificant predictors. When the network variables were intro-

duced into the regression equation in order of their predictive strength, however, the effects of network size dropped to nonsignificance. The effects of network size were actually due to number of non-kin and number of social companions within the network. There may be many reasons for this finding. We first offer an explanation based on the assumption that the causal influence runs solely from the network composition variables to happiness; later we question this assumption.

Following Arling's (1976) lead, we suggest that non-kin relations may *foster* happiness because, in contrast to kin relations, they are freely chosen and, therefore, are likely to be based on value similarity. While both kin and non-kin may provide the material, social, and emotional exchanges we asked about directly, there may be, it seems, something about non-kin relations that is especially rewarding. We suggest that the extra rewards of non-kin relations are ego-enhancing effects of value similarity. Having many relations with persons, each of whom has at least some value similarity with one's self, is likely to enhance a sense of the appropriateness of one's own values, way of life, and self—thus leading one to feel generally pleased with one's self and life in general.

Similarly, having many social companions may in itself be rewarding above and beyond the rewards of each single interaction. Having many, rather than few, persons with whom to engage in social activities would itself create opportunities for social interaction and events to look forward to; these events, in turn, may prove exciting, pleasing, or otherwise conducive to happiness.

While we have offered explanations for why these two aspects of social networks may lead to happiness, we do not wish to suggest that these are the only reasons for the relationships. The findings we have presented may be due to the influence of the social networks on well-being, as we have suggested above. However, because the data we have been examining are correlational, the direction of the causal influence is unspecified. As with all correlational analysis, we must be cognizant of several other possible explanations for the relationships found. It may be that well-being itself influences the formatization and maintenance of social networks; that is, potential network members may be attracted to happy people. Or it may be that a third variable influences both well-being and network composition. The obvious third variable is personality; a desire for social acceptance, for example, might lead an individual to score high on the happiness index and to carefully build and maintain a large non-kin network. Lastly, some combination of causal influences may be at work. It seems most realistic to assume that there are reciprocal relationships between network composition and happiness.

The challenge to researchers in this area is to design research that will permit a deeper understanding of these intricate relationships between social-support networks and well-being. A necessary first step in furthering that type of research will be to develop standardized network measures that are both comprehensive and accurate.

Acknowledgments

This research was funded by Grant #MH26802 from the Center for Studies of Metropolitan Problems, National Institute of Mental Health. Among our many co-workers we would especially like to thank Lynne McCallister and Kathleen Gerson for developing the network and the psychological well-being items, respectively.

References

Arling, G. (1976), The elderly widow and her family, neighbors, and friends. *J. Marriage & Family*, 38:757–768.

Brim, J. A. (1974), Social network correlates of avowed happiness. *J. Nerv. Ment. Dis.*, 158:432–439.

Cobb, S. (1976), Social support as a moderator of life stress. *Psychosom. Med.*, 38:300–314.

Dean, A. & Lin, N. (1977), The stress-buffering role of social support: problems and prospects for systematic investigation." *J. Nerv. Ment. Dis.*, 164:7–15.

Fischer, C. S. (1980), *Personal Communities*. Chicago: University of Chicago Press, in press.

Fischer, C. S. & Phillips, S. L. (1979), *Who is Alone? Social Characteristics of People with Small Networks*. Working Paper No. 310, Berkeley: University of California Institute of Urban and Regional Development.

Henderson, S. P., Byrne, D. G., Duncan-Jones, P., Adcock, S., Scott, R., & Steele, G. P. (1978), Social bonds in the epidemiology of neurosis: a preliminary communication. *Brit. J. Psychiat.*, 132:463–466.

Hirsch, B. J. (1979), Psychological dimensions of social networks: a multimethod analysis. *Amer. J. Commun. Psychol.*, 7:263–277.

Hirsch, B. J. (1980), Natural support systems and coping with major life changes. *Amer. J. Commun. Psychol.*

Homans, G. C. (1974), *Social Behavior: Its Elementary Forms*. New York: Harcourt, Brace, Jovanovich.

Jones, L. & Fischer, C. S. (1978), *Studying Egocentric Networks by Mass Survey*. Working Paper No. 284, Berkeley: University of California Institute of Urban and Regional Development.

Lowenthal, M. F. & Haven, C. (1968), Interaction and adaptation: intimacy as a critical variable. *Amer. Sociol. Rev.*, 33:20–30.

McCallister, L. & Fischer, C. S. (1978), A procedure for surveying personal networks. *Sociol. Meth. Res.* 7:131–147.

Miller, P. & Ingham, J. (1976), Friends, confidants, and symptoms. *Soc. Psychiat.*, 11:51–58.

Moriwaki, S. (1973), Self-disclosure, significant others, and psychological well-being in old age. *J. Hlth. Soc. Behav.*, 14:226–232.

Thibaut, J. & Kelley, H. H. (1959), *The Social Psychology of Groups*. New York: Wiley.

Relations Among Social Class, Life Events, and Mental Illness: A Comment on Findings and Methods

RAMSAY LIEM

JOAN H. LIEM

Without question the study of stressful life events has become an important line of research attracting the attention of epidemiologists, medical sociologists, community and clinical psychologists, and public-health specialists. One cannot read through the major health related journals in the behavioral and social sciences without regularly encountering references to the measurement, impact, or moderation of the impact of life events. The recent popularity of life events research probably has little to do with its theoretical or conceptual underpinnings in view of the fact that substantial discussion of the complexities of a social-stress hypothesis regarding illness and health predates the appearance of this particular body of work (Meyer, 1951; Hollingshead and Redlich, 1958). What may account for the attraction of life-events research is the methodology identified with it. The early work of Holmes and Rahe (1967), more than anything else, provided investigators with a basic approach to measurement whereby the largely proximal social field could be assessed for relatively discrete and contemporaneous occurrences capable of engendering personal stress. The availability of an apparently straightforward procedure for measuring social stressors for individuals raised the possibility that a new level of systematic and empirical examination of the social basis of health could be achieved.

Toward this end much effort has been made to predict various illness states with life-events inventories (Myers et al., 1971; Wyler et al., 1971), refine and improve measurement and scaling techniques (B. S. Dohrenwend et al., 1978), minimize threats to the reliability and validity of findings (Brown, 1974), and elaborate predictive models of stress-related health outcomes (Cobb, 1974). Each of these general areas of work continues to be a source of complex issues and problems and the subject of numerous reviews and discussions (B. S. Dohrenwend and B. P. Dohrenwend, 1974; Rabkin and Struening, 1976).

In spite of continuing challenges to the interpretation of findings from this area of research, most investigators feel that consistent if modest support for the social-stress perspective has been demonstrated by life-events research and that much is to be gained from continued efforts to improve methodologies and elaborate explanatory models.

In light of the apparent success of life-events research in demonstrating an association between discrete social stressors and multiple health outcomes, this commentary addresses the question of what contribution life-events research can make to our understanding of the broader, societal distribution of illness risk. Although this issue has received some attention, most research has been devoted to specifying the extent of a relationship between the recent occurrence of stressful life events and the appearance of symptomatology. Thus, conceptual and methodological contributions have tended to focus on the individual's immediate social environment as a source of illness-promoting stressors, leaving open the question of whether or not these social precipitants and their impact are systematically related to broader social structures and dynamics.

Where conceptual or empirical attention is paid to the societal contexts of stressful life events, a shared interest appears to be to establish some continuity between findings from the study of stressful life experiences and the principle observations in epidemiologic research, especially psychiatric epidemiology. Foremost among the latter findings is the well-known social class-mental illness relation reported by numerous investigators and reviewed by B. P. Dohrenwend and B. S. Dohrenwend (1969) and Kohn (1973). This evidence of societally distributed illness risk has generated a continuing debate regarding the processes underlying this relation (i.e., social causation vs. social drift vs. interactional social-selection models). Consequently, for some the study of stressful life events represents a research strategy that may serve to generate new explanatory evidence regarding the more global epidemiologic findings of relations between macro social structures like social class and vulnerability to disease.

This chapter examines findings from life-events research primarily in terms of their relevance to the issue of social class and mental illness. Although other parameters (e.g., race, sex) of the distribution of mental illness in the population can be evaluated in light of life-events data (B. S. Dohrenwend, 1973), this discussion will be limited to the issue of social class in view of its theoretical centrality to the dynamics of societal organization and empirical prominence as a specified correlate of mental illness.

Social Class, Life Events, and Psychiatric Impairment

In this discussion social class is assumed to be a manifestation of ongoing relations between groups in society influenced by differential access to economic, political, and social advantages. This view of social class, while incorporating an aspect of social attribution in the form of prestige or status, associates a dynamic life space with class position. Rather than treating class membership as principally a social indicator of ascribed status, this approach makes salient the existence of concrete differences in the makeup of the ongoing life circumstances of persons occupying different positions in the class structure. The issue for this discussion is whether or not the kinds of stressful life experiences commonly assessed in the literature and the contextual factors that may influence the impact of such events are manifestations of class-related life conditions that help to account for differences in the risk of mental illness across classes.

The current findings in life-events research and related areas of study make plausible two alternative and compatible models of the mediation of the social class-mental illness relation by processes involving the occurrence of life events and the conditioning of their impact. The first and most straightforward position is that the day-to-day experience of members of the lower classes is more likely to involve exposure to stress-inducing, discrete events than is the experience of members of the privileged classes. This perspective emphasizes a quantitative difference in the frequency of life events for different class positions and assumes that the higher rate of mental illness associated with lower class life is partly the outcome of greater numbers of stressful life events in the experience of lower-class persons.

The second model focuses on the context in which life events occur as a potential source of factors that may exacerbate or moderate the perception of and the short- and long-term responses to these events. This line of inquiry maintains the view of life events as objective, social occurrences but with stress values contingent on complex characteristics of the person's life circumstances. Here we are concerned with evidence that class variation in such factors as support and coping resources lead to predictably higher levels of stress impact for life events in the lower classes thereby contributing to the greater illness risk in these groups. In statistical terms, social class is treated as a moderating variable in this model of class, life events, and illness relationships. Nevertheless, it should be apparent that the existence of class differences in conditions that moderate the impact of life events by no means rules out class differences in frequencies of life events as part of the explanation for class-distributed illness rates.

This chapter also discusses the evidence for the direct mediation of the social class-mental illness relation by stressful life events and the moderation of the impact of life events by class conditions. Data from life-events research augmented by work in several related areas are the primary sources of data for this discussion. Methodological implications of the existing evidence for a relationship among social class, life events, and psychiatric health are then evaluated. Finally, the special utility of the intensive study of single events is discussed as one strategy for investigating in more detail the processes underlying the relationships among social class, stressful life experiences, and health outcomes.

Direct Mediation of the Social Class-Mental Illness Relation— Elsewhere (Liem and Liem, 1978b), we have discussed the direct mediation of the social class-mental illness relation by stressful life events. The primary sources of support for the position that high levels of social stress (including situational stressors) accompany lower-class occupancy and contribute to high rates of mental illness are some of the early epidemiologic studies, a limited number of more recent life-events investigations, estimates of the distribution in the population of single life events such as unemployment, and analyses of aggregate measures of life events and mental health.

One of the earliest, well-known documentations of an inverse relationship between rates of psychiatric hospitalization and social class comes from the work of Faris and Dunham (1939). In this research mental illness indexed by aggregate hospital admissions was found to be concentrated in geographic locales exhibiting social characteristics often associated with low socioeconomic status. While the investigators speculated that social isolation in these areas accounted for this pattern of findings, the importance of this research lies more with its early identification of a possible relationship between social-class conditions and utilization of psychiatric services than with its post hoc description of mediating factors.

Subsequent epidemiologic studies have replicated this basic finding of class-correlated indices of mental illness employing widely differing research methodologies and designs (B. P. Dohrenwend and B. S. Dohrenwend, 1969; Kohn, 1973). Few, however, have provided systematic evidence bearing on the qeustion of class-correlated frequencies of social stressors as intervening in this relationship. In their classic New Haven study, Hollingshead and Redlich (1958) rely on case material and a survey of New Haven households stratified by socioeconomic status to propose that presses, or externally originating stressors, typify the life circumstances of the lowest status group whereas stresses, or internally generated conflicts and frustrations, are more characteristic of the privileged. Social stressors, therefore, figure centrally in the efforts of these contributors to explain their findings of highest prevalence and incidence rates in the lowest class based on a treatment census.

Of the research in the epidemiologic tradition, the work by Langner and Michael (1963) most directly confronts the issue of a stress-mediated social class-mental illness relationship. Based on treated and untreated prevalence data collected in the Midtown Manhattan study (Srole et al., 1962), these researchers examined relationships among 14 adult and childhood stressors, SES, and degrees of psychiatric impairment. They found modest support for their hypothesis that higher levels of situational stress in the childhood as well as the contempory experience of lower class-persons contribute to the high levels of rated impairment among respondents from this class. Findings were most pronounced for symptoms judged to be psychotic. Although the underlying processes for the impact of childhood vs. adult stressors would clearly be different, these findings are commonly cited in support of the social-stress mediation hypothesis.

Two other studies are pertinent to this issue. Rogler and Hollingshead (1965) reported both high, sustained levels of social stress among lower-class schizophrenics in Puerto Rico and massive situational stress during the year preceding the onset of symptoms. The latter finding is especially noteworthy in view of the common observation in life-events studies that life events occurring in the year prior to the assessment of health status are most predictive of impairment. Some indirect support indicating that the specific event of unemployment may be an important correlate of psychiatric impairment is reported by Jaco (1960). He found that differences in rates of disorder for unemployed vs. employed persons were substantially greater in the predicted direction than for respondents ordered by customary social-class criteria. This observation is provocative in light of more recent findings regarding (*a*) the causal role of unemployment in the onset of psychiatric impairment and, (*b*) the class distribution of this stressful life event.

Using aggregate time series data, Brenner (1973) has published what is by now a well-known series of findings that strongly indicate an ecological relationship between psychiatric first admissions and state and national indices of employment and unemployment. These findings have been corroborated in part by others (Catalano and Dooley, 1977; R. Liem, 1977; Marshall and Funch, 1979) and have contributed to substantial research interest in unemployment as an important precursor of psychological impairment.

The intuitive assumption that unemployment is class distributed is born out by formal estimates of national and local patterns of unemployment. For example, national data from the U.S. Bureau of Labor Statistics (Stellar, 1979), reveal that from 1968 to 1978 blue-collar workers have on the average experienced approximately twice the amount of unemployment as white-collar workers. Furthermore, unemployment has regularly been least frequent among professional and managerial workers, increasing steadily as one moves through clerks and salespersons, to craftpersons and foremen, and then to operatives, service workers, and nonfarm laborers. The ratio of unemployment rates of professionals/managers to nonfarm laborers over this ten-year period ranges from 1:4 to 1:6. In a random sample of screening interviews with 1100 unemployed men in two of the largest Division of Employment Security offices in the Greater Boston Area during the summer of 1979 (for purposes of selecting participants for a research project reported below), we found that 50% of these persons were semi- and unskilled blue-collar workers, 15% were skilled blue-collar workers and craftpersons, 20% were nonprofessional white-collar workers, and 15% were professional and managerial workers. Using rough estimates (Stellar, 1979) of employment levels in Massachusetts by occupation, we found the unemployment rate among professionals/managers to be by far the lowest for all groups of workers, i.e. one-half the rate for skilled blue-collar workers, and one-fourth the rate for nonprofessional service workers and semi-skilled and unskilled nonfarm laborers. Various estimates of unemployment rates for different occupational strata, therefore, appear to substantiate common-sense expectations and lend plausibility to the hypothesis that class-distributed prevalence rates of mental illness may be partly accounted for by similarly distributed risk of job loss.

It may also be the case that high risk for unemployment goes hand in hand with a high probability of experiencing large numbers of other life events as well. Catalano and Dooley (1977) report a correlation of $r = 0.77$ between aggregate measures of unemployment and aggregate frequenceis of life events over a two-year period for a single Standard Metropolitan Statistical Area in a midwestern urban locale. They propose that part of the mediation of illness risk and macroeconomic conditions may result from a tendency for areas with an unstable economic base also to be settings where other kinds of stressful life events predominate. These results have largely been replicated as recently reported by Dooley and Catalano (1979).

Epidemiologic research, unemployment statistics, and studies of ecological clusterings of life events, however, only suggest that a positive relationship may exist between measures of social class and overall levels of life events. They do not directly test whether or not class-correlated frequencies of life events explain empirically observed relationships between social class and indicators of mental illness. Several explicit tests of a life-event mediation of the social class-mental illness relation are available in the recent life-events literature. The earliest is the work of B. S. Dohrenwend (1973) where numbers of life events experienced were hypothesized to intervene in the relation between three measures of social status (social class, race, and sex) and ratings of psychiatric impairment. Of relevance to this discussion is the report that social class as indexed by educational level was found as predicted to be inversely related to both psychiatric impairment and life events measured in terms of life-change units. Life-change scores, as expected, were also positively correlated with impairment. A partial correlation between SES and impairment controlling for life-change scores substantially reduced the original zero order correlations although not to the level of nonsignificance. In light of the fact that a further partial correlation between life-change units and impairment remained significant with SES controlled, B. S. Dohrenwend (1973) concluded that some but not all of the relationship between impairment and social status is accounted for by status differences in the exposure to life events. The basic pattern of findings is also maintained when events judged to be outside the control of the individual are substituted for the measure of total life events. Other findings concerning the differential impact of life events by SES groups have more relevance to a later section of this paper. For the moment, it is important to note that some support is provided in this research for both a class distribution of exposure to life events and the intervention of such events in the relation between social class and psychiatric impairment.

B. S. Dohrenwend's (1973) hypothesis that frequent exposure to stressful life experiences contributes to the high rates of emotional disorder among lower-class persons was partially confirmed by Myers, Lindenthal, and Pepper (1974). When life-change scores and simple frequencies for total events and undesirable events were used in analyses among socioeconomic status, life events, and impairment, the expected inverse relationship between SES and life events was not observed. However, the picture changed when two additional methods of scoring life events were employed: a ratio of undesirable to desirable events and a summed life-change unit score based on negative weights assigned to undesirable events and positive weights assigned to desirable events. The first measure correlated significantly with SES in the predicted direction using data collected at time one in this two-stage panel study, and the second measure produced expected findings at both points in time. Parital correlations also revealed that the relationship between social class and impairment was substantially accounted for by the class distribution of life events weighted for desirability and life-change units. These findings suggest that although total events demanding readjustment are equally prevalent across status groups, for lower-class persons relatively greater demand for undesirable as compared to desirable life change is associated with a disproportionately high risk for psychiatric impairment.

The evidence in support of exposure to life events as mediating the social class-mental illness relation is also buttressed by two very recently published studies. Using data from the same research just cited by Myers, Lindenthal, and Pepper (1974), Kessler (1979) proposed a unique statistical procedure for estimating the relative contributions of the amount of exposure to and the impact of life events to the impairment levels of persons in different SES groups. We are concerned here only with exposure to life events as it explains class-related psychiatric impairment. Kessler consistently found that differential exposure to life events scored either in terms of simple frequencies or life-change units contributed to the class differences in impairment. This finding was strongest when persons in Hollingshead and Redlich's (1958) classes I to III were contrasted with those in class V. While these data are very much in line with the findings from the two studies cited above, their support for the life-event mediation hypothesis must be treated cautiously. Unlike B. S. Dohrenwend (1973) and Myers et al. (1974) Kessler (1979) included in his life-events indexes two potential sources of sustained stress, family financial status, and symptoms of physical illness. The former is potentially confounded with the index of SES and the latter with the measure of psychiatric impairment. Furthermore, both factors (especially family financial status) differ conceptually from life events as precipitators of stress. As the author describes them, family finances and physical illness are "ongoing life situations that can be stressful" (Kessler, 1979, p. 260). Life events, on the other hand are generally considered to be discrete, situational occurrences with a clear, objective onset and relatively short duration. Because the data do not distinguish the effects of the life events from those of the ongoing stressors, it may be that the latter are disproportionately responsible for the pattern of findings reported by Kessler. If so, these data would be less useful as a test of the mediation of the social class-mental illness relation by life events per se.

A major report of social factors in depression in women by Brown and Harris (1978) is also pertinent to the issue of life events as direct mediators of class-linked rates of mental illness. However, as was the case with Kessler's (1979) findings, these data are not directly comparable to those of B. S. Dohrenwend (1973) and Myers et al. (1974). On the one hand, Brown and Harris report modest but significant mediation by life events of an inverse relationship between social class position and depression, especially in women with children at home. Moreover, based on independent clinical ratings of the severity of stressful events, they find that more severe household-related occurrences, where the judged duration of the stress impact is greater than ten days, are especially important for explaining some of the variation in class-distributed depression. To a lesser degree, ongoing, marked difficulties such as deteriorated housing conditions also explain part of the relationship between depression and social-class position. This finding provides an interesting complement to the possibility that Kessler's observed mediation of the social class-mental illness relationship by life events may have been strengthened by combining ongoing life stressors with life events as predictors of impairment.

The results of this study pose another problem for interpretation, however. In rating the severity (i.e., duration of impact) of life events, coders made clinical judgments based on a wide variety of interview material descriptive of the broad situational context of the respondents. It is difficult to imagine that such judgments were not influenced by at least some class-related factors, increasing the likelihood that life events would be found to intervene in the relation of depression to social class. Furthermore, such ratings of life events imply a moderating effect of conditions in the respondent's life situation and are labeled by Brown and Harris as measures of "contextual threat." Life events scored in this manner, therefore, do not provide a clean test of the degree to which differences in the simple frequency of life events explains the inverse relationship between social class and depression. In fact, based on other data discussed below, Brown and Harris found that life events influence the relation of social class to mental illness more by virtue of their interaction with class-related life conditions than as direct intervening factors.

Comment—What conclusions can we draw at this time regarding life events as intervening in the relation between social class and global indexes of mental illness? On the one hand, the evidence we have reviewed is modestly supportive of this hypothesis, certainly to the degree that one would not be confident in ruling out this line of reasoning. The most obvious implication of this conclusion for life-events researchers is that it provides the investigator with an empirical basis for conceptualizing a link between stressful life experiences in the proximal social environment and social structure and processes at the macro level. In other words it supports one model of the mechanisms relating individual and interpersonal spheres of experience to overarching societal dynamics and, thus, encourages the researcher to adopt a broader conception of the social nature of stressful life events.

The reliability of the findings we have reviewed, however, is made somewhat tenuous by at least one study where no significant relationship between social class and life events has been observed (Markush and Favero, 1974). In another study (Gersten et al., 1977) life events were not found to aid in predicting impairment once a broad range of ongoing stressful life circumstances was controlled. Some of these stressors are clearly class related. Link (1978), however, correctly pointed out that these analyses are not a sufficient basis for completely ruling out a life-events effect given the probability of a statistical masking of this effect in regression analyses used in this research.

One reason for some inconsistency in the evidence for life-events mediation of the social class-mental illness relation may involve the construction of life-events inventories. Given that social class may be correlated with frequency of exposure not only to life events in general but also to specific events as well, the selection of events to be included in an inventory can substantially influence the likelihood of finding a mediating effect for life events. Consistency is further threatened by the fact that life-change weights assigned to events in some scoring systems may reflect class bias such that correlations of life-change scores with SES are either inflated or underestimated. Given some anarchy in the choice of measurement procedures in life-events research, these kinds of scaling issues can be expected to produce some instability in findings across studies. An extensive review of these issues by B. S. Dohrenwend et al. (1978) is discussed in greater detail in a later section of this chapter.

A further qualification regarding support for the hypothesis that life events intervene in the relation between social class and mental illness is the fact that in three of the four major studies cited above, higher levels of impairment in the lower classes appeared to result most from the effects of class conditions on the degree of *impact* of life events. These and related findings are taken up next. For the moment it appears reasonable to conclude that some of the association between social-class position and psychiatric health is mediated by differential exposure to life events even though this process may be secondary to the role of social class in conditioning the impact of stressful life events.

Social Class and the Impact of Life Events—Recent studies of stressful life events have paid increasing attention to the role of situational and person-centered factors in moderating the impact of life events. This sensitivity to the context dependency of life-events effects has produced a broad range of factors for which a plausible argument could be made that they function to condition stress responses. Among these are a number that either are frequently used to operationalize socioeconomic status or, on common-sense grounds, are most probably class distributed (e.g., financial resources, housing conditions, and access to information and services). However, with one exception, life-event studies that have explicitly examined social class as an index of conditioning factors have generally failed to specify those factors empirically.

In the research by B. S. Dohrenwend (1973) cited above, within-class correlations between total life events weighted for life-change units and psychiatric symptomatology were highly significant and quite robust only for the lower-class group ($r = 0.56$ for total life events; $r = 0.49$ for life events probably beyond the respondent's control). Higher-class respondents generally exhibit low levels of symptoms regardless of the degree of exposure to stressful life events. These findings represent some of the earliest evidence that the life-events link between social class and mental illness may involve a complex process of mediation, whereby the relations of social class generate not only unequal exposure to stressful events but also differential vulnerability to their impact.

The same conclusion was reached by Kessler (1979) using a statistical model that estimates the relative importance of class differences in exposure to and impact of life events for explaining mean differences in the self-reported distress of upper- and lower-SES groups. Impact is roughly equivalent to the unstandardized regression coefficient for life events representing the amount of change in the dependent variable (distress) given a unit of change in exposure to stressors. Impact proved to be more important than exposure for explaining class differences in impairment in three of four tests of these effects, with and without statistical controls for prior levels of distress and using different methods for scoring life events. These tests showed quite consistently, that, although the higher impairment scores of lower-class persons were partly attributable to class differences in exposure to the life events, they were even more the result of a tendency for occupants of lower- vs. upper-class positions to respond with greater stress given comparable exposure to stressors.

Kessler also noted an interesting variation in this basic pattern of findings using what he calls extreme distress scores, i.e., scores of 66 or lower on the Gurin measure of mental status (1960). Scores at this level represent the most serious distress reported by this sample of respondents. When lower-class persons reported extreme distress they tended to have experienced high exposure to life events. However, lower-class persons in general were less represented among extreme distress scorers than middle- and upper-class persons: "persons in classes IV and V (Hollingshead and Redlich, 1958) are less likely than those in classes I to III to become extremely distressed when exposed to comparable stressors" (Kessler, 1979, p. 265).

Kessler sees nothing contradictory in these two sets of findings regarding the impact of life events across classes. Lower-class persons by virtue of their life circumstances are exposed to more stressors and have fewer resources with which to manage them. Consequently, they are doubly victimized, especially by their greater vulnerability to stressors as compared to upper-class persons. However, this vulnerability to stressors rarely eventuates in extreme levels of distress unless an exceptionally large number of life events have occurred. On the other hand, although middle- and upper-class persons in general respond to moderate levels of life events with less stress than lower class persons, *some* of these persons respond with extreme distress. Severe reactions to life events, thus, are more common among more privileged groups due to the presence of this group of sensitive responders.

Kessler suggested that one reason for this finding is that lower-class persons have more experience coping with stressful events than their upper-class counterparts. Therefore, they are less likely to exhibit *extreme* responses to stressors even though their limited coping resources result on the average in a higher impact of life events for them as compared to most upper-class persons. This interpretation is provocative in that it suggests that personal resources for coping with life events (e.g., ego strength and cognitive flexibility) may be greater among lower-class persons relative to upper-class persons even though their access to external material and social resources may be more restricted. His explanation contrasts sharply with one conclusion from Kohn's extensive research (1973) in psychiatric epidemiology that experience in the workplace for lower-class persons socializes the individual in ways that promote poor adaptability in the face of class hardships.

Brown and Harris's research (1978) on depression has already been mentioned as providing indirect support for the moderation of the impact of life events by class-related factors. Given that recent, severe stressors together with marked difficulties were found to be important provoking agents in depressed women and that some class-related aspects of the life circumstances of these women may have influenced the ratings of stressors, a moderation effect of social class was essentially built into the measure of life events. What is unique about this study in a different way is that these researchers also directly studied the role of context factors in conditioning the impact of life-event stressors. Having an intimate, positive marital relationship, being employed outside the home, having three or more children within the home, and having a mother who died before one reached the age of eleven were all found to influence significantly the impact of stressors and difficulties on the respondents. The first factor was especially important in that the other three conditions predicted level of response to stress events only for women without an intimate marital relationship. Together, these four moderating factors were more important in accounting for the significantly higher levels of depression in lower-class as compared to middle-class women than the frequency of exposure to life events or difficulties. At the same time, controlling both for types of provoking agents and the moderating variables completely elimi- nated the inverse relation between social class and depression. In providing further support for the moderation hypothesis these data also suggested that both contemporary conditions of class life (e.g., the quality and composition of familial relationships) and an earlier developmental experience (loss of mother during childhood) may influence one's vulnerability to present-day situational stressors. In addition the dominance of intimacy as a conditioning variable substantiates the growing belief that social support and the structure of social networks (Cobb, 1974; R. Liem and J. Liem, 1979) are especially important determinants of stress outcomes.

In view of the rather consistent finding of a greater impact of life events in lower-class populations reported in these three studies, we performed some preliminary analyses on data we are presently collecting. These data come from an incomplete sample of respon- dents in a one-year panel study of family and individual outcomes associated with the unemployment of a family breadwinner (R. Liem and J. Liem, 1978a). Some of the details of this research are discussed in the final section of this chapter. Although our sample at present is quite modest (27 blue-collar and 16 white-collar families), we compared the correlations between the number of life events jointly reported by husbands and wives and the scores of both spouses on several scales of the Derogatis Brief Symptom Inventory (1977) for blue- and white-collar families. The scales include such components of well-being as somatic complaints, interpersonal sensitivity, depression, and hostility. The sample is unique in view of the fact that all respondents share the event of involuntary job loss. The joint corroboration of life-event reporting by husbands and wives is also not commonly used in life events research.

With these preliminary analyses we find a clear trend in the direction of stronger, positive correlations between life events and symptom scores among blue-collar as opposed to white-collar husbands, i.e., five of seven correlations are stronger in the blue- collar sample. Virtually the same pattern is found when total life events or undesirable events independently rated by two judges are used in the analyses. By and large the more consistent impact of life events on blue-collar men pertains to emotional reactivity: depression, interpersonal sensitivity, and hostility as opposed to somatic complaints. The only clear exception is anxiety. On the other hand an equally strong trend in the opposite direction is observed for wives. In six of seven comparisons correlations between total life events and scores on the symptom scales reveal stronger association for white-collar as compared to blue-collar wives. The one correlation that is stronger for blue-collar women involves interpersonal sensitivity. No clear trend is apparent for wives when frequencies of undesirable events are substituted for total life events.

These data are especially provocative in light of the different trends for men and women, a finding that cannot be compared with those of B. S. Dohrenwend (1973) and Kessler (1979) where separate analyses were not performed for men and women. We had no a priori reason to expect this interaction between sex and social class particularly in view of Brown and Harris's (1978) finding of greater vulnerability of lower-class but not middle-class women to the impact of life-event stressors. Our data are even more puzzling since the reversal in pattern is especially marked for depression. For the moment it is probably unwarranted to speculate at any length about the explanation for this finding. We will be especially interested in future analyses in looking at differences in the quality of the marital relationship for these women given the importance of intimacy as a moderating influence on stress in Brown and Harris's research. We may discover that in our sample blue-collar wives do not as a group perceive themselves to be lacking in a positive and intimate relationship with their spouses.

Social Class Differences in the Weighting of Life Events—At the present time the research we have just reviewed is the principle source of support for the hypothesis that class-related factors moderate the impact of life events and, thereby, help to explain the basic relation between social class and mental illness. However, there is at least one additional type of evidence regarding this proposition; namely research concerning class differences in the assignment of life-change weights to life events.

Briefly, the issue pertaining to the scaling of life-events measures is whether the demands for readjustment created by life events are relatively uniform across the population as a whole or are unique to different subgroups (e.g., social classes). Support for the latter alternative would be consistent with the hypothesis that social class and mental illness are inversely related in part because conditions of lower-class life promote greater vulnerability to life-event stressors. In general it would be fair to say that comparisons of life-change ratings by members of different social status groups (Paykel et al., 1971) and nationalities (Rahe et al., 1971) have revealed remarkably strong agreement about the relative ordering of the life-change impact of different events. However, the existence of considerable differences in the absolute levels of life change often attributed by different groups to the same events cautions against assuming that life events are equivalent stressful occurrences for these populations (Fairbank and Hough, 1980).

B. S. Dohrenwend and her colleagues (1978) provide data particularly relevant to the weighting of life events by different social-class groups. In a careful attempt to develop a life-events instrument maximally protected from a number of important threats to test reliability and validity, they found significant differences in the life-change ratings made by persons with different social statuses. Differences were found for approximately 40% of the 101 life events studied, about 10% of which were attributable to social-class differences.

At first glance these data appear to contradict the hypothesis that differences in life circumstances associated with class membership may influence the perceived impact of life events. However, it could be argued that these findings underestimate class differences in view of the procedure employed to collect judges' ratings of events. Dohrenwend apparently used the instructions for judges reported by Komaroff et al. (1968). They asked raters to judge the amount of change created in someone's life by each event relative to a fixed standard for the event of marriage. What is important about these instructions for our concerns is that raters were asked to "think about how much of a change these things were for all people, the average person, not just for you" (Komaroff et al., 1968, p. 123). Consequently, judges' ratings cannot necessarily be assumed to reflect the collective experience of incumbents in different social classes. To the extent that respondents followed these instructions their performance is likely to have produced underestimates of true social-class differences in the perception of life-event impacts. We concur with the conclusion of Dohrenwend that caution is well advised in assuming that life circumstances do not influence the perceived, let alone actual, life-change impacts of stressful events.

Comment—Collectively, the evidence we have examined makes a reasonable case for the existence of class-related factors that moderate the impact of stressful life events and, thus, contribute to the known unequal distribution of mental illness across social classes. This effect appears to be even more important for explaining this relation than the tendency for frequent exposure to stressors to be associated with membership in the under classes. The field of social-stress research as a whole appears to have come to a similar conclusion concerning the importance of moderating factors as evidenced by the increased frequency with which concepts like coping resources, resistance resources, and social support appear in the stress literature (Pearlin and Schooler, 1978). Very recently Antonovsky (1979) has advocated an extreme form of this approach to the study of social factors in health. In the tradition of Rene Dubos (1960) he proposed that social stressors are pandemic occurrences in the lives of most people and, therefore, cannot by themselves account for the unequal social distribution of illness in the population. What matters is differential access to resistance resources, especially those which he hypothesizes contribute to the sense of a coherent, noncapricious relationship between one's self and one's environment.

The ground work, thus, appears to have been laid for at least some shift away from the study of social stressors, per se, to an examination of the manner in which current and past life circumstances shape one's response to life events. Some of the conceptual and methodological complexities associated with this research strategy are discussed in other contributions to this monograph. One significance of this development for persons primarily interested in the social class-mental illness relation is that this new data should be of major assistance in formulating substantive hypotheses about factors underlying the conditioning effect of social class. Moreover, the emphasis on context variables should produce fresh approaches to the intransigent social causation-social selection controversy. The social-causation hypothesis, for example, could be reformulated as a process involving both direct social-class causation through the promulgation of stressors and indirect causation through the class determination of important modifying conditions. In this regard, the psychiatric epidemiologist stands to learn much from this elaboration of the basic life-events research paradigm.

From the perspective of the life-events researcher the context dependency of life-events effects has further significance. It is an indication that weak and, more importantly, inconsistent life-events findings may often result from chance variations across research

samples in the distribution of unspecified and important conditioning variables. Such factors can act to suppress zero-order correlations between life-events measures and health outcomes. Social class
is a good example of this kind of factor, given the evidence for its
role in determining life-event impacts and the general tendency
among investigators to exclude it from design considerations.

One obvious method for handling a variable like social class is to
control for it, by sampling from a homogeneous class population or
by matching for social class where impaired and normal groups are
contrasted. Controlling for social class, however, would be appropriate only if class effects were relatively minor and one wanted to
insure that more important effects of life events and other predictors
were given maximal opportunity to be demonstrated.

The moderating influences of social class, however, do not appear
to be trivial. In fact, the importance of life events in the onset of
some disorders may be class specific. In other instances the processes mediating the impact of life events may differ across classes,
this difference ultimately being of more interest than the strength of
a global correlational relationship. Rather than control for the
effects of social class, in many cases it would be more desirable to
sample for social class to insure the opportunity to perform class
comparisons. A similar recommendation has recently been made by
J. Liem (1980) in regard to class differences in the sources and
impact of disordered parent-child communication processes in
families with schizophrenic offspring. Although the evidence for
class-linked effects in this area of work is less compelling than in the
data on stressful life events, the same argument can be made that
important family correlates of the schizophrenic process may often
be obscured by the researcher's failure to make social class an
explicit grouping variable. For the moment it is difficult to imagine
how the field of life-events research would not benefit from the
regular reporting of findings by social class.

Single Event Research

We would like to conclude this chapter by briefly returning to the
problem of the limited information available from studies of social
status and life events regarding which class-linked factors in particular account most for the moderating effect of social class. Except in
Brown and Harris's (1978) research, social-class effects are generally
studied only in relation to SES measured as a sociodemographic
variable. This strategy may have been based on the lack of a solid

conceptual or empirical basis for specifying a priori which aspects of lower- and upper-class life circumstances are likely to affect the impact of life events. The difficulty of identifying specific conditioning variables is exacerbated by the wide range of potential stressors represented in most life-events inventories. There is no reason to assume that the mediation of life-event effects is the same for all classes of events. For example, the types of social network relationships that are especially helpful in easing the impact of unemployment are probably not entirely the same as those whose support we most rely on to alleviate the stress of losing a loved one (R. Liem and J. Liem, 1978a, 1979).

One method for beginning to examine the conditions through which social class manifests a conditioning influence on the impact of life events is to focus attention on a specific stressful event and to measure in some detail the process of response to that occurrence in different class populations. From a pragmatic point of view this detailing of context factors is simply not possible where large numbers of life events have occurred and often at different times in the recent past.

Limiting oneself to the study of single events, however, is not without its own costs. We suspect that some predictive power in terms of health outcomes is likely to be lost when the cumulative impact of multiple stressors is excluded from the analyses. A related problem is that the moderating effects of coping strategies and resources may be unique to specific events. Consequently, for respondents experiencing multiple events, the relative power of the coping process measured in relation to a single event for predicting global health outcomes may be limited. The reduction in predictive power resulting from these limitations of single-event studies may simply be an unavoidable compromise that must be made in order to give more attention to intervening variables and processes.

One example of this research approach is a recent study by Westbrook (1979) of socioeconomic differences in the affect arousal, attitudes, and coping strategies of women shortly after childbirth. She found evidence for class differences in negative affect arousal (e.g., greater anxiety and guilt among lower-class women), attitudes toward different aspects of the childbearing experience (more positive attitudes among lower-class women with the exception of greater concern about physical aspects of childbirth), and coping strategies (e.g., less instrumental coping and more avoidance and fatalism among lower-class women). Westbrook's interpretation of the interaction effects among these variables is that middle-class women by virtue of their "realistic" appraisal of the hardships associated with pregnancy and motherhood engage in effective, confronting coping behaviors that help to minimize subsequent stress. Lower-class women, while generally perceiving childbirth in more favorable terms, cope with their fears and anxieties about labor and bodily harm through avoidance and fatalism. This account of the processes underlying the empirical relationships depicts cognitive appraisal as influencing the choice of coping responses which in turn have a direct bearing on stress outcomes. The conditioning effect of SES, thus, is grounded in class differences in cognitive styles rather than any constraints on coping that result from class differences in access to material and social resources. Most likely both situational and personal factors account for the class effects but the exclusive person-centered data in this research rules out any test of their relative contributions. What is clear in this research, however, is that substantial contributions to our knowledge of the mechanisms underlying the conditioning effects of social class on stress can be made by single-event research designs.

We are presently engaged in similar research regarding the event of involuntary job loss. Blue- and white-collar families with and without an unemployed breadwinner are being interviewed at four different times during the year following their job loss. The panel design is intended to permit us to observe changes in the response to the event given variations in the duration of unemployment. The major categories of moderating variables in this research are social and material resources and patterns of coping behavior assessed in relation to specific family hardships. Some a priori weighting of the relative importance of these factors has been done based on the assumption that the principle sources of initial stress following unemployment can be linked to the differential loss of rewards among persons at different levels in the occupational hierarchy (i.e., greater esteem and actualization losses associated with more prestigious and self-directed occupational positions). Greater emphasis is placed in this research on measures of the social and material environment of the families than was done by Westbrook. For example, in addition to assessing stylistic tendencies to call on others for help, we measure the structure of families' social networks as an indicator of access to interpersonal support. Similarly, extensive measures of direct and indirect access to material resources are used as possible determinants of instrumental coping vs. avoidance or denial.

In short, our purpose is to study the mediation of unemployment stress particularly in relation to social-class differences in life circumstances that may serve to constrain or enhance effective coping. Structural and process measures of the family system (e.g., organization of the family routine, balance of power between spouses) serve both as outcome variables at the family level and as additional conditioning variables in relation to the mood and health states of family members. When the first wave of interviewing is completed, we will have our initial opportunity to examine our proposed model of the class mediation of the stress of unemployment.

The ultimate value of this basic research approach for disclosing the class mediation of life-events stress rests with its ability to sort out highly complex interdependencies among an equally complex set of ongoing class conditions. Whether or not this methodology proves to be appropriate to this task, there is now enough evidence of a conditioning effect of social class on life events stress based on sociodemographic measures of class to warrant detailed investigations of how this effect is produced.

Acknowledgments

Part of the work discussed in this chapter was supported by the Center for Metropolitan Studies, NIMH, Grant #1R01 MH 31316-01. We would like to thank Steve McElfresh for his help in preparing this manuscript.

References

Antonovsky, A. (1979), *Health, Stress and Coping.* San Francisco: Jossey-Bass.
Brenner, M. H. (1973), *Mental Illness and the Economy.* Cambridge, Mass: Harvard University Press.
Brown, G. W. (1974), Meaning, measurement, and stress of life events. In: *Stressful Life Events: Their Nature and Effect*, ed. B. S. Dohrenwend & B. P. Dohrenwend. New York: Wiley, pp. 217–243.
Brown, G. W. & Harris, T. (1978), *Social Origins of Depression: A Study of Psychiatric Disorder in Women.* London: Tavistock.
Catalano, R. & Dooley, D. (1977), Economic predictors of depressed mood and stressful life events in a community. *J. Hlth Soc. Behav.*, 18:292–307.
Cobb, S. (1974), A model for life events and their consequences. In: *Stressful Life Events: Their Nature and Effects*, ed. B. S. Dohrenwend & B. P. Dohrenwend. New York: Wiley, pp. 151–156.
Derogatis, L. (1977), *SCL-90 Administration, Scoring, and Procedures Manual—I*

for the Revised Version. Baltimore: John Hopkins University School of Medicine.

Dohrenwend, B. P. (1979), Stressful life events and psychopathology: some issues of theory and method. In: *Stress and Mental Disorder*, ed. J. E. Barrett, R. M. Rose, & G. L. Klerman. New York: Raven Press, pp. 1–15.

Dohrenwend, B. P. & Dohrenwend, B. S. (1969), *Social Status and Psychological Disorder: A Causal Inquiry*. New York: Wiley.

Dohrenwend, B. S. (1973), Social status and stressful life events. *J. Pers. Soc. Psychol.*, 28:225–235.

Dohrenwend, B. S. and Dohrenwend, B. P., eds. (1974), *Stressful Life Events: Their Nature and Effects*. New York: Wiley.

Dohrenwend, B. S., Krasnoff, L., Askenasy, A., & Dohrenwend, B. P. (1978), Exemplification of a method for scaling life events: the PERI life events scale. *H. Hlth Soc. Behav.*, 19:205–229.

Dooley, D. & Catalano, R. (1979), Economic, life, and disorder changes: times-series analysis. *J. Hlth Soc. Behav.*, 7:381–396.

Dubos, R. J. (1960), *The Mirage of Health*. London: Allen and Unwin.

Faris, R. & Dunham, H. (1939), *Mental Disorders in Urban Areas*. New York: Hafner.

Gerstein, J., Langner, T., Eisenberg, J., & Simcha-Tagan, O. (1977), An evaluation of the etiologic role of stressful life-change events in psychological disorders. *J. Hlth Soc. Behav.*, 18:228–244.

Gurin, G., Veroff, J., & Feld, S. (1960), *Americans View Their Mental Health*. New York: Basic Books.

Hollingshead, A. & Redlich, F. (1958), *Social Class and Mental Illness*. New York: Wiley.

Holmes, T. & Rahe, R. (1967), The social readjustment rating scale. *J. Psychosom. Res.*, 11:213–218.

Jaco, E. (1960), *The Social Epidemiology of Mental Disorders*. New York: Russell Sage Foundation.

Kessler, R. (1979), Stress, social status, and psychological distress. *J. Hlth Soc. Behav.*, 20:259–273.

Kohn, M. (1973), Social class and schizophrenia: a critical review and a reformulation. *Schizo. Bull.*, 7:60–79.

Komaroff, A., Masuda, M., & Holmes, T. (1968), The social readjustment rating scale: a comparative study of Negro, Mexican, and white Americans. *J. Psychosom. Res.*, 12:121–128.

Langner, T. & Michael, S. (1963), *Life Stress and Mental Health: The Midtown Manhattan Study*. London: The Free Press of Glencoe.

Liem, J. (1980), Family studies of schizophrenia: An update and commentary. *Schizo. Bull.*, in press.

Liem, R. (1977), *Economic change and individual psychological functioning*. Final Report, Research Grant number MH27443, Center for Metropolitan Studies, NIMH.

Liem, R. & Liem, J. (1978a), *Family and individual coping following job loss*. NIMH Grant number MH31316–01, 1978a.

Liem, R. & Liem, J. (1978b), Social class and mental illness reconsidered: the role of economic stress and social support. *J. Hlth Soc. Behav.*, 19:139–156.

Liem, R. & Liem, J. (1979), Social support and stress: some general issues and their application to the problem of unemployment. In: *Mental Health and the*

Economy, ed. L. Ferman J. Gordus. Kalamazoo, Mich.: Upjohn Institute, pp. 347–377.

Link, B. (1978), On the etiologic role of stressful life events. *J. Hlth Soc. Behav.*, 19:343–345.

Markush, R. & Favero, R. (1974), Epidemiologic assessment of stressful life events, depressed mood, and psychophysiological symptoms: a preliminary report. In: *Stressful Life Events: Their Nature and Effects*, ed. B. S. Dohrenwend & B. P. Dohrenwend. New York: Wiley, pp. 171–190.

Marshall, J. & Funch, D. (1979), Mental illness and the economy: a critique and partial replication. *J. Hlth Soc. Behav.*, 20:282–290.

Meyer, A. (1951), The life chart and the obligation of specifying positive data in psychopathological diagnosis. In: *The Collected Papers of Adolf Meyer*, vol. III *Medical Teaching*, ed. E. E. Winters. Baltimore: John Hopkins University Press. pp. 52–56.

Myers, J., Lindenthal, J., & Pepper, M. (1971), Life events and psychiatric impairment. *J. Nerv. Ment. Dis.*, 152:149–157.

Myers, J., Lindenthal, J., & Pepper, M. (1974), Social class, life events, and psychiatric symptoms: a longitudinal study. In: *Stressful Life Events: Their Nature and Effects*, ed. B. S. Dohrenwend & B. P. Dohrenwend. New York: Wiley, pp. 191–205.

Paykel, E., Prusoff, B., & Uhlenhuth, E. (1971), Scaling of life events. *Arch. Gen. Psychiat.*, 25:340–347.

Pearlin, L. & Schooler, C. (1978), The structure of coping. *J. Hlth Soc. Behav.*, 19:2–21.

Rabkin, J. G. & Struening, E. L. (1976), Life events, stress, and illness. *Science*, 194:1013–1020.

Rahe, R., Lindberg, V., Theorell, T., & Bennett, C. (1971), The social readjustment rating scale: a comparative study of Swedes and Americans. *J. Psychosom. Res.*, 15:241–249.

Rogler, L. & Hollingshead, A. (1965), *Trapped: Families and Schizophrenia*. New York: Wiley.

Srole, L., Langner, T., Michael, S., Opler, M., & Rennie, T. (1962), *Mental Health in the Metropolis: The Midtown Manhattan Study*. New York: McGraw-Hill.

Stellar, M. E. (1979), *Women and Youth in the Massachusetts Labor Force, 1979*. Boston: Publication of the Labor Area Research Department, Massachusetts Division of Employment Security.

Westbrook, M. (1979), Socioeconomic differences in coping with childbearing. *Amer. J. Commun. Psychol.*, 7:397–412.

Wyler, A., Masuda, M., & Holmes, T. (1971), Magnitude of life events and seriousness of illness. *Psychosom. Med.*, 33:115–122.

Testing Hypotheses about the Life Stress Process

The last chapter of this volume returns to a general formulation of life stress and alternative hypotheses concerning the nature of the process. Robert R. Golden and Barbara Snell Dohrenwend propose methods for testing these alternative hypotheses and for developing more precise quantitative descriptions of the process.

A Path Analytic Method for Testing Causal Hypotheses About the Life Stress Process

ROBERT R. GOLDEN

BARBARA SNELL DOHRENWEND

As the chapters in this book demonstrate, recent research on life stress has been very productive of useful constructs regarding the nature of stressful life events and of the characteristics of the individual and his or her social environment that affect the outcome of life stresses. Most of these constructs are still being empirically studied both conceptually and operationally. Although the task of conceptual and operational refinement of constructs of the life-stress process is not finished, we believe that future research on life stress should be designed to test hypotheses that integrate constructs regarding life events, personal dispositions, and social environmental situations. At the end of the first chapter, examples of such hypotheses drawn from recent publications on life stress and its consequences were presented. These hypotheses are schematized in fig. 1.

In fig. 1, a one-headed arrow from one variable to another indicates the former is a direct cause of the latter; for example, an arrow from L to C, as in hypothesis A, indicates that L is a direct cause of C. In hypothesis B there is no arrow from L to C, which indicates that, in this hypothesis, L is not a direct cause of C (only R and E are direct causes of C under hypothesis B). For hypothesis B we say that L can result in C, but only by acting through R. A two-headed arrow between two variables indicates that the correlation between the two variables is hypothesized not to be zero. The absence of a two-headed arrow between D and S in hypothesis D indicates that the correlation between D and S is hypothesized to be zero. If a two-headed arrow were present between D and S, the correlation could be any value other than zero. Also in hypothesis D there is not a two-headed arrow between L and S or between L and

FIGURE 1

Hypothesis

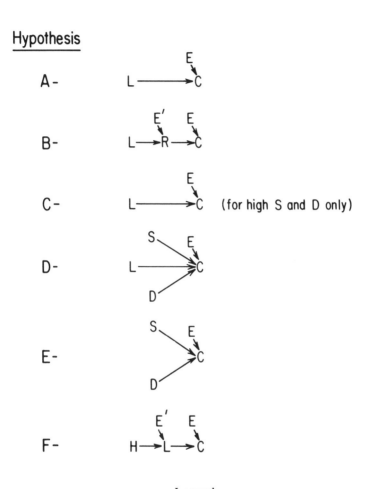

A-

B-

C-   (for high S and D only)

D-

E-

F-

Legend

C: outcome, adverse health change or exacerbation of adverse health change
L: one or more specific or general life events
D: personal disposition
R: non-pathological personal response
S: social structure or immediate social environment condition
H: previous status or symptoms of health, adverse health changes
E' or E: all other causes of the outcome C (residual causes)

Path Diagrams for Six Hypotheses About the Life Stress Process

D; hence these two correlations are hypothesized to be zero. Note that for each hypothesis the residual causes E and E' are assumed to be uncorrelated with other direct causes. We will discuss the nature of this assumption, especially with regard to its violation, below.

In order to confirm a hypothesis of life stress, it must be subjected to and pass adequate risks of refutation. This will not be a simple task since the concepts and constructs incorporated in the hypotheses about life stress are not perfectly understood and often not very easy to measure. Another source of difficulty is that these constructs are often believed or even known to be only loosely related to each other.

When statistical models are used for generation of rather than for testing of hypotheses, Richenbach (1938), the philosopher of science, suggested that the researcher should be allowed maximal freedom to develop his conjectures and theories. In the "context of discovery" he need not provide proof, evidence, data, and the like. In this activity of science one is allowed to do what he wishes (even to be irrational and inconsistent if necessary). However, in the "context of justification," he should subject his hypotheses to the strongest (but fair) tests that he can devise. According to our definition "testing a hypothesis" means to subject it to a risk or danger of refutation. In this chapter we are concerned with the problem of how we can test the verisimilitude (Popper, 1962) of the hypotheses about the life-stress process with a statistical model. That is, we will be concerned with using a particular statistical model to test hypotheses about the life-stress process in the context of justification. At the same time we test the hypotheses of life stress with the aid of the statistical model, we will wish to test the underlying assumptions of the statistical model.

Introductory Description of Path Analysis

A correlational method known as path analysis can be used to test the seven hypotheses diagrammed in fig. 1 and, thereby, to make inferences about causal relationships between constructs such as life events, personal dispositions, social structures, and adverse health changes. Path analysis was first developed by the geneticist Wright (1921, 1968), and later applied in the social sciences by Blalock (1964, 1971), Crano et al., (1972), Land (1969), Werts and Linn (1970), Goldberger and Duncan (1973), and others. This statistical method was developed explicitly to use matrices of correlations to test causal hypotheses. For a good introduction to path analysis see Li (1975).

Path analysis requires that a substantive hypothesis specify which variables are causes, which are effects, and which are both, as we have done in fig. 1. First, as an example, we will describe the algebra of path analysis for testing hypothesis B. Next, we present a general but simple path-analytic model for testing each of the six hypotheses about life stress. For present purposes we will make the assumption that we can *directly* measure each of the constructs in all six hypotheses. More complex path-analytic models that can accommodate multiple "indicators" of latent variables or constructs that are not directly measurable will be discussed. Finally, we discuss the assumptions regarding linearity and uncorrelated residual causes which underlie these path-analytic models.

We now present a simple path model to test hypothesis B. Let L denote a single measure of stressful life events, R denote a single measure of nonpathological personal response (e.g., psychophysiological strain) and C denote a single measure of adverse health changes. It will simplify the algebra of path analysis if we standardize L, R, and C such that each has a mean of zero and a standard deviation of one. According to hypothesis B, C is directly caused by R and E, and R is directly caused by L and E'. If the variables are assumed to be linearly related we can write:

$$C = p_R R + p_E E \text{ , and} \tag{1}$$

$$R = p_L L + p_{E'} E' \text{ ,} \tag{2}$$

where p_R, p_L, p_E, and $p_{E'}$ are numerical coefficients, called "path coefficients," to be estimated, as shown below. The variable E represents all causes of C other than R, and E' all causes of R other than L. That is, the variables E and E' are assumed to represent "residual causes" of C and R respectively. They can be regarded as conglomerates of all known and unknown causes of C and R other than R and L respectively.

In path analysis it is assumed, then, that each causally determined variable or effect, as indicated in the path diagram, can be expressed as a linear function of one or more conjectured causal variables, for which we have measures, and of a residual component representing all remaining causes for which we do not have a measure. In elementary path-analytic models, it is also assumed that the residual variables are uncorrelated with other causal variables, the exact form of the assumptions depending on the particular path model. In the present example we will assume that the pairs of causal variables (R, E), (L, E'), and (L, E) are uncorrelated. It is important to note, then, that the proposed statistical model will require special statistical assumptions that are neither a component conjecture nor an implication of the hypotheses of life stress. These special assumptions (uncorrelated residual terms and linearity) are made in the interest of mathematical tractability. Under these assumptions it is possible to derive formulas for estimation of the parameters (i.e., the path coefficients) of the model. Assumptions that are needed for the statistical model but are not a part of the substantive hypotheses are used in nearly all statistical models and are called "auxiliary assumptions." It follows that it is important to check or test these auxiliary assumptions, as will be discussed below.

Next we show that estimates of p_L and p_R are easily obtained. If we multiply equation 1 by R and sum over all N individuals we obtain

$$\Sigma CR = p_R \Sigma R^2 + p_E \Sigma ER .$$

Since all variables are standardized $\Sigma CR/N = r_{CR}$, where r denotes the Pearson correlation coefficient, and $\Sigma R^2/N = 1$. By assumption we have $\Sigma ER/N = r_{ER} = 0$. It follows that

$$r_{CR} = p_R. \tag{3}$$

It follows from equation 1 that $p_E = (1 - p_R)_{1/2}$.

Likewise, if we multiply equation 2 by L we obtain

$$\Sigma RL = p_L \ \Sigma L^2 + p_{E'} \Sigma E'L ,$$

$$\text{or} \quad r_{RL} = p_L . \tag{4}$$

It follows from equation 2 that $p_{E'} = (1 - p_L)_{1/2}$.

In other words, for this path model the two path coefficients p_R and p_L are simply the corresponding Pearson correlation coefficients. Also, multiplying both sides of equation 1 by L and summing over individuals, we obtain

$$\Sigma LC = p_{CR} \Sigma LR + \Sigma LE ,$$

$$\text{or} \quad r_{CL} = p_{CR} r_{LR} ,$$

since L and E are also uncorrelated by assumption. Since $p_{CR} = r_{CR}$ we obtain

$$r_{CL} = r_{CR} r_{LR}, \tag{5}$$

which is, then, a consequence for the present path model given in terms of three observable correlation coefficients. This result is known as the "chain rule" in path analysis because it can be generalized for any number of variables arranged in a "chain." It is important to note that the chain rule can be used as a means of partially testing the underlying assumptions of the present path model. That is, if the chain rule is not adequately satisfied by the data, then either the hypothesis that L causes R which causes C or the above described path model assumptions (or both) must be rejected.

A Path Model for Testing Each of the Hypotheses

Next, we present a slightly more complex path model which subsumes each of the six hypotheses given in fig. 1 as special cases, thereby allowing us to test each hypothesis against each of the others. To do this let us assume we have measures of the major variables used by the six hypotheses:

  C: outcome, adverse health change or exacerbation of adverse health change;

  L: one or more specific or general life events;

  R: nonpathological personal response;

  D: personal disposition;

  S: social structure or immediate social environmental conditions;

  H: previous status or symptoms of health; and

  E: all remaining known and unknown residual causes of C.

Let us also suppose that each of L, R, D, S, H, and E are direct causes of C to various degrees. Some of the direct causal effects may be so slight as to be negligible, others may have strong and undeniable effects. We allow each pair of the variables L, R, D, S, and H to be intercorrelated in any manner. The path diagram for this model is given in fig. 2. Unidirectional causal relationships are indicated by the six one-headed arrows, and bidirectional causal relationships or correlations by the ten two-headed arrows. The absence of a path from E to L, R, D, S, and H indicates that, by assumption, E is uncorrelated with each of these variables. The path coefficients p_L, p_R, p_D, p_S, p_H, and p_E are indicated for each of the causes of C. As in the example above, it will be useful to standardize all measures so they have zero means and unit variances.

Under the assumption of linearity we have

$$C = p_L L + p_R R + p_D D + p_S S + p_H H + p_E E. \qquad (6)$$

The path coefficients can be calculated with the same techniques used in multiple regression, where they are called "beta coefficients." This regression equation when used in the context of a path model is

FIGURE 2

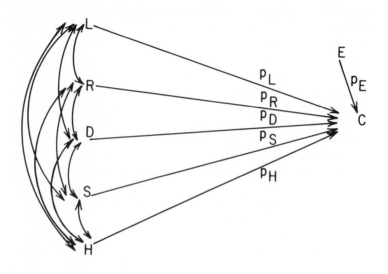

Path Diagram of the General Model

called a "structural equation," and the path coefficients are known as "structural parameters." The structural parameters are regarded as important parameters describing the causal process and are considered to have more meaning than ordinary beta weights which are used in multiple regression for purposes of predicting a criterion variable. While the form of the path model is specified by making assumptions concerning linearity and independence of residual causes, the structural parameters or path coefficients are estimated from the data. To test some of the hypotheses about life stress we desire to test statistical hypotheses about the path coefficients. For example, hypotheses A, C, D, and F each require that we reject the statistical hypothesis $p_L = O$. If we should find that p_L is zero or very nearly zero then we would not have a causal arrow from L to C in the path diagram. Likewise, if we should find that p_L is a significantly positive quantity then we would have a single or two-headed arrow between L and C in the path diagram.

Our concern is not with the size of the multiple correlation coefficient R as it would be in multiple regression analysis. Our purpose here is not to be able to predict optimally the health change but to understand better the causal process underlying the health change. We are interested mainly in which path coefficients and correlations between the independent variables are nearly zero and which are not. We can rely to some extent on the significance tests to make this determination. Further, we are concerned that the estimates of path coefficients be accurate. To summarize: we desire that the path model give an adequate approximation of the life-stress process with regard to its structure and path-coefficient magnitudes. It follows that it is most important to test the "fit" of the path model to our data. More precisely, we wish to test the auxiliary assumptions of the model. For a sufficiently large sample size it is true that if and only if the assumptions of the model are adequately satisfied, then the parameters of the model are accurately estimated.

Next, let us consider the proportion of the variance C accounted for by each of the possible sources described in the first three columns of table 1. There are five possible "direct effect" sources for which we have measures, ten possible "interaction" sources (resulting from two causal variables acting jointly) and the residual source. The variance of $C = p_L L + P_R R + p_D D + p_S S + p_H H + p_E E$ is the sum of variances of the causal variables ($p_L{}^2$, $p_R{}^2$, $p_D{}^2$, $p_S{}^2$, $p_H{}^2$, and p^2) and twice the sum of the covariance between each pair of five causal variables L, R, D, S, and H. Thus it can be shown that the variance of C (which is one) is equal to the sum of the 16 components which are given, along with descriptive names, in the first three columns of table 1. The remaining columns of table 1 indicate whether a particular component of variance is required by a particular hypothesis to be significantly positive or approximately zero. Since each of the six hypotheses requires something that none of the other five requires, we can pit the six hypotheses against each other to select the one that does best in passing the various tests. Of course, it may turn out that we will reject each of the six hypotheses if all fail the tests indicated in table 1.

To illustrate how the hypothesis tests given in table 1 were determined let us consider hypothesis E (see fig. 1). Under this hypothesis, the measured direct causes of C are S and D so the path coefficients p_S and p_D are conjectured to be positive. The variables L, R, and H play no role so each is conjectured to have a path coefficient of zero. The variables D and S are hypothesized to be uncorrelated, as indicated by the lack of a two-headed arrow

TABLE 1

Variance of the Adverse Health Change (C) Accounted for by Each Source.

Source	Variance	Description	hypothesis: A	B	C[a]	D	E	F
					Requirements for each hypothesis			
L	$p_L^{\,2}$	Direct effect of L	$+$[b]	0[c]	$+$	$+$	0	$+$
R	$p_R^{\,2}$	Direct effect of R	0	$+$	0	0	0	0
D	$p_D^{\,2}$	Direct effect of D	0	0	0	$+$	$+$	0
S	$p_S^{\,2}$	Direct effect of S	0	0	0	$+$	$+$	0
H	$p_H^{\,2}$	Direct effect of H	0	0	0	0	0	0
$L\,\&\,R$	$2p_L p_R r_{LR}$	Interaction effect of $L\,\&\,R$	0	0	0	0	0	0
$L\,\&\,D$	$2p_L p_D r_{LD}$	Interaction effect of $L\,\&\,D$	0	0	0	0	0	0
$L\,\&\,S$	$2p_L p_S r_{LS}$	Interaction effect of $L\,\&\,S$	0	0	0	0	0	0
$L\,\&\,H$	$2p_L p_H r_{LH}$	Interaction effect of $L\,\&\,H$	0	0	0	0	0	0
$R\,\&\,D$	$2p_R p_D r_{RD}$	Interaction effect of $R\,\&\,D$	0	0	0	0	0	0
$R\,\&\,S$	$2p_R p_S r_{RS}$	Interaction effect of $R\,\&\,S$	0	0	0	0	0	0
$R\,\&\,H$	$2p_R p_H r_{RH}$	Interaction effect of $R\,\&\,H$	0	0	0	0	0	0
$D\,\&\,S$	$2p_D p_S r_{DS}$	Interaction effect of $D\,\&\,S$	0	0	0	0	0	0
$D\,\&\,H$	$2p_D p_H r_{DH}$	Interaction effect of $D\,\&\,H$	0	0	0	0	0	0
$S\,\&\,H$	$2p_S p_H r_{SH}$	Interaction effect of $S\,\&\,H$	0	0	0	0	0	0
E	$p_E^{\,2}$	Residual	$+$	$+$	$+$	$+$	$+$	$+$

[a] For high S and D only.   [b] $+$ = positive.   [c] 0 = approximately zero.

between them, so the corresponding interaction term is hypothesized to be zero. Of course, all other interactions involving L, R, or H are zero.

Each of the correlations between the independent variables can be tested for significant departure from zero by use of the well known t-test (see Hayes, 1963, p. 529). In this test, the quantity

$$ t = r \left(\frac{N-2}{1-r^2} \right)^{1/2} , $$

where N is the sample size, and r is the sample value of the correlation, is distributed as the t-statistic with $N - 2$ degrees of freedom.

Each of the path coefficients can be tested for significant departure from zero by use of another t-test (see Cohen and Cohen, 1975, p. 112). The standard error of p_L , for example, is given by

$$ S_L = \left[\left(\frac{1 - R^2}{N-k-1} \right) \left(\frac{1}{1 - R^2_{(L)}} \right) \right]^{1/2} , $$

where N is the sample size, k is the number of measured direct causes of C (five in the general model), R is the multiple correlation resulting from predicting C from the five measured independent variables, and R_L is the multiple correlation resulting from predicting L from the four other independent variables (R, D, S, and H). It follows that $t = p_L / S_L$ is distributed as the t-statistic with $N - k - 1$ degrees of freedom.

It is of interest to consider the implication of this latter formula for the required sample size. To do these calculations we must have some idea as to the sizes of the correlations between the various variables. Suppose, for example, that each of the independent variables correlate 0.25 with C. (Past studies have shown this to be a realistic value to expect.) Further, suppose the independent variables are uncorrelated with each other, as indicated in several of the hypotheses of fig. 1. We have

$$ p_L = p_R = p_D = p_S = p_H = 0.25 . $$

It follows that the values of the multiple correlations are

$$ R = 0.56, \text{ and } R_{(L)} = R_{(R)} = R_{(D)} = R_{(S)} = R_{(H)} = 0 , $$

and the standard error of each path coefficient is $0.83/(N - 6)^{1/2}$. If we desire that the standard error of each path coefficient be of size 0.05 or smaller, then N must be size 282 or larger. If we can tolerate a standard error of 0.10, then the required N would be 75, a sample size which is often considerably easier to obtain. How large can the sampling error of the path coefficient be? From past empirical research it is known that the population correlations or path coefficients of important causal variables of C are likely not to exceed 0.25. Naturally, those of negligible causal variables will be closer to zero, say 0.10 or less. It follows then that the difference between two such path values, one for an important cause and one for a negligible one, is not very large. In the present model for there to be two standard errors between path coefficients of 0.10 and 0.25 we require an N of 129. The point is that it is important to use a sample size that is large enough to allow for accurate distinction between negligible population path-coefficient values of, say, 0.10 or less from sizable ones that are, say, 0.25 and larger.

Suppose we have decided which of path coefficients among L, R, D, S, and H are close enough to zero so that their corresponding direct effects can be deleted from the path diagram and path model. Next we wish to test the goodness of fit of the resulting path model to the data. We can proceed just as we did in the derivation of the chain rule. If we multiply both sides of equation 6 by each of the variables L, R, D, S, and H, sum over individuals, and divide by N we obtain

$$
\begin{aligned}
r_{CL} &= p_L + p_R r_{RL} + p_D r_{DL} + p_S r_{SL} + p_H r_{HL} ; \\
r_{CR} &= p_L r_{LR} + p_R + p_D r_{DR} + p_S r_{SR} + p_H r_{HR} ; \\
r_{CD} &= p_L r_{LD} + p_R r_{RD} + p_D + p_S r_{SD} + p_H r_{HD} ; \\
r_{CS} &= p_L r_{LS} + p_R r_{RS} + p_D r_{DS} + p_S + p_H r_{HS} ; \\
r_{CH} &= p_L r_{LH} + p_R r_{RH} + p_D r_{DH} + p_S r_{SH} + p_H ;
\end{aligned}
\tag{7}
$$

which is a system of five equations in terms of the five (already estimated) path coefficients. We can also derive similar equations for the correlations between L, R, D, S, and H. The goodness of fit tests consist of comparing the observed correlations on the left side of equation 7 with the "reproduced" or model based estimates on the right side. If the assumptions of the model are approximately true then the observed and reproduced correlations should be approximately equal.

A simple way of making the comparison between an observed and reproduced correlation is by testing for a statistically significant difference by use of the common t-test. A more accurate and sophisticated procedure which uses maximum likelihood theory has been developed by Land (1973).

It is important to note that equation 7 provides a stronger test of fit when several of the path coefficients are hypothesized to be zero than when only one or two are. In fact it is necessary to hypothesize that at least one path coefficient be zero to use this test, otherwise the system is "just determined" (number of path coefficients is equal to the number of equations) and the path coefficients have been estimated so as to perfectly satisfy equation 7. If we hypothesize that one or more path coefficients are zero, then the system is "overdetermined" and will only be satisfied by the data if the hypothesis and the model assumptions are both sufficiently valid.

At this point we might reconsider what is the maximum tolerable difference between a sample correlation and its reproduced or model-inferred value. A traditional null hypothesis test to determine whether the difference is significantly different from zero is not exactly what we desire, since we are not hopeful that literal fulfillment of the path model will ever be possible. For example, in testing hypothesis B, we cannot expect the chain rule to hold perfectly for a number of reasons. First, the strongest advocate of hypothesis B would never claim it to have perfect verisimilitude. One obvious reason that hypotheses are not perfect is that causal variables considered to have only slight effects are left out. The point here is that to the extent the substantive hypothesis is imperfect, the path model and its consequences are not perfectly satisfied. Second, we never have perfectly valid measures of the constructs of the hypothesis. For example, to the extent that the measures of different constructs lack discriminant validity, or specificity (and thereby, have correlated measurement error), the correlations between the measures will differ from those that would be obtained if perfectly valid measures were used. As we have seen above, path analysis uses the correlations between measures to estimate the path coefficients and to derive further consequences such as the chain rule. Hence, the estimation procedures and the consequences of the model will be erroneous to the extent the correlations are erroneous. Third, it is evident that assumptions regarding linearity and independence can, at best, be satisfied only approximately by actual data. Last, the observed correlations between measures will always contain some degree of sampling error.

In practice, the really important question in setting tolerance limits for the difference in the observed and reproduced correlations is one of robustness of the model. We need to know how much disagreement can be tolerated in this test without incorrectly contradicting a true hypothesis that the state of nature is adequately approximated by the idealization. By "adequately approximated" we mean close enough to justify employing the method to improve our guesses as to the causal structure and the magnitude of the path coefficients by a worthwhile amount in relation to our initial state of ignorance (Meehl, 1978). An answer to the general question of robustness is best provided by a study of the path model with real and artificial data where the causal structure is known. However, we typically do not have available the results of such studies. In absence of these ideal criteria we must rely on judicious use of a significance test and judgment in evaluating the size of the difference between the correlation and its reproduced value.

The results of the application of a path model will approximate the actual situation only to the extent that the assumptions of the model approximate the truth. It follows that checking the verisimilitude of the assumptions is a matter of critical importance. Unfortunately, two frequently used methods of checking assumption verisimilitude in path analysis, recourse to quasitheoretical argument and reliance on claims of self-evidence are inadequate. The failure to check assumption verisimilitude has been a serious defect in many path-analytic studies and has undoubtedly resulted in many highly inaccurate or spurious findings. Assumptions probably never have perfect verisimilitude. In other words, there usually is some degree of "assumption departure." However, it is only necessary that assumption departure be adequately small, or that assumptions be adequately robust in order for path coefficients to be accurate enough for a given purpose.

The single most important reason to subject a model to sufficient danger of refutation is to avoid spurious results. Results are spurious if they are artifactual, and have very little or no correspondence to the actual situation. Spurious results may have the appearance of cohesiveness and may generally make good sense, yet be unequivocally wrong. Such results are not only unfortunate in their own right, but they have a detrimental effect on the nonspurious results as well, since, of course, it is not known which are which.

We have suggested that the amount of assumption departure can be partially checked by the use of statistical tests (such as the chain rule) which are based on deductions from the assumptions of the path model. The clearance of these tests can help reduce doubts regarding estimation accuracy and spuriousness.

We have suggested that the life-stress hypotheses and the path models can be evaluated just as Sir Karl Popper proposed that all scientific theories be evaluated. He argued that " . . . the criterion of the scientific status of a theory is its falsifiability or refutability or testability" (Popper, 1962, p. 27). It follows that for a given life-stress hypothesis and path model to gain maximal scientific status they should be tested in a fair but rigorous manner.

Suppose for a given set of data the chain rule given by equation 5 holds approximately, say to within tolerance limits allowing for sampling error. Also, suppose we have several other tests such as those suggested in equation 7 which also flow from the path model and that they are also passed. In that case we can say that the substantive hypothesis from which the path model flows has been "corroborated." It is important to note that we can never "prove" that the substantive hypothesis is true or even approximately true. In fact, the logic underlying *any* form of theory testing does not allow such a statement (Popper, 1962). The logic says that if the life-stress hypothesis has high verisimilitude, if the measures are highly valid, and if the "auxiliary assumptions" of the path-analytic model are approximately correct, then certain observable conditions such as the chain rule should hold approximately, possibly within sampling error. However, even if the observable consequences hold, none of the following are a logical consequence: (*a*) the hypothesis has high verisimilitude; (*b*) the measures are valid; and (*c*) the path-model assumptions are approximately met. That is, we can only hope to show that the data are "consistent" with the substantive hypothesis, the path model, and the selected measures. We can do this by using tests such as the chain rule that flow from the model. To the extent that we have many such tests that are strong (difficult to satisfy spuriously), we can corroborate the substantive hypothesis, the path model, and the measures of the constructs.

On the other hand, suppose tests such as these are not passed. Then we have "discorroboration" of at least one of the following: the substantive hypothesis, the validity of the selected measures, or the path model (i.e., the underlying assumptions of the model). Whereas in corroboration we can not prove that everything is all right, in discorroboration we can prove that something is definitely wrong.

Some methods for correcting certain sources of discorroboration are available. For example, the auxiliary assumptions of the path model regarding linearity and uncorrelated residual variables, when sufficiently violated, result in failure of the tests even when the substantive hypothesis has high verisimilitude. If it is suspected that the linearity assumption is violated excessively a possible recourse is to transform or rescale some of the troublesome variables. To deal with correlated residual variables it is possible to modify the path model by, for example, addition of more variables and more paths to accommodate shared measurement error.

An important indication of a path model's testability is the degree to which it is "overdetermined." The number of equations required for parameter estimation is simply the number of unknown path coefficients (which is 5 in our multiple-regression model). The number of equations that must be approximately satisfied is the number of pairwise correlations that are conjectured to satisfy certain constraints. In the general multiple regression model this number is also 5. A highly testable path model is characterized by having several independent variables and a relatively small number of two-headed arrows and a small number of one-headed arrows (or path coefficients).

Each of the six life-stress hypotheses given in fig. 1 is very strong (i.e., testable), since, in each case, fifteen predictions (given in table 1) are made concerning the relationships between the six life-stress variables and since only one to three coefficients must be estimated. If each of these hypotheses is refuted by the data we may wish to consider a weaker hypothesis of life stress where some of the independent variables are hypothesized to be intercorrelated and several are hypothesized to be direct causes of the health change. However, the weaker the hypothesis, the less testable it is. In the weakest of all hypotheses, all five independent variables are hypothesized to be (a) direct causes of the health change, and (b) intercorrelated with each other. In that case, the multiple-regression model we have presented above is "just determined" since there are the same number of equations as unknowns. The path model must be overdetermined to be testable and this is the case only if we hypothesize that some of the path coefficients or correlations are zero.

We could also hypothesize that the same causal network and/or path coefficient magnitudes hold for different health outcomes, different populations, or for repeated measurement periods over time. Suffice it to say here that a method developed by Jöreskog (1973) allows for parameter estimation and testing of such models. With such analytic extensions it also becomes possible to consider the constructs as latent and only measureable indirectly through multiple "indicators" such as is done in factor analysis. That is, one or more latent factors can be incorporated in the path model and the conjectures regarding the corresponding latent path coefficients and the causal relationship between these factors can be tested. Such sophisticated analysis could come after the more elementary analysis described above. For a clear review of the literature and an introduction to latent variable path models, see Bentler (1980).

Measuring Strength of Association

Suppose that we conclude by means of the path model that certain of the hypothesized independent variables have direct causal effects on health change. Suppose, for example, that we find the path coefficient p_L for life events is significantly greater than zero and of the same or greater order of magnitude as the other path coefficients. We will have found then that, compared to the other variables of the hypotheses, the life-events variable is a relatively important one. We might then be interested in the magnitude of the association between life events and adverse health outcome. The square of the path coefficient p_L is the proportion of the variance in C that is uniquely accounted for by L—that which would exist if all other causal variables of C are somehow held constant. While the proportion of variance is often used to describe the magnitude of statistical associations it usually is not as appealing intuitively as are measures given in terms of probabilities, odds, risk, and the like. To know that life events has a path coefficient of 0.3 (meaning that 9% of the variance in C would remain if all other sources were held constant) does not describe the magnitude of the association nearly as well as, for example, the statement that the presence of certain life events doubles the chances of adverse health changes.

In general, then, we are suggesting that the next step be the dichotomous assessment of the magnitude of the relationship between each related independent variable, such as life events and the dependent variable, adverse health change. Let us assume that the life-events measure and the health-change measure are both dichotomous. For this situation, we will describe the "relative difference" measure of association first developed by Sheps (1958, 1961) (see also Fleiss, 1972).

We consider here only the simplest case where both the life event and the adverse health change are measured in a dichotomous fashion or can be dichotomized in a meaningful way. Let L denote the presence of the life event, L denote its absence; let C denote the presence of the adverse change and C denote its absence. Let the joint event probabilities for each of the four cells of the life events by health change fourfold table be denoted as in table 2. For example, the proportion of all people where both the life event and the health change are present is denoted by $p(L, C)$. A measure of the association between the life events variable and the health change

TABLE 2

The Cell and Marginal Probabilities of Life Event by Health Change
Fourfold Table.

	C	$\overline{C}$	
L	$p(L,C)$	$p(L,\overline{C})$	$p(L)$
L	$p(\overline{L},C)$	$p(\overline{L},\overline{C})$	$p(L)$
	$p(C)$	$p(\overline{C})$	1

$$p(L,C) + p(L,\overline{C}) + p(\overline{L},C) + p(\overline{L},\overline{C}) = 1.$$

variable can be specified in form of a mathematical function of the four proportions $p(L,C)$, $p(L,\overline{C})$, $p(\overline{L},C)$, and $p(\overline{L},\overline{C})$, which sum to one.

For the purpose of this discussion, let us consider the example in which the life-events variable is the recent exit of a person important to the individual and the adverse health change is depression (Paykel, 1974). One parameter which we may consider as a measure of the strength of association between these two variables is the difference between two conditional probabilities:

$$p(C/L) - p(C/\overline{L}),$$

which has been called the "attributable risk." The conditional probability $p(C/L)$ is defined to be $p(L,C)/p(L)$, and $p(C/\overline{L})$ is defined to be $p(\overline{L},C/p(\overline{L})$. In our example, the attributable risk is the proportion of all depressed people who have recently experienced an exit less the corresponding proportion for all people who have not recently experienced an exit. The attributable risk can be criticized in the following manner. Consider only those individuals who have recently experienced an exit and are depressed. We cannot assume that *all* of these individuals are depressed *because* they recently experienced an exit; in all likelihood, some would have been depressed without an exit. The attributable risk does not take into account the cause of depression and a measure that does would be preferable.

We will consider two types of individuals who recently experienced an exit (those in the first row of table 2). The first type of individual is defined to be one who is depressed but where the exit was not a necessary cause of the depression; that is, the depression resulted from one or more causes other than an exit. All individuals of the first type are depressed and are in the (L,C) cell of table 2. The second type of individual experiencing an exit is the complementary class of the first type. When individuals of the second type are depressed, their depression was caused, at least in part, by the exit; that is the exit was a necessary cause of the onset of depression. Individuals of the second type are in either the (L,C) or the $(L,\overline{C})$ cells of table 2. Before proceeding it will be useful to note that (a) each individual experiencing an exit is either of type 1 or of type 2 and not both, and (b) all type 1 individuals are depressed and only some of type 2 are depressed. Typically, we do not know which of the two types a particular individual experiencing an exit is. It is possible, however, to use a simple model to estimate from data given in the form of table 2 the proportion of all people of type 2 that are depressed, and we suggest that this proportion be used as a measure of the strength of association between being depressed and experiencing an exit. The measure of association we propose, then, is the proportion of all people experiencing an exit who are also depressed, where the depression is caused, at least in part, by the exit.

Let the unknown rates of the two types of individuals who recently experienced an exit, as described above, be denoted by P_1 and $P_2 = 1 - P_1$. That is, P_1 is the proportion of all people who have experienced an exit, but became depressed for other reasons; $P_2 = 1 - P_1 =$ the complementary proportion of all people who have experienced an exit, of whom some are depressed but only because of the exit. In table 2 all of the first type of individuals are in the (L,C) cell whereas some of the second type of individuals are in the (L,C) cell and the remainder of the second type are in the $(L,\overline{C})$ cell. All individuals who have experienced an exit are either of the first type or of the second type. The proportion of all people who have experienced an exit who are depressed is

$$p(C/L) = \frac{p(L,C)}{p(L)} = p_1 + rP_2 = p_1 + r(1 - p_1), \qquad (8)$$

where r is the proportion of the second type who are depressed. That is, the proportion of all people who have experienced an exit who are depressed is the rate of the first type of individual, P_1, since all of this type are depressed, plus the rate of the second type of individual, P_2, times the proportion of the second type who are depressed, r. Our purpose is to estimate r, the proportion of the second type of individuals whose depression is due at least in part to an exit.

If we consider the group of all people who have experienced an exit and the group of all people that did not experience an exit, it is not unreasonable to assume that the rate of depression due to causes other than an exit is the same for the two groups. In the group who have an exit, this rate is simply P_1. From table 2 we see that in the group without an exit this rate is $p(C/\overline{L}) = p(\overline{L},C)/p(\overline{L})$. It follows from this assumption that

$$P_1 = p(L,C)/p(L). \tag{9}$$

Solving equation 8 for r we obtain

$$r = \frac{p(L,C)/p(L) - P_1}{1 - P_1}. \tag{10}$$

Substituting equation 9 into equation 10 and simplifying we obtain

$$r = \frac{p(L,C)\, p(\overline{L}) - p(\overline{L},C)\, p(L)}{p(\overline{L})\, p(L) - p(\overline{L},C)\, p(L)}. \tag{11}$$

The above expression for r can also be written in terms of the conditional probabilities $p(C/L) = \dfrac{p(L,C)}{p(L)}$ and $p(C/L) = \dfrac{p(\overline{L},C)}{p(\overline{L})}$ as

$$r = \frac{p(C/L) - p(C/\overline{L})}{1 - p(C/\overline{L})} \tag{12}$$

If $p(C/L) \geq p(C/\overline{L})$, r is positive and varies between zero and one. If $p(C/L) \leq p(C/\overline{L})$ is negative then the health change and life event variables are negatively correlated.

To summarize: formula 12 gives an estimate of the proportion of all people who have experienced an exit whose subsequent depression is caused, at least in part, by the exit.

Formulas 11 and 12 can only be used when both variables are dichotomous. A corresponding measure for the case where the variables have several categories or are continuous has not been developed.

Concluding Remarks

The path-analytic methodology described in this chapter has been used extensively in various areas of social science research. We suggest that it will prove useful as a method of testing alternative hypotheses concerning the life-stress process. These attempts may reveal very important considerations regarding its application that are not mentioned here. The present chapter is written in the context of discovering how we might go about testing hypotheses about life stress. The researcher of life stress is invited to apply the present methodology in an empirical context and judge its usefulness for himself.

We have shown that path models, like many other statistical models, are based on auxiliary assumptions. When such a model is used for testing a substantive hypothesis the results of the analysis will approximate the actual situation to the extent, and only to the extent, that the assumptions of the model approximate the truth. It follows that checking the assumptions is a matter of critical importance.

Finally, we have given a description and derivation of the relative difference measure first developed by Sheps. We suggest that it is a useful, intuitively appealing measure of the strength of association between the adverse health change variable and another variable believed to cause the adverse health change.

References

Bentler, P. M. (1980), Multivariate analysis with latent variables: causal modeling. *A. R. Psychol.*, 31:419–456.

Blalock, H. M., Jr. (1964), *Causal Inferences in Nonexperimental Research.* Chapel Hill: University of North Carolina Press.

Blalock, H. M., Jr. (1971), *Causal Models in the Social Sciences.* Chicago: Aldine-Atherton.

Cohen, J. & Cohen, P. (1975), *Applied Multiple Regression/Correlation Analysis for the Behavioral Sciences.* New York: Wiley.

Crano, W. D., Kenny, D. A., & Campbell, D. T. (1972), Does intelligence cause achievement? A cross-lagged panel analysis. *J. Ed. Psychol.*, 63:258–275.

Fleiss, J. L. (1972), *Statistical Methods for Rates and Proportions.* New York: Wiley.

Goldberger, A. S. & Duncan, O. D. (1973), *Structural Equation Models in the Social Sciences.* New York: Seminar Press.

Hayes, W. J. (1973), *Statistics for Psychologists.* New York: Holt, Rinehart and Winston.

Jöreskog, K. G. (1973), A general method for estimating a linear structural equation system. In: *Structural Equation Models in the Social Sciences*, ed. A. S. Goldberger & O. D. Duncan. New York: Seminar Press, pp. 85–112.

Land, K. C. (1969), Principles of path analysis. In: *Sociological Methodology 1969*, ed. E. F. Borgatta & G. W. Bohrnstedt. San Francisco: Jossey-Bass, pp. 3–37.

Land, K. C. (1973), Identification, parameter estimation, and hypothesis testing in recursive sociological models. In: *Structural Equation Models in the Social*

Sciences, ed. A. S. Goldberger & O. D. Duncan. New York: Seminar Press, pp. 3–37.

Li, C. C. (1975), *Path Analysis – A Primer*. Pacific Grove, Calif.: Boxwood Press.

Meehl, P. E. (1978), Theoretical risks and tabular asterisks: Sir Karl, Sir Ronald, and the slow progress of psychology. *J. Consult. Clin. Psychol.*, 46:806–834.

Paykel, E. S. (1974), Life stress and psychiatric disorder: applications of the clinical approach. In: *Stressful Life Events: Their Nature and Effects*, ed. B. S. Dohrenwend & B. P. Dohrenwend. New York: Wiley, pp. 135–149.

Popper, K. R. (1962), *Conjectures and Refutations*. New York: Basic Books.

Richenback, H. (1938), *Experience and Prediction*. Chicago: University of Chicago Press.

Sheps, M. C. (1958), Shall we count the living or the dead? *New Eng. J. Med.*, 259:1210–1214.

Sheps, M. C. (1961), Marriage and mortality. *Amer. J. Pub. Hlth.*, 51:547–555.

Werts, C. E. & Linn, R. L. (1970), Path analysis: psychological examples. *Psycholog. Bull.*, 74:193–212.

Wright, S. (1921), Correlation and causation. *J. Agri. Res.*, 20:557–585.

Wright, S. (1968), *Evolution and the Genetics of Populations*, vol. 1, *Genetic and Biometric Foundations*. Chicago: University of Chicago Press.

Afterword

Recent Directions in Life Stress Research from a Public Health Perspective

RICHARD DAY

In a seminal article on the epidemiology of illness conditions, Casse (1976) observed that:

> throughout all history, disease, with rare exceptions, has not been prevented by finding and treating sick individuals, but by modifying those environmental factors facilitating its occurrence. This formulation would suggest that we should focus efforts more directly on attempts at further identification and subsequent modification of these categories of psychosocial factors rather than on screening and early detection. [P. 121]

For those of us adhering to a psychosocial perspective, stressful life-event research has always been a critical component of the effort to identify environmental factors that contribute to the etiology and onset of psychiatric illnesses. Yet, recent empirical studies (Andrews and Tennant, 1978b; B. S. Dohrenwend and B. P. Dohrenwend, 1979) have failed to unambiguously establish the causal significance of stressful life events for psychiatric illness. The issues here are both methodological and substantive in nature.

Over the past fifteen years, an enormous amount of data has been collected on the relationship between stressful life events and psychiatric illness. Along with this proliferation of studies, the field of life-stress research has become strewn with methodological pitfalls just waiting for the unwary investigator. The data reported in different studies have been collected using a wide variety of techniques that range from simple self-administered checklists (Holmes and Rahe, 1967), on the one hand, to detailed and lengthy interviews on the other (Brown and Harris, 1978b). To further complicate matters, Naugebauer (1980) points out that substantive research has proceeded well in advance of reliability studies, and he questions both the appropriateness of design and the statistics in the work that has already been done. It is common to use periods of recall that extend over twelve or more months when we know that the reliability of our respondents' memory for events is usually limited to about six months (Jenkins et al., 1979). Even though investigators have utilized numerous scales, we still cannot say what characteristics of life events (e.g., degree of required readjustment, upsettingness, undesirability, threat, etc.) make them "stressful" or account for their relationship to illness (Shrout, 1980). Turning to the dependent variable, there are numerous unresolved issues involving the determination of the date of onset of the patient's psychiatric condition, and it is frequently unclear whether developing symptoms, becoming ill, or taking on the patient role is being associated with the occurrence of stressful life events (Andrews and Tennant, 1978a, 1978b; Mechanic, 1968). Moreover, the methods utilized in different studies to assess the nature of the patient's clinical state vary to the same extent as the techniques for collecting information about experienced life events. Finally, the results emerging from most research on stressful life events have not been of the sort that inspire other investigators to undertake proper replication studies.

Even though much of the current data remains open to competing interpretations, it does seem clear that the relationship between stressful life events and psychiatric illness is far more complex than originally expected. The substantive results from the most sophisticated studies often approximate Paykel's (1974) findings concerning the relationship between "social exits" and clinical depression. Here Paykel (1974) notes that although retrospective research indicates that among psychiatric patients a greater than expected frequency of "exits" is experienced prior to the onset of depression when compared to a nondepressed control population, "only a small proportion of exits, less than ten percent, appear to be followed by clinical depression" (p. 139). In a similar fashion, retrospective studies (Brown et al., 1973a, 1973b) have implicated stressful life events in the etiology of neuroses, but prospective studies (Theorell, et al., 1975) have indicated that only a minute proportion of events occurring in the general population are followed by the advent of neurotic conditions. Perhaps, the most judicious evaluation of the current data was put forward by Andrews and Tennant (1978): "Life (events) may best be regarded as but one of many social and environmental factors non-specifically related to formal psychiatric illness" (p. 548). Paykel (1978) comes to a similar conclusion:

It is clear that the event is only responsible in part for the onset of illness, and the proportion of causation that can be attributed directly to it may not be large. The event must be regarded as interacting with a host of other factors in determining whether the outcome is an illness, and which specific illness. [P. 251]

From a public-health perspective, results of this sort provide very little in the way of practical information that can be used in the design of primary, secondary, or even tertiary intervention programs. Perhaps, the only studies emerging from the life-event field that promise to have an immediate application are the work of the London-based group of investigators (Brown and Birley, 1968; Birley and Brown, 1970; Leff et al., 1973) on the involvement of stressful life events in schizophrenic relapse episodes and the ability of neuroleptic medications to forestall their effects.

In the light of this situation, we cannot help but recommend the direction taken in the present collection of papers. I am referring specifically to the emphasis placed on the necessity of integrating social support/network and personal dispositional factors into future studies involving stressful life events. The importance of this step has been the subject of much discussion by investigators in the field, but the problems of operationalizing the critical variables and the impulse to work with more parsimonious research designs apparently has inhibited progress in this direction. The marginal yield from less ambitious prior studies has provided additional impetus, however, and this approach is rapidly gaining recognition as the most profitable line of future research for life stress investigators. Paykel (1978) for example, suggests that "it is not merely the event" that is significant "but the soil on which it falls" (p. 251). His subsequent remarks concerning the types of factors that must be considered in future studies (e.g., social support, personality factors, the qualities of the event itself, etc.) are strikingly similar to the factors mentioned by B. S. Dohrenwend and B. P. Dohrenwend in the first chapter of this volume.[1] An additional source of influence underlying the new direction of the field can be found in the series of studies by Brown and his colleagues (Brown et al., 1975, 1977; Brown and Harris, 1978b) on the social factors implicated in the development of depression.

[1]In addition to the variables listed above, we should also keep in mind that biological and genetic factors may play a significant role in determining the individual's vulnerability or resistance to the stressful aspects of life events and other stimuli originating in social relationships (Levi, 1972; Seyle, 1956).

Again, from a public-health point of view, the answer to how these variables are related to life events (e.g., in an interactive or additive fashion, see Tennant and Bebbington, 1978; Brown and Harris, 1978a) probably will be less significant than a careful documentation of their association with the development and onset of psychiatric illness. In any case, this emphasis on the need to study the "protective" and "vulnerability" factors (Cassel, 1976) operative in the life-stress process may well provide the data required to design primary and secondary intervention strategies that can be implemented with clinical and general populations. As an illustration of the type of work that may be possible in the future, we should mention the experimental program being carried out by Leff and his associates in London with the families of schizophrenic patients (personal communication). Past research (Vaughn and Leff, 1976a, 1976b; Leff and Vaughn, 1980) has implicated a triangle of factors including stressful life events, the use of neuroleptic medications, and the atmosphere of the family environment with the frequency of schizophrenic relapse episodes. Although it is unrealistic to advise the patient to "refrain from experiencing stressful life events," and often difficult to guarantee compliance with a schedule of recommended medications, we can attempt to modify the characteristic emotional atmosphere in the home, turning a potential vulnerability factor into what may become a protective factor. Unlike stressful life events, the family support system is a potentially accessible factor, changes in which may provide both the patient and the family with additional resources to withstand the impact of other life-stress variables.

In order not to appear unduly optimistic, let me emphasize the amount of developmental and basic research that must be done before such programs may be realistically contemplated. At the same time, it is clear that a new and more sophisticated perspective is emerging in the field of life-stress research, a perspective that ultimately holds out the promise of improved practical strategies for intervening in the development and onset of psychiatric illness.

References

Andrews, G. & Tennant, C. (1978a), Being upset and becoming ill. *Med. J. Austral.* 1:324–327.

Andrews, G. and Tennant, C. (1978b), Life stress and psychiatric illness. *Psychol. Med.*, 8:545–549.

Birley, J. G. & Brown, G. W. (1970), Crises and life changes preceding the onset or relapse of acute schizophrenia: clinical aspects. *Brit. J. Psychiat.*, 116:322–327.

Brown, G. W. & Birley, J. (1968), Crises and life changes and the onset of schizophrenia. *J. Hlth Soc. Behav.*, 9:203–214.

Brown, G. W. & Harris, T. (1978a), Social origins of depression: a reply. *Psychol. Med.*, 8:577–588.

Brown, G. W. & Harris, T. (1978b), *The Social Origins of Depression: A Study of Psychiatric Disorder in Women.* London: Tavistock.

Brown, G. W., Harris, T., & Copeland, J. (1977), Depression and loss. *Brit. J. Psychiat.*, 130:1–18.

Brown, G. W., Harris, T., & Peto, J. (1973b), Life events and psychiatric disorders, part II: nature of the causal link. *Psychol. Med.*, 3:159–176.

Brown, G. W., NiBhrolchain, M., & Harris, T. (1975), Social class and psychiatric disturbance among women in an urban population. *Sociology*, 9:225–254.

Brown, G. W., Sklair, F., Harris, T., & Birley, J. (1973a), Life events and psychiatric disorders, part I: some methodological issues. *Psychol. Med.*, 3:74–87.

Cassel, J. (1976), The contribution of the social environment to host resistance. *Amer. J. Epidemiol.*, 8(2):107–123.

Dohrenwend, B. S. & Dohrenwend, B. P. (1978), Some issues in research on stressful life events. *J. Nerv. Ment. Dis.*, 166:7–15.

Holmes, T. H. & Rahe, R. H. (1967), The social readjustment rating scale, *J. Psychosom. Med.*, 11:213–218.

Jenkins, C., Hurst, M., & Rose, R. (1979), Life changes: do people really remember? *Arch. Gen. Psychiat.*, 36:379–384.

Leff, J., Hirsch, S., Gaind, R., Rohde, P., & Stevens, B. (1973), Life events and maintenance therapy in schizophrenic relapse. *Brit. J. Psychiat.*, 123:659–660.

Leff, J. & Vaughn, C. (1980), The interaction of life events and relatives' expressed emotion in schizophrenia and depressive neuroses. *Brit. J. Psychiat.*, 136: 146—153.

Levi, L., ed. (1972), *Stress and Distress in Response to Psychosocial Stimuli.* Stockholm: Almquist and Wiksell.

Mechanic, D. (1968), *Medical Sociology.* New York: Free Press.

Paykel, E. S. (1974), Life stress and psychiatric disorder: applications of the clinical approach. In: *Stressful Life Events: Their Nature and Effects*, ed. B. S. Dohrenwend & B. P. Dohrenwend. New York: Wiley, pp. 135–149.

Paykel, E. S. (1978), Contribution of life events to psychiatric illness. *Psychol. Med.*, 8:245–253.

Selye, H. (1956), *Stress of Life.* New York: McGraw-Hill.

Tennant, C. & Bebbington, P. (1978), The social causation of depression: a critique of the work by Brown and his colleagues. *Psychol. Med.*, 8:565–575.

Theorell, T., Lind, E., & Flonderus, B. (1975), The relationship of disturbing life changes and emotions to the early development of myocardial infarction and other serious illnesses, *J. Epidemiol.*, 4:281–293.

Vaughn, C. & Leff, J. (1976a), The influence of family social factors on the course of psychiatric illness. *Brit. J. Psychiat.*, 129:125–137.

Vaughn, C. & Leff, J. (1976b), The measurement of expressed emotion in the families of psychiatric patients. *Brit. J. Clin. Soc. Psychiat.*, 15:157–165.

Notes on Contributors

BARBARA SNELL DOHRENWEND was Professor and Head of the Division of Sociomedical Sciences at Columbia University School of Public Health when she died of cancer on June 28, 1982. She obtained her doctorate in psychology from Columbia University and was on the faculties of New York University and the City College at the City University of New York before coming to Columbia. She served on the Study Section of the Center for Epidemiologic Studies of the National Institute of Mental Health and was a past chairperson of the Society for Life History Research in Psychopathology. She was President of the Division of Community Psychology of the American Psychological Association, served on the Task Panel on the Nature and Scope of the Problems of the President's Commission on Mental Health, and was a member of the Task Group on Behavioral Effects of the President's Commission on the accident at Three Mile Island.

At the time of her death, Dr. Dohrenwend was on the editorial board of the *Journal of Health and Social Behavior* and the *American Journal of Community Psychology* and *Health Psychology*. She was also on the Council of the Medical Sociology Section of the American Sociological Association, a member of the Section Committee of the Section of Epidemiology and Community Psychiatry of the World Psychiatric Association, and a member of the World Health Organization Panel on Mental Health.

Alone, and together with her husband, Dr. Bruce P. Dohrenwend, she wrote extensively in the area of stressful life events and illness. She was the recipient of several major grants to study stress situations, and was a joint winner with Dr. Bruce Dohrenwend of the 1980 Distinguished Contributions Award of the Division of Community Psychology of the American Psychological Association, and the 1981 Rema Lapouse Mental Health Epidemiology Award of the American Public Health Association.

BRUCE P. DOHRENWEND is the Foundations' Fund for Research in Psychiatry Professor at Columbia University where he is head of the Social Psychiatry Research Unit. In addition, he is Chief of the Department of Social Psychiatry at the New York State Psychiatric Institute and Director of the Research Training Program in Psychiatric Epidemiology at Columbia University, a program supported by a grant from the National Institute of Mental Health. He is also Principal Investigator on several NIMH research grants.

In the past, Dr. Dohrenwend, who obtained his Ph.D. degree in social psychology from Cornell University, has served on the Study Section of the Center for Epidemiologic Studies of NIMH, as a member of the Task Panel on the Nature and Scope of the Problems of the President's Commission on Mental Health, and as the head of the Task Group on Behavioral Effects of the President's Commission on the Accident at Three Mile Island. He has been as associate editor of the *Milbank Memorial Fund Quarterly,* the *Journal of Health and Social Behavior,* and the *American Journal of Community Psychology.* He was also a member of the Committee to study "Research on Stress in Health and Disease" of the Institute of Medicine of the National Academy of Sciences.

Dr. Dohrenwend has authored and edited, alone and with his wife, Dr. Barbara Snell Dohrenwend, numerous papers and several books on life events, stress, and illness. They were joint recipients of the 1980 Distinguished Contributions Award of the Division of Community Psychology of the American Psychological Association, and the 1981 Rema Lapouse Mental Health Epidemiology Award of the American Public Health Association. Dr. Dohrenwend received a Research Scientist Award from the National Institute of Mental Health in 1971 and renewals of that award in 1976 and 1981. Dr. Dohrenwend's address is Columbia University, 100 Haven Avenue, Tower 3-19H, New York, NY 10032.

GEORGE W. BROWN is in the Department of Sociology, Bedford College of the University of London, Inner Circle, Regent's Park, London NWI 4NS.

RICHARD DAY is a member of the Division of Mental Health, World Health Organization, 1211 Geneva 27, Switzerland.

DIANNE TIMBERS FAIRBANK is on the Life Change and Illness Research Project, Neuropsychiatric Institute, Center for the Health Services, University of California, Los Angeles, CA 90024.

CLAUDE S. FISCHER is a member of the Sociology Department at the University of California, Berkeley, CA 94720.

DAVID C. GLASS is in the Psychology Department, Laboratory Office Building, State University of New York, Stony Brook, NY 11794.

ROBERT R. GOLDEN is at the School of Public Health at Columbia University, Division of Biostatistics, 600 West 168th Street, New York, NY 10032.

SUSAN GORE is at The Center for Survey Research, University of Massachusetts, 100 Arlington Street, Boston, MA 02116.

JOHN E. HELZER is in the Department of Psychiatry, Washington University School of Medicine, 4940 Audobon Avenue, St. Louis, MO 63110.

RICHARD L. HOUGH is at the Neuropsychiatric Institute, Center for the Health Services, University of California, Los Angeles, CA 90024.

RICHARD S. LAZARUS is in the Department of Psychology at the University of California at Berkeley, 4105 Tolman Hall, Berkeley, CA 94720.

HERBERT M. LEFCOURT is in the Department of Psychology at the University of Waterloo in Waterloo, Ontario, Canada N2L 3G1.

JOAN H. LIEM is in the Department of Psychology at the University of Massachusetts, Harbor Campus, Boston, MA 02125.

RAMSEY LIEM is in the Department of Psychology at Boston College in Chestnut Hill, MA 02167.

KAREN A. MATTHEWS is in the Department of Psychiatry and Epidemiology at the University of Pittsburgh, 3811 O'Hara Street, Pittsburgh, PA 15261.

RICHARD NEUGEBAUER is at the Gertrude H. Sergievsky Center at Columbia University's College of Physicians and Surgeons, 60 Haven Avenue, New York, NY 10032.

SUSAN L. PHILLIPS is at the insitute of Urban and Regional Development at the University of California, Berkeley, CA 94720.

RICHARD H. RAHE is at the United States Navy Regional Medical Center, Long Beach, CA 90822.

PATRICK E. SHROUT is in the Division of Biostatistics of Columbia University School of Public Health, k600 West 168th Street, New York, NY 10032.

5 6 6175